ROUTLEDGE LIBRARY EDITIONS: THE ENGLISH LANGUAGE

Volume 19

AN HISTORIC TONGUE

AN HISTORIC TONGUE
Studies in English Linguistics in Memory of
Barbara Strang

Edited by
GRAHAM NIXON AND JOHN HONEY

Routledge
Taylor & Francis Group
LONDON AND NEW YORK

First published in 1988

This edition first published in 2015
by Routledge
2 Park Square, Milton Park, Abingdon, Oxon OX14 4RN

and by Routledge
711 Third Avenue, New York, NY 10017

Routledge is an imprint of the Taylor & Francis Group, an informa business

© 1988 Graham Nixon and John Honey

All rights reserved. No part of this book may be reprinted or reproduced or utilised in any form or by any electronic, mechanical, or other means, now known or hereafter invented, including photocopying and recording, or in any information storage or retrieval system, without permission in writing from the publishers.

Trademark notice: Product or corporate names may be trademarks or registered trademarks, and are used only for identification and explanation without intent to infringe.

British Library Cataloguing in Publication Data
A catalogue record for this book is available from the British Library

ISBN: 978-1-138-92111-5 (Set)
ISBN: 978-1-315-68654-7 (Set) (ebk)
ISBN: 978-1-138-91732-3 (Volume 19) (hbk)

Publisher's Note
The publisher has gone to great lengths to ensure the quality of this reprint but points out that some imperfections in the original copies may be apparent.

Disclaimer
The publisher has made every effort to trace copyright holders and would welcome correspondence from those they have been unable to trace.

AN HISTORIC TONGUE

Studies in English Linguistics
in Memory of Barbara Strang

Edited by
GRAHAM NIXON
and JOHN HONEY

ROUTLEDGE
London and New York

First published in 1988 by
Routledge
11 New Fetter Lane, London EC4P 4EE

Published in the USA by
Routledge
in association with Routledge, Chapman & Hall, Inc.
29 West 35th Street, New York NY 10001

© 1988 Graham Nixon and John Honey

Printed and bound in Great Britain by Mackays of Chatham PLC, Kent

All rights reserved. No part of this book may be reprinted or
reproduced or utilised in any form or by any electronic, mechanical, or
other means, now known or hereafter invented, including
photocopying and recording, or in any information storage or retrieval
system, without permission in writing from the publishers.

British Library Cataloguing in Publication Data

An Historic tongue: Studies in English
   linguistics in memory of Barbara Strang.
   1. English language   2. Historical
   linguistics
   I. Nixon, Graham   II. Honey, John
   III. Strang, Barbara
   420   PE51
   ISBN 0-415-00310-5

Library of Congress Cataloging in Publication Data

Data applied for

Contents

Contributors	vii
Preface	viii
Foreword *Sir Randolph Quirk*	ix
In Memoriam Barbara Strang	xi
PART I: Old to Middle English Period	1
1. The Difficulty of Establishing Borrowings Between Old English and the Continental West Germanic Languages *E.G. Stanley*	3
2. Cyn(e)wulf Revisited: The Problem of the Runic Signatures *Roger Lass*	17
3. Snuck: The Development of Irregular Preterite Forms *Richard M. Hogg*	31
4. Ambiguous Negations in Chaucer and Queen Elizabeth *Sonia Baghdikian*	41
5. Goodbye to All 'That'? The History and Present Behaviour of Optional 'That' *Joan Beal*	49
6. The Rise of the *For NP to V* Construction: An Explanation *Olga Fischer*	67
7. Negation in Shakespeare *N.F. Blake*	89
8. Englishmen and Their Moods: Renaissance Grammar and the English Verb *John O. Reed*	112

PART II: Middle to Modern English Period 131

9. The Great Vowel-Shift and Other Vowel-Shifts
   John Frankis 133
10. Thematic Genitives
    Noel E. Osselton 138
11. The Discourse Properties of the Criminal Statute
    Michael Hoey 145
12. *Varietas Delectat:* Forms and Functions of English Around the World
    Manfred Görlach 167
13. 'Talking Proper': Schooling and the Establishment of English 'Received Pronunciation'
    John Honey 209
14. The Methods of Urban Linguistic Surveys
    Graham Nixon 228
15. A Bibliography of Barbara Strang
    Richard N. Bailey 242

Contributors

Sonia Baghdikian
Université Libre de Bruxelles

Professor Richard N. Bailey
University of Newcastle-upon-Tyne

Joan Beal
University of Newcastle-upon-Tyne

Professor N.F. Blake
University of Sheffield

Olga Fischer
University of Amsterdam

John Frankis
University of Newcastle-upon-Tyne

Professor Manfred Görlach
University of Cologne

Michael Hoey
University of Birmingham

Professor Richard M. Hogg
University of Manchester

Professor John Honey
Leicester Polytechnic and University of Bophuthatswana

Professor Roger Lass
University of Cape Town

Graham Nixon
University of Sheffield

Professor Noel E. Osselton
University of Newcastle-upon-Tyne

John O. Reed
Kyushu University, Japan

Professor E.G. Stanley
Pembroke College, Oxford

Preface

Following Barbara Strang's untimely death in 1982 a number of her former colleagues, students, and fellow scholars in related disciplines responded to an initiative from Graham Nixon (who had taken his MA under Barbara at Newcastle) to offer a volume of essays in her memory. John Honey (likewise a product of that course) joined the enterprise later as co-editor, and he alone takes responsibility for the compilation of the biographical essay which prefaces this book, and which was compiled on the basis of information and impressions from several sources, including Colin Strang, Jean Bone (whose long friendship with Barbara began during their student days in London), Richard N. Bailey and Kelsey Thornton.

These essays, all on topics on which Barbara took a lively interest, are offered in humble tribute to a remarkable scholar and teacher, and a wonderful person, whose influence lives on both in her own publications and in the creative work she inspired in others.

The Editors

Foreword

Sir Randolph Quirk
President of the British Academy

It is difficult to do justice in a few words to a treasured friendship that extended over a period of thirty-five years. It is next to impossible when, as in the present case, the need arises to convey the abiding sense of *privilege* felt in enjoying this long friendship. Even the briefest acquaintance with Barbara was enough to show that she combined a rare and precious set of qualities. Sparkling intellect and originality. Profound moral strength. Unshakable dedication to the most demanding standards of scholarship. Generosity. Loyalty. And sense of fun.

She and I graduated in the same year in the same university but we did not actually meet until I had pored over her weighty MA thesis on Kentish — awesome in quality as well as in scale. From then on we established the agreeable habit of reading each other's work in manuscript, of regularly exchanging views, and (especially when we were colleagues in Durham and Newcastle) of debating the goals of the subject 'English'. These discussions, at once deliberative and convivial, were further enriched after Barbara's marriage to Colin, when my sense of privilege was enhanced by awareness of a philosophical dimension added to the philological one.

Even during the last decade or so of her life, when we were separately busy in widely separated universities, our mutual trust and close relationship happily persisted. I still miss the monthly occasions when she would emerge from the night train en route to a UGC meeting and join me for a dietarily frugal but conversationally copious breakfast in my Bloomsbury office.

Few people can have left a more beloved and deeply revered memory than this noble colleague.

BARBARA STRANG
1925–1982

In Memoriam Barbara Strang

Barbara Strang was born Barbara Mary Hope Carr in 1925, the only child of Frederick and Amy Carr, and grew up in Shirley, Surrey. Her father was an engineer who suffered unemployment in the 1930s, and Barbara was proud of her humble origins. Though not Catholics, her parents made sacrifices to give her a good schooling at Coloma Convent of the Ladies of Mary in Croydon. The school was evacuated to Wales for the early years of the war, and when Barbara entered King's College, London, in 1942, she spent her first undergraduate year in the college's wartime refuge in Bristol before studies were resumed in the Strand. It was at King's that Barbara was introduced to the Anglican liturgy, whose linguistic influence on her was lasting.

Graduating in 1945, she proceeded to the research degree of MA under Professor C.L. Wrenn, submitting for her thesis an extended study of historic Kentish dialects. Three years as an assistant lecturer at Westfield College helped to convince Barbara, and one of her mentors at that time, Marjorie Daunt, that her first tenured post should be in a mixed academic community rather than another cloistered single-sex institution such as the Oxford women's college for whose English language post she was runner-up in 1950. It was a happy chance which took her instead in that year to a lectureship at King's College, Newcastle, then a part of the University of Durham and later to become the University of Newcastle-upon-Tyne, which she served, as one of its most outstanding teachers and scholars, for the rest of her life.

It was here that she met Colin Strang, lecturer in an adjoining department (Philosophy), whom she married in 1955; his father, (Sir) William Strang, who had himself risen from modest origins to become head of the Foreign Office, had been created a peer in the previous year, and Colin, who became Professor of Philosophy at Newcastle in 1975, succeeded as the second Baron Strang in 1978. It was in many ways an ideal partnership, and a source of great strength to Barbara. Their only child, Caroline, was born in 1957.

Barbara quickly established herself as a deeply impressive teacher. But the content of her teaching was to prove no less significant. From a background in conventional philology, she had at an early stage begun to develop that unique integration of descriptive and historical approaches to the study of English Language which was to become the hallmark of the Newcastle Department. In close partnership with Randolph Quirk, at first Reader and soon Professor of English Language in the Durham Colleges, she developed a teaching programme which contributed to her rising reputation in the fast-developing field of linguistics. That reputation was further enhanced in 1962 by the publication of her first book, *Modern English Structure*, which rapidly became a standard work. Her promotion by Newcastle to a new Chair in English Language and General Linguistics in 1964 gave her the opportunity to gather around her a small team of able colleagues in a School which began to be known internationally, and to attract postgraduate students and academic visitors from far afield. A single term's leave in late 1968 to accompany her husband for part of his visiting semester at Harvard enabled her (sitting, he recalls, 'on a balcony in a bathing costume') to produce the first draft of *A History of English*. Published in 1970, it represents the inspired synthesis of 20 years of deep learning and lively interaction with her students, and was immediately recognised as destined to become — as it has indeed become — *the* History for our generation.

During the 1970s she was increasingly involved in university administration. She was frequently on Senate, and the respect in which she was held in the counsels of the university led to a demand for her services in a wider sphere. She served on the University Grants Committee from 1975 to 1980 and thereafter on its Hong Kong counterpart. All these roles were ideally suited to her grasp of complex details — often quarried from the unlikely content of official documents — and to her love of planning. Despite these demands on her time, and a substantial teaching programme, she was heavily involved in a number of long-term research topics which included linguistic analysis of the work of writers such as Swift and Spenser, Shakespeare and Clare. The Tyneside Linguistic Survey, established on her initiative, is the subject of a separate contribution in this volume. Later, when the possibility of early retirement began to open up, a work on dialect in English literature and a history of English rhythm and metre were among the projects for which she was formulating plans.

Such a national and international reputation naturally led to

In Memoriam Barbara Strang

attractive offers of senior posts elsewhere, but her loyalty to the University of Newcastle, the city, and the county, proved even stronger. 'I told them I would only come if they would let me live in Northumberland,' was her explanation to her colleagues of her rejection of one dazzling offer. Her home and family, her students and colleagues, and the richness of local historical associations and of resources for dialect study, were part of the bond which held her. Another was the opportunity for horse-riding, into which she had been initiated by a contemporary and friend at King's College, London, and which replaced her child-hood enthusiasm for ballet dancing. Having fulfilled her long-held ambition to own her own horse, she derived enormous pleasure from regularly riding on the Town Moor and with the Morpeth Hunt, almost always in the company of her daughter.

To everything she undertook Barbara brought intelligence and determination, and it is understandable that this led to an often gruelling personal timetable and ultimately told on her health, though there was little warning of the cerebral haemorrhage which struck her down at home on 11 April 1982. She died the next day, at the age of 56. As the *Times* said in its obituary, her early death robbed the international community of English language scholarship of one of its most considerable figures.

Barbara's most obvious memorial is in her own publications: her books and articles and, no less important to the development of the discipline, her reviews. Professor Richard N. Bailey has provided for this volume as complete a list as is possible of all these. Another memorial is the influence of Barbara on the work of other practitioners of English linguistics, both among her students and colleagues at Newcastle and indeed all over the world, and this volume is a tangible, though of course not necessarily representative, embodiment of that.

A memorial of a third kind is constituted by the memories which her colleagues, students and friends will carry with them for the rest of their lives. If she had published nothing, and if her administrative achievements had been negligible, the immediate influence of Barbara on those around her was of that deeply formative kind which is the mark of the really great teacher. To have been taught by her was a truly memorable experience, as many of the public and private tributes at the time of her death attested. The first reaction to her teaching was commonly awe; the next stage reflected admiration, affection, and gratitude. These feelings were intensified for many who experienced the personal acts of kindness and special concern which it was so characteristic of her to bestow. Typical was her willingness to find time, even at moments of great pressure in her own crowded timetable, for a first-year student struggling (for example) with the intricacies of language, so that she could help him to discover with her its delights. Not that the awe would necessarily diminish on close contact: despite her humanity, there was about her a certain austerity, and a sometimes formidable composure. 'Perhaps,' wrote a close colleague, 'the root of her love of teaching lay in the fact that it allowed the expression of her care and concern which she always seemed to feel, but was not always able to express.' And there were other, very palpable ways in which that kindness and concern were manifested. Not many even of the recipients were aware that studentships and grants for postgraduate work in English Language and in Philosophy were funded by Barbara and Colin Strang personally, and it is a fitting tribute that the University has recognised this in the re-designation of what are now the Strang Studentships. All this helps to explain why, the length and breadth of the British Isles and around the world, there are former students now in many walks of life who look back on the experience of having been taught by Barbara Strang as among the most inspiring events of their lives.

PART I
Old to Middle English Period

1

The Difficulty of Establishing Borrowings Between Old English and the Continental West Germanic Languages

E.G. Stanley
Pembroke College, Oxford

Barbara M.H. Strang, in *A History of English* (London, 1970) § 184, provides her readers with a succinct account of linguistic borrowing within the West Germanic group of languages. She had a special interest in linguistic contacts of different periods, and that emerges from other passages of this book and from various other writings.

In § 184 she follows a long line of scholarly speculations on the history of OE *heretoga* 'dux, comes, ealdorman, eorl', and its West (and thence North) Germanic equivalents. The word in West Germanic had been the subject of a protracted controversy between E. Schröder and R. Much, neither of them really sufficiently at home in the Old English material some of which they used.[1]

Barbara Strang (1970: § 184) sums up what she accepts of the arguments for English:

> Occasionally borrowing can be traced between the Germanic languages. One of the most interesting cases is *here-toʒa* (literally, 'one who draws the army [after him]', 'a general', also used to translate L *consul*). This was first used by Alfred, then in later poetry (where it is one of the survivals into ME). The source of this is WG, and it may have been brought to England by one of Alfred's Continental aides. In turn, WG got it from EG, where it was used in the Gothic Bible as a calque of Greek *strategos*, 'army leader'. Having adopted it, OE characteristically used it as a model for a new formation, *folctoʒa*, in which the first element is translated as *people* (*folk*) or *army*, and means 'the whole people considered in its capacity to form a (national) fighting force'.

Difficulty of Establishing Borrowings Between Languages

In fact, no such calque occurs in the Gothic Bible, but was invented by Schröder as a link in his chain of argument, involving the hypothesised East Germanic origins of the calque.[2] It is said, Germanic *strategoi*, roughly contemporary with Wulfila, fought in Imperial armies; the invented Gothic calque is irrelevant to the problem of establishing borrowings between the early West Germanic languages. For the history of the relationship of Old English to Old Saxon the distribution of OE *heretoga*/OS *heritogo* and OE *folctoga*/OS *folctogo* is important. Schröder suggested that OE *folctoga* was modelled on *heretoga*, and that furthermore the Old Saxon poet of *Heliand* borrowed OS *folctogo* from the *folctoga* of the Old English poets, and used the word once for Herod and three times for Pilate (both of whom he more often called *heritogo*).

As Schröder knew from the dictionaries more or less as fully as we know it from the concordances now,[3] OE *folctoga* occurs only in poetry (fifteen times), *heretoga* occurs rarely in verse (twice in Alfred's *Metres of Boethius* and once in the Exeter Book *Gifts of Men*) but often in prose (161 times, according to the Venezky–Healey *Concordance*). The occurrence in *Gifts of Men* 76 is of interest because the word is varied by the unique *fyrdwisa*, which confirms that the Anglo-Saxons who used them fully understood the elements from which such compounds are constructed.

The compound *folctoga* comes in verse most of which would not generally be accepted as of the time of King Alfred or later, including, *Genesis A*, *Exodus*, *Daniel*, *Beowulf*, *Andreas*, *Juliana*, *Guthlac B*, as well as *Judith* and *Solomon and Saturn* which would be more generally accepted as late. This is not a good basis for Schröder's suggestion that OE *folctoga* was coined on the model of *heretoga*:[4] if, in the ninth century, the *Heliand* poet had an ear for Old English poetry he may have known that the Old English poets did not use the word corresponding to OS *heritogo* but had a word that would correspond to an OS *folctogo* for which he quite happily used *heritogo* more often. On the other hand, it seems no great stroke of poetic genius to coin *folctogo* if one had *heritogo* in ordinary use, and an Old Saxon would not need to go to Old English verse to coin it, quite independently. Schröder's other assumption, that OE *heretoga* is from West Germanic words such as OS *heritogo*, was not, as he thought, strengthened by finding the rare form *heretoha*,[5] and Much lost no time before he pointed that out.[6]

Difficulty of Establishing Borrowings Between Languages

The use of *heretoga* in the Vespasian Psalter Gloss of the middle of the ninth century was overlooked by Schröder as well as by Much.[7] Before any Alfredian text, the gloss has Ps. 67:28 (the earliest of many similar Old English psalter glosses):

ðer   se gungesta in fyrhtu aldermen
Ibi Beniamin adulescentior in pauore principes Iuda

heretogan heara aldermen   7 aldermen
duces   eorum principes Zabulon et principes Neptalim.[8]

Also highly relevant, and overlooked by Schröder and Much, though recorded in Bosworth–Toller, s.v. *teón* (from *teóhan*), II, is a use in the Old English translation of Bede of *teon* + *here* 'to lead an army': 'þa he þæt þa longe tiid dyde, þa gelomp þætte Penda Mercna cyning teah here 7 fyrd wið Eastengle 7 þider to gefeohte cwom',[9] not a slavish translation such as might involve unidiomatic calquing: 'Quod dum multo tempore faceret, contigit gentem Merciorum duce rege Penda aduersus Orientales Anglos in bellum procedere' where it would be unwarranted to see *teon here 7 fyrd* as arising from the double title of Penda *dux rex Merciorum*.[10]

The distribution of the word *heretoga* in the Anglo-Saxon charters is puzzling. According to the Venezky–Healey *Concordance* it comes only seven times, each time as part of the opening formula in documents by Oswald Bishop of Worcester and later Archbishop of York, each time with reference to the permission or leave granted by Ealdorman Ælf(h)ere of Mercia in addition to that of the king (and others): in Robertson charters 34, 42, 46, 55, 56, 57, and 58, all of them in Hemming's Cartulary (in the case of Robertson 46 also British Library Additional Charter 19792), in that part of Hemming given the letter G by N.R. Ker.[11] The documents have reference to transactions datable as follows: 34 AD 962, 42 AD 966, 46 AD 969, 55 AD 977, and 56, 57 and 58 AD 975–8.[12] In the Latin charters in Hemming's Cartulary Ælf(h)ere's rank is given as *dux* or *comes*, and in English *ealdorman* (Robertson 36; and from Cotton MS Claudius C.ix Robertson 51 twice, from Textus Roffensis Robertson 59 twice; in a will British Library Additional MS 15350 of AD 968–71,[13] and in the legal text 'IV Edgar', 15.1).[14] Wulfstan the homilist, in the annal in Cotton MS Tiberius B.iv, AD 975,[15] assigned to him on grounds of style, calls him *Ælfere ealdorman*. Why did seven of Oswald's charters call the ealdorman *heretoga*? I do not believe that the reason is recoverable, and regard it as too easy to shrug it off as mere whim or fashion, as Schröder does.[16]

If we had more early West Mercian texts like the Vespasian Psalter gloss and more texts from the area of the West Mercians, though the texts may be West-Saxonised as the Bede and the Oswald Charters are, we might have evidence for the use of *heretoga* and *teon here* that might lead us to look to pre-Alfredian Mercia rather than to the continent for the use in English of *heretoga* for *dux*, a use with abundant parallels in the cognate West Germanic languages, but not necessarily borrowed from them into English. We have not the evidence to assert with Schröder that *heretoga* was not indigenous in England and was never truly naturalised, especially not for the first half of that assertion. For the second half, it is significant that the use, particularly frequent in Ælfric, of *heretoga* for biblical figures, for Moses above all others, and for other non-Germanic army-leaders was well established in 'classical Old English' prose; but it is rare for English generals.

OE *heretoga* and its relationship to OS *heritogo* may serve as an introduction to the more complicated problems of the dependence, if any, of *Christ III* on the Old Saxon *Heliand* (or perhaps on the source of *Heliand*). Some treatment has recently been given to the subject of such dependence by Roland Zanni in a work with a serviceable bibliography and also an account of the scholarship of the subject, but without perhaps sufficient evaluation of and discrimination between the various contributions and their methodologies.[17] The problem of the indigenousness of *Christ III* is more complicated than that of *heretoga* because it at once got entangled with the now settled problem of the unity of *Christ*, as a single poem by Cynewulf or in three parts of which Cynewulf wrote (and 'signed') only the second. Some of the early defenders of the unity of *Christ* thought that they had to demolish the view that only *Christ III* (or even only parts of *Christ III*) contained features pointing to Old Saxon origins. Now that the text in the Exeter Book is generally accepted as consisting of three separate parts, the demonstration of different origins of the three parts has ceased to be entangled with Cynewulf's authorship. The indigenousness of *Christ III* or its debt to Old Saxon verse is of interest in its own right. The methodology of the demonstration either way is of interest.

Christ III was regarded as having a close connection with Old Saxon verse by O. Grüters, first published as a *Teildruck* of his Bonn dissertation of 1904, and published in full in 1905.[18] Grüters's study was methodologically too weak to bear the weighty conclusions supposedly drawn from it. Some lines in *Christ III*, for example 1379-1427 (I use ASPR numbering throughout), seemed to him significantly dense with what might be Old Saxonisms. G. Binz, writing in 1907, had no difficulty in showing that Grüters's work was unsatisfactory, but Binz himself also wished to show that *Christ III* is, at least in part, dependent on Old Saxon.[19] Of course, he did not wish it to appear that he in his analysis of the Old Saxonisms in *Christ III* was indebted for the idea, though not the methodology, to Grüters, and so he takes care to point out at the start that his, Binz's, demonstration of Old Saxonisms in *Christ III* had not derived its impetus from Grüters; he himself had given expression to the idea in 1904, the year of the *Teildruck* in fact.

Both Binz and Grüters had the example of Sievers and *Genesis B* before them, an example which still reverberates in its triumphant effects in Barbara Strang's § 184: Sievers's boldly asserted and rigorously proved theory of Old Saxon origins for that part of the Old English poem had been rejected by inferior scholars like George Stephens in *Academy* 21 October 1876, 409, as Grüters reminds his readers (p. 2), but the discovery of the Vatican fragments of the Old Saxon *Genesis* vindicated Sievers's brilliant philological deductions. As late as 1948, F. Mossé, at the end of an article on possible Old Saxonisms in *Christ III*, still toys with the possibility that a lucky find may bring proof; but he despairs of such luck:

A moins de quelque heureux hasard qui fasse découvrir un jour le texte vieux-saxon qui a servi à l'auteur anglais de *Christ III*, il ne sera jamais possible d'administrer la preuve de l'emprunt. Pris séparément, chacun des faits que nous venons d'évoquer serait un témoignage insuffisant. Réunis, ces phénomènes qui vont tous dans le même sens, celui de calques involontaires, concourent à fournir une présomption qui n'est peut-être pas négligeable.[20]

Binz relied on words found in Old English only in *Christ III* but more common in Old Saxon. Zanni's monograph gives an historical account of Old Saxonisms discussed in this connection by Binz and others. Binz, however, failed to avail himself of all the lexicographical tools at his disposal, relying too much on Grein's *Sprachschatz* without checking Bosworth–Toller for prose uses.[21] The reviewers had little difficulty in disposing of Binz to their satisfaction.[22]

By the time Binz's material was sifted little remained for continued discussion; but some items, especially the following, were still considered of interest: *crybb, tom, mur.* Mossé still relied on such material in his acceptance of cumulative evidence for philological deductions. It seems doubtful if, when each strand of evidence has been found weak, after proper scrutiny, such evidence can nevertheless combine to give support to the edifice of Old Saxon origins. The case of *Genesis B* was quite different even before the great discovery of 1894. Various classes of borrowings from Old Saxon do not admit of doubt: e.g. *giongorscipe, giongordom*; *romigan*; *hearran hyldo*; *fyrnum, þicce.*[23] Even if in one or two cases the evidence is less convincing because a newly adduced use in Old English reduces it to some extent, e.g. *strið*,[24] or in a more English form, e.g. not *-abal* but *-afol*,[25] the language of *Genesis B* is uniquely different from ordinary Old English as used in verse or prose, that it is significant that a relatively high proportion of its unique features are close to the language of *Heliand.*

Having scrutinised Binz's listings and removed from them item after item as unproven, his critics went over to the attack by seeking proof of English indigenousness of *Christ III* by making the most of those linguistic items which were English and not Old Saxon. In this they may have built upon Sievers's methodology for *Genesis B*. He had been able to contrast the many locutions based on Old Saxon with the few exclusively English in that poem. The distribution was quite different from that in *Christ III*, and it seems a singularly unconvincing procedure to single out *holm* 'sea' (978), as Brown did (p. 95), and regard it as 'a piece of positive evidence against Binz's theory'. W. Krogmann, pointing out that *neorxnawong* (1405) is exclusively English, uses that as evidence.[26] The absence in this poem on Judgement Day of an Old English form of OS *mutspelli* (OHG *muspilli*) is regarded by Krogmann (pp. 26–7) as evidence for the indigenousness of *Christ III*: but forms of the word — so prominent in the minds of *Germanisten* — occur only three times in West Germanic, twice in *Heliand* and once in the Old High German poem that goes under the name of the word,[27] and four times in Old Icelandic literature where it is used rather differently. With such a rare word we can deduce very little from non-occurrence other than that it was not equally prominent in the minds of authors in the Germanic languages. Differently questionable is Krogmann's rejection (pp. 18-21) of Binz's highly unlikely derivation (pp. 187-8) of *feorhgomum* (1548) as having the second element from OS *goma* 'entertainment, banquet' and the first element perhaps OS *fern* (< Latin *infernum*) 'hell'. Krogmann triumphantly points to OFris *gōm* 'punishment',[28] and adds: 'Damit ist auch die letzte Stütze Binz' zusammengebrochen.' The proposed etymology of *feorhgomum* looks away from the obvious sense of the words in Old English: *feorh* 'soul, life' and *goma* 'palate' in pl. 'jaws', leading to an adequate, early representation of hell-mouth as the jaws in which the soul enters, 'soul-jaws', or perhaps, thus Bosworth-Toller, 'fatal or deadly jaws'. (For another depiction of hell-mouth in Old English verse, cf. *Andreas* 1703 *in helle ceafl* 'into the jaws of hell'.) For *Genesis B* this kind of etymology often works well; for example, OE *sælð* 'happiness' is not uncommon, but at 784 the word seems to be OS *selida* 'dwelling'; OE *wǣr* is common as a noun 'agreement' or as an adjective *wǣr* 'prepared'; but *Genesis B* 475 has *wǣr* corresponding to OS *uuār* 'true'. Such etymologies provide a demonstration of Neo-Grammarian skills: after discovering concealed meanings in some words of *Genesis B* the Germanic philologist may therefore be tempted to look for similar concealed Old Saxonisms in *Christ III* if he believes that the poem is of Old Saxon origins.

A complex example of a claim to have detected concealed borrowings from Old Saxon in *Christ III* occurs at line 1440.[29] It may be most convenient to begin with OS *felgian*, thought to underlie the verb in the *Christ* reading: *fylgdon me mid firenum*. In Old Saxon verse *felgian* 'lay, charge, impose (something) upon (a person)' occurs only at *Heliand* 1340, 4968, 5116, and probably 5299.[30] The readings are: *felgiad iu firinspraka endi fiundskepi* (1340 M, C similar): '(they) subjected you to wicked speech and hostility'; *Thar im ok en uuif bigan / felgian firinspraka* (4967b-8a M, C similar): 'Then a woman did also subject him to wicked speech'; *felgidun imu firinuuord fiundo menegi* (5116 M, C similar): 'the multitude of enemies subjected him to wicked words';

> ledian hiet ina lungra mann,   endi lastar spracun,
> folgodun im firinuuord,   thar hie an feteron geng
> bihlagan mid hoscu.   (5298–5300 C, not in M)

where MS *folgodun* is usually emended to *felgidun,* '(Herod) commanded strong men to lead him, and they spoke evil, subjected him to wicked words, where, derided with mockery, he went in fetters'. In the 'Formelverzeichnis' to his edition (s.v. *lästern,* p. 430), Sievers drew attention to the phrase *fylgean mid firenum* in *Christ III.* The etymology of *felgian* is not obvious, and certainly not close to that of OE *folgian, fyl(i)gan* 'follow'. Of cognates (or probable cognates) only OHG *felgen* has senses in any way comparable with those of OS *felgian.*[31] In Old Saxon the word is used in formulas invoking evil, and these rare formulas include explicitly 'evil speech' or 'evil words'. The verb in the Cotton MS at 5299 is significantly different; there is confusion with *folgon* 'follow', cf. OE *folgian, fylgan.* Not everyone favoured the emendation of the Cotton text at 5299; C.W.M. Grein, whose cautious editing of Old English texts has had a lasting influence on Anglo-Saxon textual scholarship and has made it more conservative than is customary in most branches of Germanic studies, suggests that *lastar-spracun* is a compound instr. pl. with *firinuuord* nom. pl.: 'and wicked words pursued him with evil utterances'.[32] That may well be how the Cotton text could be made sense of, but in view of line 5116 a form of the verb *felgian* probably underlies 5299, the reading *folgodun* providing evidence perhaps that *felgian* + dat. of the person + *firin*-compound acc. was obsolescent.

The reading at *Christ III* 1440 is different. Hofmann regards it as the result of an Anglo-Saxon's misunderstanding of an Old Saxon poetic formula, i.e. *felgidun mi firinuuord* 'they subjected me to wicked words'. The text makes sense as it stands, however: 'Then I received before the people the hatred of enemies; they pursued me with iniquities; they did not shrink from hostility, and with scourges they struck.' (For a similar use in verse of *fylgian* 'pursue', cf. *Pharaoh* 3: 'þa hy folc godes / þurh feondscipe fylgan ongunn[on]', 'when through enmity they did pursue God's people'.) The context of *Christ III* 1440a is significantly concerned with the iniquity of hating Christ and giving expression to that hatred in physical violence causing corporal pain (*licsar* 1429), buffeting (*hearmslege* 1434) of head and countenance, spitting from the mouth of the ungodly (*arleasra spatl / of muðe* 1435-6), the drink of vinegar and gall (1438), then the lines (1439-41a) just quoted in translation. The poem goes on to *þæt sar* 'the pain' at 1441b, referring to the crowning with thorns (1443b-45) as well as perhaps to the torments of the preceding lines; and the crowning with thorns is indeed accompanied by *hosp ond heardcwide* 'abuse and obloquy' (1443a) in the text as we have it.

The text as we have it: but here too bringing into line with a hypothesised Old Saxon original is proposed. P.J. Cosijn proposed emendation of MS *heard cwide* to *hearmcwide*.[33] The compound *heardcwide* is *hapax legomenon*; *hearmcwide* (OS *harm-quidi*, cf. OHG *harmquiti* once) occurs more often. Because of *Heliand* 5303a (only four lines after MS *folgodun im firinuuord* emended to *felgidon*, as we have seen) *hosc endi harmquidi* Hofmann sees further evidence in *Christ III* 1443 *hosp ond heardcwide* (emended to *hearmcwide*) for Old Saxon origins of the Old English poem. Hofmann points to *Christ III* 1120 *hysptun hearmcwidum*, and after changing *heardcwide* to *hearmcwide* at 1443 he regards *hosp ond hearmcwide* as an accommodation into an English poetic formula of an Old Saxon poetic formula (attested three times in *Heliand*: 1896, 3528, 5303).[34] Though Old English has *husc* (and also *husclic, husclice, huscword*), there is no reason to think that to an Anglo-Saxon the etymologically closer *husc* would seem closer to OS *hosc* than would *hosp*, especially when the OS *to hosca hebban* (four times in *Heliand*) corresponds, as Sievers pointed out, to OE *habban on hospe*, and OS *te hosce don* corresponds to OE *to hospe don*, and similar phrases. The Venezky-Healey *Concordance* reveals some ten uses of such locutions as these (excluding many more with *geworden*). In many cases we are dealing with literal translations of the common *factus est opprobrium* as OE *gedon is hosp*, and as we consider formulas in Old English and Old Saxon we cannot easily distinguish the stock of poetic formulas common to the Germanic languages from the common debt the Anglo-Saxons and the continental speakers of West Germanic owe to the vocabulary of Christianity. Seeing that literate West Germanic authors shared not only in a community of faith but also, as a result of belonging to the same language group with common poetic traditions, in a community of literary expression, we cannot use *isolated* locutions, as do Binz, Mossé and Hofmann, to prove for *Christ III* what the *widespread* Old Saxonisms of *Genesis B* had enabled Sievers to demonstrate with a high degree of certainty — long before the discovery of 1894 proved him right.

On the other hand, a comparative study of these closely related languages may reveal possible meanings. Old English has *heoloðcynn* at *Christ III* 1541, a *hapax legomenon*. Grein, *Sprachschatz* (1864), renders it 'incolae tartari'; the next word is *heoloþ-helm* 'unsichtbar machender Helm'. A.S. Cook[35] accepted that as 'dwellers in hell' in the glossary and he gives a reference to *heoloþhelm* in his notes. The word *heoloþhelm* is used of the devil at *Whale* 45 *heoloþhelme biþeaht helle seceð* 'covered with a helmet of invisibility he goes to hell'. The common OE poetic word *hæle(ð)* is not found as the first element of a compound, and *Genesis B* 444 *hæleðhelm* has rightly been explained as translating *heliðhelm* of the lost Old Saxon original.[36] The word occurs at *Heliand* 5452. *Heliand* twice has *helidcunni*, at 1411 in collocation with *forhelan* 'conceal' and varying *liudi dernea* 'hidden or insidious people'; but at 2624 the sense 'concealed, insidious' is not involved, and though in Old Saxon too the common word *helið* 'man' nowhere else forms a compound, the compound here must stand for *heliðo cunni* 'mankind' used at 1682 and 5096 (though the compound should not be emended away). In Old Saxon the compound is ambiguous; in Old English the different vowels of *heoloð-* and *hæleð-* leave no room for ambiguity. Binz (p. 187) regards *heoloðcynn* at *Christ III* 1541 as the result of confusion because the Old English translator of Binz's hypothetical Old Saxon source gave to the first element of a supposed underlying *heliðcunni* the sense that element has in *heliðhelm*. Since that sense fits the Old English context well, and since the word occurs nowhere else in Old English, a language in which the common *hæle(ð)* does not form compounds, it is to be regarded as right. This unique Old English use provides no evidence either for Old Saxon origins of *Christ III*, nor even for Old English origins of *Heliand*.[37]

We may return to Barbara Strang, § 184:

> The chances of our being able to detect an inter-Germanic compound borrowing are extremely slender; the amount of evidence we have indicates that these words must have wandered about a good deal between the various Germanic languages. Throughout the period, English contributed at least as much as it received in this matter.

Notes

1. The most important articles are: E. Schröder, '"Herzog" und "Fürst". Über Aufkommen und Bedeutung zweier Rechtswörter', *Zeitschrift der Savigny Stiftung für Rechtsgeschichte* Germanistische Abteilung 44 (1924), 2-9; answered by R. Much, '"Herzog", ein altgermanischer Name des dux', in the same journal, 45 (1925), 1-12; Schröder again, 'Herzog', *Nachrichten der Gesellschaft der Wissenschaften zu Göttingen*, Philologisch-Historische Klasse, subsection IV, 1932, 182-95; and Much again, 'Der Streit um das Wort Herzog', *Teuthonista*, 9 (1933), 105-16. C.T. Carr, *Nominal Compounds in Germanic*, St Andrews University Publications No. XLI (1939), 5-6, provides a brief summary of aspects of the controversy; he inclines towards Schröder's side of the argument, and finds support in the acceptance of his views in several works of reference, T. Frings, *Germania Romana*, Halle 1932, F. Holthausen, *Altenglisches etymologisches Wörterbuch*, Heidelberg 1934, and the eleventh edition of F. Kluge, *Etymologisches Wörterbuch der deutschen Sprache*, revised by A. Goetze, Berlin and Leipzig 1934.

2. Cf. S. Feist, *Vergleichendes Wörterbuch der gotischen Sprache*, Leiden 1939, 479b.

3. J. Bosworth and T.N. Toller, *An Anglo-Saxon Dictionary*, Oxford 1882-98; Toller, *Supplement*, Oxford 1908-21; C.W.M. Grein, *Sprachschatz der angelsächsischen Dichter*, revised by J.J. Köhler and F. Holthausen, Heidelberg 1912-14; J.B. Bessinger, Jr., and Philip H. Smith, Jr., *A Concordance to The Anglo-Saxon Poetic Records*, Ithaca and London 1978; R.L. Venezky and A. diP. Healey, *A Microfiche Concordance to Old English*, Toronto 1980.

4. *Nachrichten* 1932, pp. 187-8.

5. *Zeitschrift der Savigny Stiftung* 44, 5, and again *Nachrichten* 1932, p. 190.

6. *Zeitschrift der Savigny Stiftung* 45, 4-5, and again *Teuthonista* 9, 106-7. Cf. E. Sievers, *Angelsächsische Grammatik*, 3rd edn, Halle 1898, § 214 Anm. 3; and see now K. Brunner's revision of Sievers, *Altenglische Grammatik*, Tübingen 1965, § 214 Anm. 4; A. Campbell, *Old English Grammar*, Oxford 1959, § 447. Cf. A. Campbell, in D.H. Wright and A. Campbell, *The Vespasian Psalter*, Early English Manuscripts in Facsimile, XIV (1967), 83.

7. H. Sweet lists it in the right place of the glossary in what was the standard edition. *The Oldest English Texts*, EETS, o.s. 83 (1885), 582/2; also C. Grimm, *Glossar zum Vespasian-Psalter und den Hymnen*, Anglistische Forschungen 18 (1906), 117.

8. See Sweet, p. 279; Sherman M. Kuhn, *The Vespasian Psalter*, Ann Arbor 1965, 62.

9. Edited by T. Miller, EETS, o.s. 95 (1890), 208, lines 17-18. The passage is referred to significantly in H.R. Loyn, 'The Term *Ealdorman* in the Translations Prepared at the time of King Alfred', *EHR* 68 (1953), 515. Loyn provides a good survey of Alfredian terms, and suggests that *heretoga* is used for *dux* quite specifically in the *dux*'s function as military leader.

10. *Ecclesiastical History* iii. 18, edited by B. Colgrave and R.A.B. Mynors, Oxford 1969, 268, lines 7-9.

11. A.J. Robertson, *Anglo-Saxon Charters*, Cambridge 1939. See N.R. Ker, 'Hemming's Cartulary', in R.W. Hunt, W.A. Pantin and R.W. Southern (eds), *Studies in Medieval History Presented to F.M. Powicke*, Oxford 1948, 49-75, especially 54-5.

12. P.H. Sawyer, *Anglo-Saxon Charters*, Royal Historical Society Guides and Handbooks 8 (1968), Nos 1299, 1309, 1326, 1332, 1373, 1374, 1372.

13. D. Whitelock, *Anglo-Saxon Wills*, Cambridge 1930, No. 9, and see her notes pp. 124, 176.

14. F. Liebermann, *Gesetze der Angelsachsen*, I, Halle 1903, 214.

15. J. Earle and C. Plummer, *Two of the Saxon Chronicles Parallel*, i (Oxford 1892), 121. See K. Jost, 'Wulfstan und die angelsächsische Chronik', *Anglia* 47 (1923), 105-23. For Ælfhere's relationship to Ælfwine of *The Battle of Maldon* (Ælfhere died in 983, the battle took place in 991), see Margaret A.L. Locherbie-Cameron, 'Ælfwine's Kinsmen and *The Battle of Maldon*', *N & Q* 223 (1978), 486-7.

16. *Zeitschrift der Savigny Stiftung* 44, 4, 'das ist aber ebenso eine Laune oder Mode, wie wenn eben diesem Aelfhere z.B. in [Birch] Nr. 1182 "Eadgarus basileus" vorausgeht.' The reference is to Sawyer No. 1310, Robertson 43 of A.D. 966, also from Hemming G. Instead of asserting whim or fashion for *basileus*, Schröder might have consulted A.S. Napier and W.H. Stevenson, *The Crawford Collection of Early Charters and Documents*, Anecdota Oxoniensia IV. vii (1895), 110-11, 137; and cf. F.E. Harmer, *Anglo-Saxon Writs*, Manchester 1952, 455.

17. *Heliand, Genesis und das Altenglische: Die altsächsische Stabreimdichtung im Spannungsfeld zwischen germanischer Oraltradition und altenglischer Bibelepik*, Quellen und Forschungen zur Sprach- und Kulturgeschichte der germanischen Völker, n.F. 76 (200), Berlin and New York 1980.

18. 'Über einige Beziehungen zwischen altsächsischer und altenglischer Dichtung', *Bonnger Beiträge zur Anglistik* 17 (1905), 1-50.

19. Binz added a footnote to say that he intended to write shortly on the influence which he assumed Low German had had on *Christ III* to his review of A.J. Barnouw's *Textkritische Untersuchungen nach dem Gebrauch des bestimmten Artikels und des schwachen Adjectivs in der altenglischen Poesie*, Leiden 1902, in *Zeitschrift für deutsche Philologie* 36 (1904), 273. (I do not know if it would have been impossible for Binz to have got that footnote in after he had read Grüters's *Teildruck*.) See G. Binz, 'Untersuchungen zum altenglischen sogenannten Crist', *Festschrift zur 49. Versammlung Deutscher Philologen und Schulmänner in Basel im Jahre 1907*, Basle 1907, 181-97.

20. F. Mossé opens his article (in which he still supports Binz), 'Poésie saxonne et poésie anglaise à l'époque carolingienne (à propos de *Christ III*)', *Études Germaniques* 3 (1948), 157-65, with the glorious example of Sievers on *Genesis*; he recalls the objections and reservations of E. Hönncher, 'Studien zur angelsächsischen Genesis: Zur Interpolation der angelsächsischen Genesis Vers 235-851', *Anglia*

7 (1884), 469-96 — but Hönncher never questioned Sievers's linguistic analysis and conclusions, and since the article appeared originally as a Leipzig doctoral dissertation directed by Sievers it would have been surprising had he done so — as well as the objections and reservations of B. ten Brink, *History of English Literature* (translated by H.M. Kennedy), London 1883, i, 83-5 and 377-9; in the former passage ten Brink, in fact, accepts Sievers, but with some reservations; in the latter passage ten Brink again accepts Sievers's views, but ascribes *Genesis B* to an Old Saxon translator working in England, not an Englishman translating Old Saxon. In this belief he is followed by Timmer (and also by Barbara Strang § 184); but I remain unconvinced. Modern translators have as their ideal to render, for example, Modern Dutch or Modern German into idiomatic Modern English, avoiding especially all 'false friends' (i.e. expressions in the foreign language which look like English expressions but which are very different in sense), rendering longer customary usages not word for word but by their equivalents in sense (e.g. the owls carried to Athens in Greek become in English coals carried to Newcastle). Much medieval translation is not like that. Instead, foreign expressions are accommodated into the translation language with less regard to the idiomatic usage of that language, stretching the receiving language not merely beyond custom but even beyond comprehensibility at times.

21. C.W.M. Grein, *Sprachschatz der angelsächsischen Dichter*, Cassel and Göttingen 1861-4; the revised edition by J.J. Köhler and F. Holthausen appeared in 1912-14, at Heidelberg. J. Bosworth and T.N. Toller, *An Anglo-Saxon Dictionary*, Oxford 1882-98. Toller's *Supplement* was published (Oxford) 1908-21.

22. See especially L.L. Schücking, *Archiv* 120 (1908), 209-12; the review-article by C.H. Gerould, 'Studies in the *Crist*', *Englische Studien* 41 (1909), 1-19; and Carleton Brown, *Englische Studien*, 45 (1912), 94-8. They reviewed Binz's article issued as a separate.

23. See the still very useful original paper by E. Sievers, *Der Heliand und die angelsächsische Genesis*, Halle 1875. Cf. B.J. Timmer's introduction to his edition, *The Later Genesis*, Oxford 1948, 27-38.

24. See Timmer, pp. 27-8: S.J. Crawford (ed.), *Exameron Anglice*, Bibliothek der angelsächsischen Prosa x (1921), reprinted Darmstadt 1968, variant from Corpus Christi College Cambridge MS 302 of line 328.

25. See Timmer, p. 32: Wulfstan's *Institutes of Polity*, ed. K. Jost, Swiss Studies in English 47 (1959), 40, I a, 3 line 2; *weoroldafol* occurs more frequently. Cf. Feist (see n. 2), p. 1*a*, but, in fact, though the word is orthographically un-English in the form *abal*, Old Saxon or Old High German cognates do not survive.

26. 'Die Bodenständigkeit des Crist III', *Zeitschrift für Mundartforschung* 21 (1953), 1-28; see p. 25.

27. The title was given by the first editor, J.A. Schmeller: 'Muspilli Bruchstück einer alliterirenden Dichtung vom Ende der Welt. Aeltestes Denkmal hochdeutscher Poesie', *Neue Beiträge zur vaterländischen Geschichte, Geographie und Statistik* 1 (1832), 89-117. Schmeller, in

his translation into Modern German, does not translate the word, but gives it as *Muspille* (p. 110), with a long explanation (p. 111).

28. See W.L. van Helten, *Zur Lexicologie des Altwestfriesischen*, Verhandelingen der Koninklijke Akademie van Wetenschappen te Amsterdam, Afdeeling Letterkunde, Nieuwe Reeks I, 5 (1896), 24. The word occurs in *Dat boeck des keysers Rodulphi*, ed. K. von Richthofen, *Friesische Rechtsquellen*, Berlin 1840, 428a line 15; H.S.E. Bosvan der Heide, *Het Rudolfsboek*, in (J.M.N. Kapteyn's) Friesch-Saksische Bibliotheek, III (Assen 1937), 102 line 187. Binz's etymology is, in fact, from Grein's *Sprachschatz* (1861), s.v. *feorhgôme*.

29. See D. Hofmann, 'Die altsächsische Bibelepik ein Ableger der angelsächsischen geistlichen Epik?', *Zeitschrift für deutsches Altertum* 89 (1959), 173–90; cf. W. Krogmann, 'Crist III und Heliand', in W. Schröder (ed.), *Festschrift für Ludwig Wolff zum 70. Geburtstag*, Neumünster 1962, 111–19. Zanni has an account of the supposed borrowing, pp. 73–9.

30. *Heliand* is quoted from E. Sievers's edition, Halle 1878, the Munich MS (M) rather than the Cotton MS (C); cf. E.H. Sehrt, *Vollständiges Wörterbuch zum Heliand und zur altsächsischen Genesis*, Göttingen 1925 (reprinted 1966).

31. Cf. R. Grosse (E. Karg-Gasterstädt and T. Frings), *Althochdeutsches Wörterbuch*, iii/9–10, cols 720–1, esp. 4 '*imprecari*'.

32. 'Zur Kritik und Erklärung des Heliand', *Germania* 11 (1866), 215. Hofmann (p. 176) interprets the Cotton reading as arising from a misunderstanding of an original form of *felgian* along the lines of Grein's interpretation, except that he does not use Grein's interpretation *lastar-spracun*. Presumably he would begin the sentence with *Folgodun*.

33. 'Anglosaxonica. IV', *Beiträge zur Geschichte der deutschen Sprache und Literatur* 23 (1898), 114, accepted by Hofmann, p. 176.

34. See Sievers, *Heliand*, p. 448, s.v. *spott*, with a reference to *Christ* 1443 *hosp ond heardcwide* (unemended).

35. *The Christ of Cynewulf*, Boston 1900, 2nd edn 1909.

36. See Grein, *Sprachschatz* (1864), p. 22; Timmer has a good note in his edition, p. 106, though no West Mercian stage need be assumed in the phonological history of the text.

37. The latter assumption is made by Krogmann, 'Der Schöpfer des altsächsischen Epos. Fortsetzung', *Zeitschrift für deutsche Philologie* 78 (1959), 34. Cf. Hofmann, pp. 178, 185.

2
Cyn(e)wulf Revisited: The Problem of the Runic Signatures

Roger Lass
University of Cape Town

1

The four 'signed' Old English poems attributed to 'Cynewulf'[1] (solely on the basis of their problematic runic 'signatures' themselves) are one of the perenially fascinating curiosities of Old English literature, both because of the rarity of any kind of 'signature'[2] at all in Old English texts (Woolf, 1955:8f), and because of the problems involved in interpreting them. In this paper I will not offer a final solution to the Cynewulf problem, but rather attempt to clear something of a path through the interpretive jungle, and dispose of some of the worst interpretations.

The 'signatures' consist of groups of runes in epilogue-like portions of four poems: *Christ II* and *Elene* (Exeter Book) and *Juliana* and *Fates of the Apostles* (Vercelli Book). These epilogues are distinguished from the preceding text by a shift from relatively impersonal heroic-style narrative to a personal concern with eschatology and individual salvation. But before going into the texts themselves in any detail, it is worth saying a word about MS runes in general, and some possible interpretations of the particular individual runes that appear.

2

The interpretation of MS runes should on the face of it not be too difficult; we have the remains of what is apparently a fairly stable and uniform tradition in the numerous *fuþorcs* or runic alphabets that have been preserved in MSS (see Derolez, 1954 for a survey), as well as (for the Old English tradition, which is all I'm concerned with here) a poem that explains the runes.

Manuscript runes were generally used in two ways: either phonetically, representing the first letter of their names (as generally in epigraphy) or 'ideographically' (logographically), standing for a word (their name: see below). Examples of the latter use are the *ēþel* rune in *Beowulf* 520 *swæsne* . ᛟ ., 913 . ᛟ . *scyldinga*, 1702 . ᛟ . *weard*; or the *man* rune in *The Ruin* 232 . ᛗ . *dreama*, etc. We may have examples of both uses in the Cynewulf runes, as we will see.

The Cynewulfian epilogues represent what Derolez (1954: xxxi) calls an 'autonomous tradition' of runic writing: MS as opposed to epigraphic runes. This tradition is late, post-dating the introduction of the Latin alphabet for writing Germanic vernaculars, and had become, by the time of the earliest MSS, 'a fossil ... a curiosum incapable of further evolution' (Derolez, lvii). It seems likely in fact (cf. Derolez, xxiii) that by the time our texts were written,[3] however well-known the names of the runes and their significations might have been to the reading public,[4] their use represented a kind of (self-conscious?) 'archaising'.

From the combined evidence of the MS *fuþorcs* and the *Rune Poem* (8th–9th c.: cf. Dobbie (1942:xlix f), which is basically of the 'A is for Apple' type, we can derive an apparently nearly unanimous tradition concerning the names and letter-values of the runes. Derolez appears to have examined all the extant English *fuþorcs*, and a composite drawn from his work yields the following archetype for the relevant runes (here given in their usual *fuþorc* order:

Rune	Name	Meaning
ᚠ	*feoh* (usually Angl. *feh*)	cattle, wealth
ᚢ	*ūr*	aurochs
ᚳ	*cēn*[5]	torch
ᚣ	*ȳr*[6]	bow (?)
ᚹ	*wyn* (often Kt. *wen*)	joy
ᚾ	*nēd* (sometimes *nead, nyd*)	necessity, hardship
ᛖ	*eoh* (often Angl. *eh*)	horse
ᛚ	*lagu*	water

On the basis of this evidence, and that of the *Rune Poem*, there seems no real possibility of ascribing any other names to the runes (though people have wanted to: see the comments below on various interpretations). What evidence there is fixes the traditional (usually common Germanic) ascriptions quite firmly, though there are some difficult cases. The *Rune Poem* in any case backs up the *fuþorcs* by giving descriptions of what the runes represent. Most of the names are unproblematical anyhow; only *cēn, ȳr,* and *ūr* cause any difficulty.

One problem with *cēn* is that the word (like *ūr* and *ȳr*) seems to exist in Old English only as a rune name (Sisam, 1953:20), and to fit some of its contexts in the epilogues only with difficulty. Further, the Germanic tradition is not unanimous on the name of this rune, the Old Norse texts giving *kaun* (< */kaun-a-z/*'ulcer'?), while the OE name is probably < */ke:n-a-z/* 'torch' (no cognates outside Germanic, but cf. OHG *kien*, MLG *kēn*; for discussion Elliot, 1963:57 and refs). But the description in the *Rune Poem* (16ff: text from Dobbie, 1942) is unambiguous:

ᚳ byþ cwicera gehwam   cuþ on fyre,
blac and beorhtlic,   byrneþ oftust
ðær hi æþelingas   inne restaþ.

Ȳr is generally assumed to mean 'bow', but the passage in the poem is unclear (84ff):

ᚣ by æþelinga   and eorla gehwæs
wyn and wyrþmynd,   byþ on wicge fæger,
fæstlic on færelde,   fyrdgeatwa sum.

All this says is that it's a piece of war-equipment, not specifically a bow; indeed, if *on wicge* means what it looks like, i.e. 'on (a) horse', rather than what it might be a misspelling of, *on wīge* 'in battle', bow seems unlikely. Brooks (1961:126) suggests, rather plausibly, that it may be a sharp-pointed weapon of some type, on the basis of the term *æxe-yre* in one of the OE chronicles. I will look at the relevance of this in considering the individual signatures; we will be forced, at any rate, to accept 'bow' or some other weapon name as the basic sense of *ȳr*.

The last rune which causes some trouble is *ūr*, which according to tradition and the *Rune Poem* must mean 'aurochs' (*Bos primogenius*, the European bison: ON *úrr*, OHG *ūro*). The poem has (4ff):

   ᚻ byþ anmod   and oferhyrned,
   felafrecne deor,   feohteþ mid hornum,
   mære morstapa;   þæt is modig wuht.

The problem is that only one of the signatures seems to allow this reading, no matter how hard we try. But there is a way out via homophony, as we will see.

Many variant meanings have been proposed for these 'difficult' runes; some, which are homophones or near-homophones, like *cēne* 'bold' for *cēn* may be at least provisionally acceptable (though see below); others, which are simply other words beginning with the same letter, are not — no matter how tempting they might be because of the sense they yield. The trouble with the various *ad hoc* interpretations that have been proposed (for an imposing list see Cook, 1900:155f) is that many fit only one signature; and it is only natural to assume that if the signatures are in fact some kind of acrostic, and in at least three out of four cases (except for *Juliana*: see below) also ideographic, they would defeat their own apparent purpose if the runes were not unambiguously interpretable by any reader. And this proposes a known and accepted meaning for each rune.

3

Now to the four signatures. All appear in passages that serve as epilogues to their poems, and all are non-narrative; they are sombre, elegiac pieces, dominated by a mixture of naturalistic depression at the thought of approaching death and eschatological terror. Let us look first at what is perhaps the most doubtful of the lot (due to the mutilated MS),[8] and which also stands apart from the others because of the self-conscious way it announces itself as a puzzle. This is the one in *Fates*. After the fates of the apostles have been recounted, the poet asks the reader who has enjoyed the poem to pray for him when he has to leave this earth, and let his body *wælræf wunigean, weormum to hrofre* (95). Then, apparently so the clever reader can figure out who to pray for, he writes (96ff):

   Her mæg findan   foreþances gleaw,
   se ðe hine lysteð   leoðgiddunga,

hwa þas fitte fedge. . ᛦ . þær on ende standeþ,
eorlas æs on eorðan brucað;   ne moton hie awa ætsomne
woruldwunigende. . ᛒ . sceal gedreosan
. ᚾ . on eðle,   æfter tohweorfan
læne lices frætwa,   efne swa . ᛚ . toglideð.
þonne . ᚻ . ond . ᛗ .   cræftes neotað
nihtes nearowe,   on him . ᛏ . ligeð,
cyninges þeodom.   Nu ðu cunnon miht
hwa on þam wordum wæs werum oncyðig.

If this were the only signature, would we call him 'Cynewulf'? The text says FWULCYN, which is impossible (*/fw/ is not a legal OE cluster),[9] but surely WULFCYN would be a reasonable first approximation.[10] (What happens — theologically — if a misled reader prays for 'Wulfcyn'?) It is also worth noting that this text (properly reordered) and *Christ II* read CYNWULF, while *Juliana* and *Elene* have CYNEWULF. What *was* his name? (Actually, if the first element is PGmc */kuni-/, we would expect *Cyne-*, since deletion of unstressed vowels is general only after heavy syllables; and there appears to be no OE word whose first syllable goes back to PGmc */ku:ni/*.)

Assuming however that we have an anagram of CYNWULF, how do we read the 'difficult' runes? To begin with, *ūr* must probably be treated as a (partial) homophone of the first person possessive pronoun (plural), since no reading of 100b–101a with 'aurochs' seems possible: 'Joy shall fall/aurochs in (our) native land'? Obviously not. But 'Our joy shall fall...' is fine.[11]

Now what about *cēn* and *ȳr*? If we accept the conjecture (J.C. Pope, personal communication) that these runes are to be read 'I, Cynewulf', then what about the plural *neotað*? We could of course emend to *neoteð* (and indeed the scribe's *standað* for *standeð* in the same poem, l. 86, makes one want to). But there is no evidence for runes being read this way, and I would not want to emend on such tenuous grounds.

Brooks (1961:125f) suggests (illegitimately, by my argument at the end of § 2) that *ȳr* can be read here as 'horn' (i.e. inkhorn), and renders the passage attractively as 'while torch and ink-horn employ their function with labour in the night'. But his other conjecture, that if *ȳr* can be a pointed weapon, then it might be extended to mean 'quill' or 'pen-knife', is a bit better. This of course stands or falls on how one interprets the *ȳr* section of the *Rune Poem*; but that's vague enough to allow this reading to be possible, maybe.

4

Now let us look at the other slightly 'abnormal' passage, in *Juliana*. This is unusual, not in tone, or in being an anagram, but in the grouping of the runes. After declaring his need for divine help, the poet writes (699b ff; text from Woolf, 1955):

> Min sceal of lice
> sawul on siðfæt,   nat ic sylfa hwider,
> eardes uncyðþu;   of sceal ic þissum
> secan oþerne   ærgewyrhtum
> gongan iudædum.   Geomor hweorfeð
> . ᚳ . . ᚣ . 7 . ᚾ .   Cyning biþ reþe
> sigora syllend, þonne synnum fah,
> . ᛗ . . ᚹ . 7 . ᚢ .   acle bidað
> hwæt him æfter dædum   deman wille
> lifes to leane;   . ᛚ . . ᚠ . beofað,
> seomað sorgcearig.   Sar eal gemon,
> synna wunde   þe ic siþ oþþe ær
> geworhte in worulde ...

The passage makes no sense at all if we assume that the runes in the first two groups are being used ideographically: 703b–704a for instance would read 'Sadly will journey torch, bow and necessity'; the later 'horse, joy and aurochs' isn't any better as subject of *bidað*. So the usual type of solution is to take these two groups as simply alphabetic (as in epigraphic runes) — even though 7 'and' gives us some trouble (more of which below). If we do this, the first two groups give us real words: CYN and EWU respectively (with *and* suppressed). (Note that this is the only place in the four signatures where *ūr* could be read 'aurochs' — since if we read the runes alphabetically their meaning makes no difference anyway).

So, taken alphabetically, the tricky passage reads: 'Sadly will journey CYN ... the giver of victory will be fierce when (the) EWU, terrified, sin-stained, await ...' Sisam suggests (1953:21) that we could read CYN in an extended sense as 'the race of men', and EWU as 'sheep'; but *ewu* appears to mean 'ewes' in

Old English, not 'sheep' generically. I don't think, however, that this is an insuperable difficulty; though Sisam (*ibid*) gives up on this one and claims that 'the runes have only their value as letters spelling his name'. But it could be argued that the substitution of ewes for the more traditional general sheep in this kind of context (e.g. of the type *Grex perditus factus est populus meus*: Jer. 50:6) is pardonable in difficult conditions, like those of an acrostic (or whatever this is). And it might even be more effective — frightened ewes being even more frightened than frightened rams, or sheep of mixed sexes.

So let's accept CYN and EWU. We still have a problem with the final group, which reads, if we follow the same strategy, LF. Since this is rubbish, we must change tack; leaving aside contentious novelties like Trautmann's *lic-fæt* (Tupper 1912:136), which is unsupported by tradition and uninterpretable without it, we must still read a compound here. And what we get is *lagu-feoh*. While this is a *hapax*, Tupper (*loc. cit.*) nonetheless makes a good case for accepting it with the sense 'watery estate', i.e. 'earth'. I see no reason why a kenning shouldn't be acceptable here.[12]

The only other solution would seem to be Sisam's, that each group of runes be allowed to represent the name CYNEWULF, so that the three relevant lines read:

Geomor hweorfeð / CYNEWULF ...
CYNEWULF acle bidað ...
CYNEWULF beofað ...

This of course makes a mess of the verb concord: why one plural and two singulars? Of course, *hweorfeð* could be agreement to the nearest noun of a set of conjuncts, or to CYN as a singular; and *bidað* could be agreement to the number of the conjoined nouns together, or to EWU; and *beofað* ought to be singular no matter how we read LF. (Or we could, with the arrogance of editors who *know* what the text must mean, emend to *beof[i]að*.)

In addition, of course, there's no evidence for this way of reading runes; the other signatures don't work this way, and we still have the problem of *and*. (Though with an interpretive strategy this unconstrained, we could just suppress this, I suppose, or claim that it's there 'for metrical reasons'.)[13] Anyhow, under the CYNEWULF reading for each group, the second must be ungrammatical; or is this a pointer to the trick? Unfortunately, however, for all our interpretations, it seems to be the case that when we get rune-groups of the form R_1 (R_2) & R_3, we have to read them just that way (e.g. *Husband's Message* 51a, Riddle 24, 8a, Riddle 64 throughout). So this is still a problem.

Of all the solutions offered, the best seems to be that of taking the first two groups as CYN and EWU, and the last as LAGU-FEOH. But the intrusive *and* is a nuisance, and makes me suspect that this is not the way it was meant to be read, and that we're all missing the point. Shall we simply agree to call it a *locus desperatus*?

5

The next passage is at the end of *Christ II*, in a description of the Last Judgement (798ff; text from Krapp and Dobbie, 1961):

> þonne . ᚳ . cwacað,   gehyreð cyning mæðlan,
> rodera ryhtend,   sprecan reþe word
> þam þe him ær on worulde   wace hyrdon,
> þendan . ᛗ . ond . ᛏ .   yþast meahtan
> frofre findan.   þær sceal forht monig
> on þam wong stede   werig bidan
> hwæt him æfter dædum   deman wille
> wraþra wita.   Biþ se . ᚹ . scæcen
> eorþan frætwa. . ᚳ . wæs long
> . ᚾ . flodum bilocen,   lifwynna dæl,
> . ᚠ . on foldan.

Cēn in the first line is a bit difficult. As early as 1840 (cf. Cook, 1900:154) Kemble suggested *cēne* as the reading for the rune here; but unfortunately the rune name has no final *-e*, and *cēne* < */koːni/* always does. This prevents us, I think, from assuming the potential *ūr*-type homophony here.[14] A pity, though, because *cēne* used substantively ('the bold ones') is just what we need here, i.e. the bold quaking on hearing the voice of the judging God. If *cēn* is read as the rune name, we get a rather obtuse and (I think) un-Cynewulfianly vague image: the *cēn* hearing the King speak must be something like the soul, under the similitude of a windblown flame. But I suppose it's possible.

Now to *ȳr*. The way it is combined with the *nēd* rune almost tempts one toward Kemble's *yrmðu* (cf. Cook, 195); the *fuþorcs* don't distinguish long and short vowels, so the only obstacle is the unanimity of tradition against nonce-readings. If we take *ȳr* as 'bow' or some unspecified weapon, perhaps we could read *yr ond ned* as a kenning for 'fighting' or 'strife'? On the same lines we could borrow a leaf from Sisam, and read 'CYNEWULF ond NED', perhaps as a hendiadys for 'oppressed Cynewulf'. But Occam says no.

6

Now to the last of the four signatures, the one at the end of *Elene* (1256b ff; text from Gradon, 1958):

      A wæs secg oð ðæt
cnyssed cearwelmum, . ⊓ . drusende
þeah þe he in medohealle maðmas þege,
æplede gold. . ⊓ . gnornode,
. ✝ . gefera nearsorge dreah,
enge rune þær him . M . fore
milpaðas mæt, modig þrægde,
wirum gewlenced. . Þ . is geswiðrad,
gomen æfter gearum, geoguð is gecyrred,
ald onmedla. . ⊓ . wæs geara
geogoðhades glæm; nu synt gcardagas
æfter fyrstmearce forð gewitene,
lifwynne geliden swa . ᚾ . toglideð,
flodas gefsed. . ᛉ . æghwam bið
læne under lyfte ...

Cēn can be read as it was (if a bit reluctantly) in *Christ*, as a metaphor for the life of man. But here the image isn't so strained, since the flame is required only to be dying, not hearing God's voice. The image itself is in fact rather commonplace, but clear. *Ȳr* is also less of a problem here than in the others, and whether we read it as 'bow' or 'unspecified (sharp?) weapon' it makes equal sense. There is no need for alternatives like 'horn' — even if it is perhaps easier to imagine a (non-ink-) horn lamenting literally than a weapon. But this is a poem; and what could be more fitting in an elegiac passage like this, lamenting vanished glory and creeping age, than a disused weapon complaining of its uselessness, watching others going off to battle on resplendent horses?[15] In this case we should read .✝. *gefera* as 'necessary companion' or 'companion in (cases of) need' rather than 'inevitable companion', as Gradon does in her note to this line. And *ūr* again must be read as the pronoun, which gives an unforced sense: 'Ours was once the gleam of youth.'

So this is apparently the least equivocal of the four passages. But how are we to interpret this clarity in relation to the others? Should we say that this is 'the one that worked', and that the others are just more or less lame attempts at the same thing? This is not an easy question to answer, and in fact I won't answer it; but a little speculation on the purposes of the signatures might not come amiss. The real question is: to what extent are they serious requests for adjuvant prayer, and to what extent are they puzzles? Or better, is there any reason why the two functions can't sit happily together?

Now given the context, there is no doubt that the requests for prayer are serious; Cynewulf's orthodoxy and sincerity of faith aren't in question, and there is (though in Latin, not in the vernacular) a tradition of colophons including authors' names, and asking for just such prayer. Now it would seem on the face of it that if the signatures were primarily meant to identify the author, to tell the reader who to pray for (if he's so inclined), then they shouldn't be puzzles. Sisam writes (1953:25) that the poet 'might miss his purpose, which was nothing less than his own salvation, if he puzzled the simplest mind about his name. If, then, very acute modern critics are baffled by his signatures, it is likely that the puzzle is of their own making.'

There are two points here, one right and the other wrong. The wrong one is the first, and deserves detailed comment. What Christian is entirely dependent on the prayers of others for his salvation? Would a poet who went so far as to instruct a *mon se mæra* (*Christ* 441a) concerning the Mystery of the Ascension be so in doubt about the quality of his life and faith (and so shaky on Christian doctrine) as to rest all his hopes for salvation on the prayers of his readers? Salvation comes by prevenient Grace (though of course prayers help). I think we can take it that Cynewulf knew better than that.

For what it's worth, my own idea is that at least one of the reasons for the puzzle-like quality of the signatures has to do with the quality of the prayer he wanted to elicit. Might it not be possible that the prayers of a reader who went to the trouble to work out the puzzle might be 'better' prayers, i.e. serious and concentrated, not merely ritual and offhand? If he had just written at the end 'Cynewulf made this; please pray for him', or something of the sort, might it not just be too easy, and allow the reader to pray without 'collection', inattentively? The fact that it requires some effort for the reader to find out who to pray for might just provoke a greater attentiveness. If this is tenable, then it's not counterproductive to introduce the puzzle element, but quite the reverse.

Another aspect of course is simply that these are medieval poems, and medieval men — often, I suspect, with purely secular motives like pride of craftsmanship — just *liked* acrostics, and felt nothing the slightest bit out of place in introducing them into the most serious religious contexts. (This kind of cleverness in serious religious settings is no problem in any age: are Bach's fugues in his sacred works less clever than those in the 48, or in bad taste because they're not? Is Herbert's *Easter Wings* ruined by its ingenious typography?) And this particular acrostic tradition is a pervasive one, and survives quite late. In the fifteenth century, for instance, we find a similar authorial acrostic in the totally serious (and not dissimilar) context of Villon's *Ballade... Pour Prier Nostre Dame* (Jannet, 1876:56):

Vous portastes, Vierge, digne princesse,
Jesus regnant, qui n'a ni fin ne cesse.
Le Tout-Puissant, prenant nostre Foiblesse,
Laissa les cieulx et nous vint secourir;
Offrist a mort sa tres clere jeunesse;
Nostre Seigneur tel est, tel le confesse.

But as to Sisam's point about our bafflement being of our own making: this is most likely correct. Knowing as little as we do about the tradition, about Old English, about runes, and so on, it seems fair to say, when the signatures get too difficult and the easy out of 'corrupt text' isn't available, and we have to stand on our heads to make sense of them — that the fault lies not in them but in ourselves.

Cyn(e)wulf Revisited

Notes

1. My interest in the Cynewulf signatures was sparked off, more years ago than I like to remember, by an Old English seminar at Yale taught by John Pope. This paper owes something to one written for that seminar, and to Professor Pope's comments; as well as to subsequent frustrated brooding on the subject.

2. 'Signatures' in inverted commas because it's not quite clear that that's what they are (though it's likely). In any case, they are an odd sort, and require (now, and I'd bet then) some work to unravel.

3. C.1000 for the Exeter Book (Krapp and Dobbie, 1961:x); late 10th century for the Vercelli Book (Brooks, 1961:xii).

4. Whatever the merits (and I think they are, in general, slight) of claims for 'oral formulaic' origin for OE poetry, it is clear that MS runes — especially in their self-conscious use in the Exeter Book riddles and the Cynewulf texts — depend on being seen for their effect, and are directed to (silent) readers, not hearers. Cf. n. 11.

5. In one MS (B.M. Cott. Galba A 2) the name of this rune is spelled *coen*, which suggests not *cēn* 'torch', but a Northumbrian form (with missing *-e*) of *cēne* 'bold' < */ko:ni/. Cf.§ 5.

6. This rune probably represents the *u*-rune ⊓ with a subscript *i*-rune; an early use of First Grammarian-type diacritics. (Cf. Hockett, 1959: § 3.1). At any rate this is not an 'original part of the Germanic *fuþark* (which goes back at least to North-West Germanic: cf. Antonsen, 1975), but must post-date the phonologisation of *i*-umlaut.

7. Largely on Old Norse evidence. Arntz (1944:207) gives 'Norw. ᛦ *ȳr* "Eibe", Isl. ᛦ *ȳr* "Bogen" (aus Eibenholz)"; ON *ȳr* is cognate with OE *ēoh* 'yew', which was the name of the English rune ᛇ (of problematic value: cf. Elliott, 1963:58f). Elliott (36) suggests that *ȳr* was borrowed from North Germanic as the name of the new /y/ rune.

8. For textual history, Cook (1900:152f). The text given below is from Brooks (1961), which differs from Cook only in restoring *tohweorfan* (101b) for Sievers's *tohreosan*, which Cook adopts.

9. Brooks (1961:124) reads 98b as saying that ᚠ stands at the end (of the name), thus alerting the reader to the fact that the runes are partially out of order.

10. There is nothing wrong with anagrammatic rearrangements of runes like this; a number of the Exeter Book riddles seem to require it (cf. the solutions and discussions of Riddles 19, 24, 64, 74 in Wyatt, 1912). And this epilogue, with the *Her mæg findan* opening and the closing *Nu ðu cunnon miht* is reminiscent of an OE riddle; cf. the ending of Riddle 32, *Rece, gif þu cunne,/ Wis worda gleaw, hwæt sio wiht sie*. It's not without interest in this connection that in the 19th century, when the Exeter Book poem now known as *Wulf and Eadwacer* was thought to be a riddle, its solution was argued by some to be 'Cynewulf'. And it was thought that Riddle 93 also referred to him. (For details of this episode, Wyatt, 1912:xx ff.)

11. I wonder how this could possibly work with an audience *hearing* the poem (cf. note 4)? Presumably the first couple of lines could alert the hearer to some sort of trickery like runes, and 98b *Feoh þær on*

ende standeþ might give it away (so Sisam, 1953:25f). But would they have the *fuþorc* enough at their fingertips to spot *which* other words are meant to be runes, and do the necessary computation while listening? I doubt it. Any attempt to figure out how this kind of thing might be effectively read aloud argues that it's meant to be read silently. (Though cf. Sisam's contention, *loc. cit.*, that since *cēn* and *ȳr* are unambiguously rune names, this makes it easier to imagine.) But surely in order (say) to be able to understand something like the *Rune Poem*, the audience would have to know these names as 'real' lexical items, with denotata; and the 'fact' that they exist in Old English (now) only as rune names might be a contingency of text survival, not a fact about the OE lexicon.

12. For runes used at least as the first elements of compounds, see the examples cited above, and . ✝ . *gefera* (*Elene* 1260a, discussed below).

13. A variant of Sisam's approach was suggested to me by J.C. Pope: read 'CYN, EWU, and CYNEWULF', 'the last two runes completing the whole name'. I.e. if LF is garbage, what can I do with it to make sense of it along with CYN and EWU, which aren't? This is better than Sisam, but still too complicated and indirect.

14. The fact that *cēne* begins with a velar and *cēn* (if from */ke:n-a-z/*) with a palatal is probably not a problem. The *c*-spelling for both suggests this (and cf. Lass and Anderson, 1975:139ff). The late OE *fuþorc* did in fact have a separate rune for a velar /k/ (or [k], if you think palatals and velars were non-distinct; for the view that the palatal/velar contrast in OE was phonemic, Penzl 1947; for the claim that it wasn't, Lass and Anderson, Chapter IV). But this velar rune does not as far as I know appear in the poetic corpus.

A worse problem, here and in the other signatures, is the supposed homophony of 'aurochs' and 'ours'. The possessive pronoun was normally spelled *ūre*, and was thus at best a semi-homophone for *ūr* (about as good, say, as *butt* and *butter* for a non-rhotic speaker of English). There are, though, attested occurrences of *ūr*, notably in *Vespasian Psalter* (see Brooks's note to *Fates* 101). If Cynewulf was originally Anglian (Mercian), this would make such a usage plausible; but the absence from any Cynewulf text of such diagnostic *VP* features as second fronting makes this a bit dubious (would a WS scribe have caught all of them? And could a non-Anglian audience be expected to see the point?). But one could always argue that the monosyllabic form could have been a poetic *koiné* form, which poets from anywhere could use if they wanted to work with runes, and needed to use ⊓ . But there is in fact a good argument for an Anglian provenance for Cynewulf: the rhymes, involving pre-velar vowels, in the odd rhymed passage in *Elene* 1236ff (cf. Sisam, 1953:2 and Gradon, 1958:13f).

15. Arntz (1944:207) translates 1259b 'der (unbenutzte) Bogen trauerte', which seems to capture the proper sense.

References

Antonsen, E.H. (1975) *A Concise Grammar of the Older Runic Inscriptions*, Tübingen
Arntz, H. (1944) *Handbuch der Runenkunde*,[2] Halle
Brooks, K.R. (1961) *Andreas and the Fates of the Apostles*, Oxford
Cook, A.S. (1900) *The Christ of Cynewulf*, Boston
Derolez, R. (1954) *Runica Manuscripta*, Bruges
Dobbie, E.V.K. (1942) *The Anglo-Saxon Minor Poems*, New York
Elliott, R.W.V. (1963) *Runes*, Manchester
Gradon, P.O.E. (1958) *Cynewulf's Elene*, London
Hockett, C.F. (1959) 'The Stressed Syllabics of Old English', *Language* 35, 575-97
Jannett, P. (1876) *Oeuvres complètes de François Villon*, Paris
Krapp, G.P. and Dobbie, E.V.K. (1961) *The Exeter Book*, New York
Lass, R. and Anderson, J.M. (1975) *Old English Phonology*, Cambridge
Penzl, H. (1947) 'The Phonemic Split of Germanic *k* in Old English', *Language* 23, 34-42
Sisam, K. (1953) *Studies in the History of Old English Literature*, Oxford
Tupper, F.W., Jr. (1912) 'The Cynewulfian Runes of the Religious Poems', *Modern Language Notes* 27, 131-7
Woolf, R. (1955) *Juliana*, London
Wyatt, A.J. (1912) *Old English Riddles*, Boston and London

3
Snuck: The Development of Irregular Preterite Forms

Richard M. Hogg
University of Manchester

In recent and primarily American dialects of English the regular verb *sneak* has acquired, alongside the expected preterite and past participle form *sneaked,* the irregular form *snuck*[1] = /snʌk/. The final volume of *A Supplement to the Oxford English Dictionary* (Burchfield, 1985) gives as the earliest example a quotation dated 1887 from *Lantern* (New Orleans) which is as follows:

> He grubbed ten dollars from de bums an den snuck home

Some other examples, none of which is dated earlier than 1932, are:

> They had all snuck in and were having a good time, making trouble (J.T. Farrell, *Young Lonigan*, 1932)

> I snuck in there and grabbed it (R. Chandler, *Farewell, my Lovely*, 1940)

> I have come around the back way and snuck up, as we say in Nebraska, on my subject (*Vassar Quarterly*, 1979)

These examples surely confirm an intuitive feeling that the form is highly colloquial, perhaps somewhat facetious or whimsical, and possibly most widespread in children's language. This might well be the reason why the form is not to be found in the list of irregular verbs given in Bloch (1947), and although I am not here primarily concerned with the sociolinguistics of the form, it is important for the discussion which follows to note the social contexts in which the form is used.

Snuck

The question, rather, to which I wish to address myself is how, purely linguistically, did the form arise. Showing as it does a movement away from the unmarked regular preterite of weak verbs towards the marked irregular preterite formation of strong or ablauting verbs, *snuck* most obviously presents itself as some kind of analogical formation. Admittedly, whatever the analogy might be, it seems rather peculiar, since it involves the replacement of a regular form by an irregular form, but for the moment we need only note that this may well be peculiarly characteristic of modern American English, compare here American *dove* against British English *dived*. But assuredly there is nothing in the rather obscure history of *sneak* that would suggest that the ablauting form is an historical relic, since it is most probable that *sneak* is to be related either to the Old Icelandic weak verb *snikja* or to a reconstructed Old English verb *snǣcan*, cf. Skeat (1910:576). Although the weak verb would be a derivative of *snāc*, the preterite singular of the strong verb *snīcan* 'to creep', this is of little help, since *snāc*, if it had survived, would have given Modern English *snoke* (although see below for further comment). In any case, if *snuck* were an historical relic, we might expect occasional forms to have been preserved from before this century, but this, apparently, is not the case.

Therefore it does indeed appear to be the case that we must regard *snuck* as the result of some analogy, and the most obvious analogy is one formed on the basis of some other irregular verb type. The problem here, however, is that there does not seem to be any irregular verb type which could serve as an appropriate analogical model. Of the verb types listed by Bloch (1947), only the following three types have a preterite in /ʌ/.

1. /i/—/ʌ/, e.g. *cling, slink, dig, stick*, etc.;
2. /æ/—/ʌ/, *hang* (only);
3. /ay/—/ʌ/, *strike* (only).

None of these provides a perfect analogical proportional model for *sneak*, which has, in Bloch's phonemic system, a present—preterite alternation /iy/ — /ʌ/, although probably the type (1) verbs, with present tense /i/, are nearest to fulfilling the necessary conditions for the analogy. Even worse is the fact that all the irregular verbs which do have /iy/ in the present tense have a preterite vowel which is radically different from that of *snuck*, thus we find *bled, ate, saw, sought*. Perhaps the most surprising fact here is that *sneak* did not analogise to the type *creep—crept*, since, as Samuels (1972:160ff) shows, this irregular formation has prospered up to the modern period.

Since even the most probable irregular alternation, that of the type exemplified by *slink—slunk*, is very far from being a convincing proportional model for the analogical formation *sneak—snuck*, we must look further afield for the answer. One suggestion that has been made to me is that in view of the rather facetious nature of *snuck*, it may be that the form is an analogical creation modelled on one or other of the two monosyllabic taboo words (in American English) which end in /ʌk/. Three difficulties arise here. Firstly, since English appears to be rather well endowed with monosyllabic taboos ending in /k/, it is rather surprising that there is not some variation in the form, giving, for example, **snock*. Secondly, although the words concerned are both verbs, they are both regular verbs, and hence the analogy would have to be to the present tense, not to the preterite, and this would have given **snuck—*snucked*. Thirdly, one of the two taboos is surely too violently rejected for it to be admissible as a proportional model, although admittedly the other, namely *suck*, has precisely the facetious, 'giggly' quality that might have encouraged the development of *snuck*.

The unsatisfactory character of the two suggestions so far offered prompts a third, which relies at least to some extent on each of the other two. If we consider the irregular verb *slink—slunk* and bring in the taboo form *suck*, we can observe that not only do both forms have rather similar phonetic structures, it is also the case that the forms have similar pejorative connotations. Therefore there is at least the possibility that we have before us a phonaesthetic category in the sense of Firth (1964:184) and Samuels (1972:46). Now this possibility is an appealing one, for both a semantic reason and a phonological reason. Semantically, as I understand the position and as the citations above would seem to suggest, *snuck* emphasises the quickness and furtiveness of the action denoted by the verb, and this would clearly tie up with a phonaestheme which was realised by a set of words including *slink* and *suck*. Phonologically the phonaestheme is easily characterised, as /sCV(N)k/, and if that is so, then the rejection and replacement of *sneaked* is straightforwardly explicable on the phonological level, for, firstly, its shape is /sCVGkC/[2] and, secondly, as *sneaked* has a long vowel (or diphthong) as opposed to the short vowel of *snuck*, and if the phonaestheme represents semantically quickness and furtiveness, it is quite clear that that would be more appropriately represented by the short vowel form.

But this, perhaps, is not quite the end of the story, for there are in English five other verbs which form their preterites with unexpected /ʌ/. These are: *hang, string, stick, strike, dig*. In order to provide a full account of *snuck*, it seems necessary to me to place that form in the context of these other forms. Interestingly, these five verbs are at least chronologically homogeneous, since the formation of preterites in /ʌ/ is for all of them a sixteenth century phenomenon. And alongside these apparently analogical forms, of course, there exist preterites of original strong class III verbs such as *drank, clung, rang*, and *wrung*. Such forms undoubtedly provided the proportional base for the sixteenth century analogical formations, and as we shall see below, the variation between *a* and *u* in the preterite of such forms is of considerable importance.

Of these five forms with non-historical /ʌ/, the first to transfer from the regular conjugation was, apparently, *hang*, and in this case the motivation for the change is quite clear. Alongside the native form *hang(en)* there existed in northern dialects of Middle English a present form *hing* which was derived from Old Icelandic *hengja*, and in those dialects the verb was remodelled on the pattern of *sing* as *hing, hang, hung*. Then the new irregular past forms were borrowed into the emergent standard dialect, which, however, caused syncretism between the present and preterite forms, since the resultant paradigm was *hang, hang, hung*. Now, as Ekwall (1975:§ 225) points out, there was in Early Modern English amongst irregular verbs belonging to the original strong class III, i.e. verbs of the same type as *sing*, systematic confusion of *a* (original preterite) and *u* (original past participle) forms, with the result that either *a* or *u* forms could be used in the preterite. Thus in Shakespeare one can find both *began* and *begun* in the preterite. Since syncretism of present and preterite forms is obviously, on general linguistic grounds, less desirable than syncretism of preterite and past participle forms, it is reasonable to suppose that the confusion of *a* and *u* was exploited in order to eliminate the undesirable syncretism and so produce the paradigm *hang, hung, hung*.

String with its preterite *strung* is equally simply explained.

When first used as a verb in the sixteenth century it is surely quite natural that the irregular conjugation should be adopted, given the frequency and strength of the class III conjugation and the phonological parallelism between *string* and the original verbs of that conjugation.

Although the remaining three verbs, namely *stick, strike* and *dig*, are clearly more relevant to any explanation of *snuck* than the two we have discussed so far, since, like *snuck*, they lack the post-vocalic nasal which is characteristic of the original class III verbs, they are, unfortunately, less susceptible to a straightforward analogical explanation. Thus, for example, O.E.D. simply and unrevealingly cross-references *dig* and *stick* as parallel analogical formations. Ekwall (1975) is slightly more ambitious, for he suggests that *stuck* is formed on the pattern of *sink, sank, sunk*, etc. (§ 273), that *dug* is an analogy on *spun* (§ 228), and that *struck* is due to special dialectal phonological developments (§ 215). Let us consider each of these separately.

Part of the difficulty with suggesting that *sink*, etc. is the proportional base for the analogical formation of *stick—stuck* is that the phonological patternings are insufficiently close, because of the absence in *stick* of the post-vocalic nasal which was characteristic of the preterites with *u*. But at least of equal importance is the fact that such an explanation fails to provide any motivation for the rejection of the earlier preterites of *stick*. Now the Middle English verb *strike* is a result of the merger of the Old English weak verb *stician* and a cognate strong verb **stecan*, with the result that in the fifteenth century the most common forms of the verb were: present — *stike*, preterite — *stiked, sta(c)k*, past participle — *sticked*. The preterite form *sta(c)k* is a regular development of the class IV/V verb *steken* < **stecan*.

Now the crucial form here, I would argue, is the irregular preterite *stak* with the ablauting vowel /a/. As far as class III verbs are concerned, as we have already noted, this /a/ came to be confused with /u/ from the past participle in the sixteenth century (and Ekwall (1975:§ 225) points out that *u* forms were preferred up to the nineteenth century). The only other irregular verbs where /a/ marked the preterite were in classes IV and V. Here too /a/ began to be avoided from the sixteenth century onwards. In almost all cases /a/ was lengthened to /a:/ which was taken over from the Middle English preterite plural, and in the case of class IV verbs where the past participle had the ablauting vowel /ɔː/ or /oː/, even the lengthened low vowel /aː/ was eliminated in favour of the vowel of the past participle, hence *broke* rather than *brake* as the preterite of *break*, and even more revealingly, there is a contrast in Modern English between original class V verbs such as *gave* and original class IV verbs such as *stole*.

Even if it is unclear why preterites in *a* should have suffered such a thoroughgoing rejection in the sixteenth century, it is quite clear that such a rejection did in fact take place. This, of course, means that *stak*, with /a/ in the preterite, must have been in a perilous position and hence open to some kind of analogical reformation. True, there was always the possibility of using the regular preterite *sticked*, and why that form did not come to predominate is ultimately unanswerable. On the other hand, if we consider the possibilities amongst the irregular preterites, it is soon quite obvious why neither /aː/ nor /oː/ would be chosen. For in order to provide a proportional model for the analogy it would be necessary that either the preterite plural with /aː/ or the past participle with /oː/ was in common usage, and in the case of *stick*, because of the fact that it is the result of the merger of a weak and a strong verb, this was not the case — for example, the past participle was usually *sticked*. The consequence of this is that it would be necessary to look elsewhere for a solution, and the only irregular verbs which provided a possible model were the class III verbs, where *a* and *u* forms alternated quite freely in the preterite. Although, as we have observed, the phonological similarities of, say, *sink* or *stink* were hardly close enough in themselves to force a remodelling of *stick*, it seems quite reasonable to suggest that, given the further motivation of the strong tendency to avoid preterites in /a/, *stick* could be so remodelled in the absence of any alternative possibility.

Let us now consider the development of *struck* as the preterite of *strike*. Originally this verb was a member of the irregular class I, i.e. parallel to *drive, drove, driven*, and, since the class I verbs have remained relatively stable in the history of English, the emergence of *struck* is rather puzzling. Ekwall (1975:§ 215) suggests that the regular Early Modern English form /stroːk/ was developed in some dialects as /struːk/ and that /uː/ was then shortened to /u/ and lowered in the seventeenth century, eventually to /ʌ/. Both the raising of /oː/ to /uː/ and the placing of shortening before the development of

/ʌ/ raise difficulties. Firstly, the evidence for raising of /oː/ is solely from cases with post-vocalic /r/, as Luick (1964:§ 511) shows, and so cannot reasonably be used to support a putative development to /uː/ in the case of /stroːk/. Secondly, Luick (1964:§ 525.2) also shows that shortening of /uː/ before /k/ always seems to have taken place after, not before, the lowering and unrounding of /u/ to /ʌ/, which thus makes, in this account, the actual present-day form inexplicable.

Nevertheless, even if a purely phonological explanation is untenable, the evidence of spellings in contemporary texts shows quite clearly that /stroːk/ developed to /struk/ in the sixteenth century or slightly later and that perhaps for some time there was an alternative form /struːk/. But what I want now to suggest is that the shift is explicable on non-phonetic grounds. The first point to note is that, as we have already noted, in the sixteenth century /u/ began to be perceived as a primary marker of past tense. To add to this, we should note the possibility of homophonic clash between /stroːk/ as the preterite of *strike* and as the cognate verb *stroke* 'rub softly'. Although I have argued elsewhere that it is all too easy to over-estimate the importance of homophonic clash, see Hogg (1983), this instance seems to me at least plausible. Now such a homophonic clash would provide the motivation for finding a new form and the increasing use of /u/ as a marker of past tense would provide an easy means by which a new form might be created. Some support for this suggestion is received from the fact that in the case of *strike* the past participle *stricken* is preserved for much longer than in other cases, and this can only reasonably follow from a situation where the major problem area in the conjugation of the verb lay in the preterite. Admittedly, this explanation cannot deal with the form /struːk/, if that ever existed, but in any other plausible account that form remains unexplained in any case.

The final form to consider is *dug* as a replacement of earlier *digged*. *Dug* occurs as a past participle from the sixteenth century and as a preterite from the eighteenth century. It is difficult to believe that this development is no more than a simple case of analogy, as is suggested both by Ekwall and the O.E.D., cf. above, since the verb is somewhat remote phonologically from any of the available class III verbs — Ekwall mentions *spun*, the O.E.D. mentions *stuck*. But Ekwall's point (1975:§ 225) that forms in *u* for both the preterite and the past participle become more and more common up to the eighteenth century seems to me to be very relevant. Surely what is happening, and I have already suggested this in a rather mild variant, is that /u/ (or later /ʌ/) is becoming seen as a standard marker of past forms, or, to use a term which Smithers (1954) borrowed from Bantu linguistics, /u/ is an ideophone representing pastness. The form *dug*, therefore, may best be viewed as an idiosyncratic ideophonic transfer from *digged*. This, of course, is scarcely an explanation in any theoretical sense, but it may be the best we can do, and it has the merit of fitting coherently into the pattern of the other changes which we have observed.

We can, therefore, conclude that in the three most difficult cases, namely *stuck*, *struck* and *dug*, it would seem necessary to invoke the notion of /u/ (>/ʌ/) as an ideophonic marker of past forms regardless of the vowel of the present tense. This makes these forms rather less eccentric than they first appear to be, since from the sixteenth century to the end of the eighteenth century, as we have noted, /u/—/ʌ/ was being increasingly used in the preterite of a large number of irregular verbs.

Now I have argued above that the shift from *sneaked* to *snuck* is essentially a phonaesthetic development. But that argument failed to answer the question of why it was precisely the form *snuck* that was chosen, for, phonaesthetically speaking, almost any short vowel would have served the purpose equally well. But once we take the above ideophonic factors into consideration, then it becomes much easier to see why it was that the form *snuck* was favoured. Yet, there is still a problem. The earliest O.E.D. citation for *snuck* is 1887. On the other hand, Ekwall (1975:§ 225) notes that a reaction against forms in *u* sets in in the nineteenth century. Obviously, there is a chronological mismatch. Yet this is explicable. Firstly, although I have not looked at the relevant grammar books in sufficient detail, I have the feeling that the decline of forms in *u* was most probably one of the few visible consequences of the prescriptive grammatical tradition. And if this is the case, then there is every reason to suppose that such prescriptive norms would have affected the development of *snuck*, which clearly is non-standard in origin. Secondly, and this point relates to the first, given that *snuck* is non-standard in origin, there is no reason to suppose that the O.E.D. citations given above reflect accurately the chronology of the emergence of *snuck* into non-standard varieties of the language. The form could well have led an underground existence for a long time previously. Thus the chronological mismatch is far more likely to be apparent than real.

Apart from the simple fact that if the arguments above are correct we now know a little more about the origins of *snuck*, this paper has two more wide-ranging conclusions, one for the theoretical linguist, one for anyone, linguist or not, who cares to read this paper. The theoretical linguist, who, even if he does recognise such phenomena as phonaesthemes and ideophones, appears to consider them as being peripheral to normal linguistic activity, should note that we have here yet another case where such phenomena play a far from unimportant role in the development of the language. And everyone, linguist or not, who, like me, finds *snuck* a delightful and appealing form which has, as it were, snuck surreptitiously into the language, should note that the form is in defiance of all prescriptive norms, being, as it is, both non-standard and grossly irregular. And in the past few years, as is well exemplified by a number of the articles in Michaels and Ricks (1980), see also works such as Simon (1982), more and more voices have been raised in denigration of non-standard varieties of the language. I can scarcely claim here to have redressed the balance, but *snuck* is at least a helpful reminder of what Barbara Strang (1970:xv) so graphically described as 'the ceaselessly, oceanically, heaving, swelling, flowing, ungraspable mass that historians corset into manageable chunks on to which quasi-scientific labels can be stuck'. I like to think that she would have approved if I had changed the *t* of the last word of that quotation into an *n*.

Notes

1. I am most grateful to Dr R.W. Burchfield for allowing me to see and make use of the uncorrected galley proofs of Volume 4 of *A Supplement to the O.E.D.*, from which all the examples of *snuck* have been taken. Dr Burchfield also made some useful suggestions informally, which I have made use of in the writing of the paper, and D. Gary Miller pointed out to me the American taboo words discussed below. But neither can be held responsible for the faults which remain in this paper.

2. I use here the kind of structural analysis to be found in Bloch (1947). No doubt there are better analyses available, but they would not affect the point at issue.

References

Bloch, B. (1947) 'English Verb Inflection', *Language 23*, 399–418

Burchfield, R.W. (ed.) (1985) *A Supplement to the O.E.D., Volume 4*, Clarendon Press: Oxford

Ekwall, E. (1975) *A History of Modern English Sounds and Morphology*, trans. A. Ward, Blackwell: Oxford

Firth, J.R. (1964) *Speech and The Tongues of Men*, Oxford University Press: London

Hogg, R.M. (1983) 'The Sound of Words: Some Phonological Influences on Vocabulary', *Bulletin of the John Rylands Library, Manchester 66*, 88–103

Luick, K. (1964) *Historische Grammatik der englischen Sprache*, Blackwell: Oxford

Michaels, L. and Ricks C. (eds) (1980) *The State of the Language*, University of California Press: London

O.E.D. [1933] = J.A.H. Murray, H. Bradley, W.A. Craigie and C.T. Onions (eds) *The Oxford English Dictionary*, Clarendon Press: Oxford

Samuels, M.L. (1972) *Linguistic Evolution*, Cambridge University Press: Cambridge

Simon, J. (1982) *Paradigms Lost*, Chatto and Windus: London

Skeat, W.W. (1910) *An Etymological Dictionary of the English Language*, [4] Clarendon Press: Oxford

Smithers, G.V. (1954) 'Some English Ideophones', *Arch. Ling. 6*, 73–111

Strang, B.M.H. (1970) *A History of English*, Methuen: London

4

Ambiguous Negations in Chaucer and Queen Elizabeth

Sonia Baghdikian
Université Libre de Bruxelles

The present article is based on a study of negative realisations in Chaucerian English, more specifically in Chaucer's *Boece*. Where enlightening, a comparison is drawn with the Latin text from which the translation was made, viz. Boethius' *De Consolatione Philosophiae*.

As we were studying all the negative sentences that occurred, we came across several examples which were ambiguous and where the comparison with the Latin text proved revealing. Occasionally it was also interesting to compare the examples with the translation of the same Latin text into Early Modern English, that is, in Queen Elizabeth's *Englishing of Boethius' De Consolatione Philosophiae* (1593).

As a starting-point Klima's (1964) theory on negation seemed to be best suited for a detailed analysis of the sentences to be examined. Klima assumes that there are two types of negation, one in which the scope of the negation extends over the whole sentence and another one in which the scope of the negation is restricted to one constituent only. And he adduces ways for ascertaining which type of negation is which.

Klima applies his theory to examples from present-day English; however, it can be shown with examples from historical data that this theory sometimes fails to resolve ambiguous cases.

There are examples in Chaucer's *Boece*, which can be taken as instances of either Sentence Negation or of Constituent Negation, and which are consequently ambiguous.

This can occur firstly when the negation is realised by the special negatives *nothing, nought,* and *none,* for example:

— Semeth it thanne that folk foleyen and erren, that enforce

> hem to have nede of *nothyng*? (III P2, 90)
> Latin: Num enim uidentur errare hi qui nihilo indigere nituntur? (54)

> — Thanne is evel *nothing*... (III P12, 151)
> Latin: Malum igitur nihil est ... (80)

Nothing occupies the place of a constituent that could be positive as well. The possibility of *having need* in the first example is not negated. A similar example is found in the following sentence, where *nothing* is subject:

> — The whiche men *nothyng* elles ne broght hem to the deeth, but oonly ... (I P3, 58)
> Latin: Quos *nihil* aliud in cladem detraxit nisi quod ... (36)

In the same way, *noght* can be interpreted as filling the place of a positive word in:

> — it ne scholde nat only semen litel, but pleynliche ryght *noght* (II P7, 112)
> Latin: non parua sed plane nulla esse uideatur (62)

> — For eyther alle thinges ben refferrid and brought to *noght*, and floteren without governour, despoyled of oon as of hire propre heved (III P11, 210)
> Latin: nam uel ad nihil unum cuncta referuntur et uno ueluti uertio destituta sine rectore fluitabunt ... (115)

The focus of the negation is not the nexal verb. 'Alle thinges' undergo the process of being 'brought to' something, only that 'something' is 'noght'.

> — the wil nys but in idel and stant for *naught*. (IV P2, 28)

where Latin does not have *nihil*, but has an equivalent phrase:

> Latin: voluntas frustra sit (16)

> — evel is *nawght*... (IV P2, 213)
> Latin: malum nihil est (119)

> — thanne schal it seme that thilke thing is comen or woxen of *nawght* (V P1, 54)
> Latin: id de nihilo ortum esse uidebitur (30)

In the last example, there is no question of negating the fact of originating.

If we consider these examples with *nothing* or with *nought*, we can see that the presence of *nothing* or of *nought* in the sentence does not entail the *neither*-tag, which is one of Klima's criteria; the sentences need not necessarily be interpreted as negative. A clause of the type '*and so* + aux. + subj.' can be appended, which points to the positive interpretation. *Nothing* or *nought* are here taken as representatives of Constituent Negation.

The problem with *nought* is that *nought*, also written *nawt* at that time, could either be an indefinite negative pronoun equivalent to *nothing*, or it could be a simple negative particle. In the latter case, it developed into *nat* or *not* in Early Modern English. The occurrence of these two possible and necessarily unambiguous interpretations can be exemplified thus:

> — it *ne* oweth *nawht* to lattere thinges (V P6, 286)

which becomes in Queen Elizabeth's translation of the same Latin text, thus in Early Modern English:

> QE — the force of his knoledge ... owes *nothing* to the comming (V P6, 151)

In this last example, moreover, it can be noticed that multiple negation has disappeared in Queen Elizabeth's translation, the light *ne* particle (second element of the negation) has been dropped, although the negative is the special negative *nothing*, making it clearer that *nawt* in Chaucer's text is a special negative.

The comparison between the two translations leads to a different conclusion in the following example:

> — Is *noght* this the gerdouns (I P4, 24)

which becomes in Queen Elizabeth's text:

> QE — Is *not* this the shop (I P4, 7)

In a number of other examples, *noght* has already lost its 'special negative' value and has become a simple negative element having a bearing on the whole sentence, for example:

— y *ne* myghte *noght* knowen what that womman was ... (I P1, 76)

which becomes in Queen Elizabeth:

— I ... could *not* knowe what she was ... (I P i, 37)

In this case, though the morphological form *noght* is still close to the indefinite pronoun, it no longer has its value. Such a change happened gradually as we can see from a series of examples ranged according to the scope of the negation, and where comparison with the Latin text is the keystone to the interpretation.

— thow *ne* doutest *noght* that this world be governed by God ... (I P6, 27)

In Queen Elizabeth:

— thou doutst *nat* the world by God be rulde (I P6, 16)

And again in Chaucer:

— your richesses ne mowen *noght* passen unto moche folke ... (II P5, 29)

which becomes, in Queen Elizabeth:

— Riches ... may *not* passe to many ... (II P5, 14)

This is also the case in the following example where *ne* has already been dropped:

— sorwe hath *noght* so dullid my wyt (I P4, 188)

In Queen Elizabeth:

— sorow hath *not* so duld my senses ... (I P4, 89)

A similar problem of ambiguity arises in the case of catenative verbs, and here again, the Latin text can be helpful, for example:

— For as knowledge bringes no necessity to doo so, foreknowledge compels *nothing* to be don (V P4, 53)

Latin has a positive clause standing for the infinitive, which supports the interpretation of the English example as being an instance of Sentence Negation:

— ita prae scientias futurorum *nihil* his quae uentura sunt necessitatis importat (61)

According to Klima, who analyses a similar kind of example, 'at least one of the structures represented by that sequence of words, is a case of sentence negation [which] is seen from the presence of the *neither*-tag with that sentence...' (1964:285).

In some cases, the sentence can be interpreted as positive with a restriction: one element in the sentence is negated:

— Ne certes thou *ne* hast *nat* comen to fleten with delites, and for to welken in bodily lust (IV P7, 90)

where the form of the negative *ne ... nat* should be unambiguous, that is, it points to a general negative; *nat* no longer has any close connection with the indefinite *noght, nothing*.

But in fact, it is not denied that you have come; only the purpose of the action is negated, although the sentence lends itself at first sight to a sentence negation interpretation, given the form of the negation. Queen Elizabeth's translation has this displacement of the negation:

QE — For you cam *not* to vs in the aduancement of vertue, to make vs overflow with delites, or drownd in pleasure, but that we should make a sharp battell against all fortune ... (IV P7, 36).

This occurs again in

— he *ne* travaileth hym *nat* for to geten power (III P9, 96) which becomes in Queen Elizabeth's translation:

— ... *nothing* carith for powre (III P9, 40)

from the Latin clause:

— ... de potentia *nihil* laborat (51)

Here it is clear that the general negative (clustering around the verb) in Chaucer's text is a form of displaced negative, since both the original Latin text and Queen Elizabeth's text more accurately have a special negative.

One example is particularly interesting: *nat* is placed in initial position in the sentence and thus negates the whole sentence, which reflects the order in deep structure.

— For although that for that thing is ben to comen therfore ben thei purveied, and *nat* certes for thei ben purveied therfore ne bytide they nat ... (V P 3, 76)

Again, the same kind of syntactic ambiguity occurs in the case of non-finite verbal forms which are embedded in larger structures, for example:

— thei hadden power *noght* to han bytyd (V P6, 214)
— ... that rejoysseth hym of the duellynge of his citizeens and *nat* for to putten hem in exil (I P5, 22)

This last example could be taken as an instance of Sentence Negation: *nat* would then negate the main verb 'rejoysseth'.

This can be brought into relation with an *adverbial phrase* being negated, yielding Constituent Negation, for example:

— For which thyng oon of the familiars *noght* unskilfully axed thus ... (I P4, 199)

— For which thyng *nat* unskilfully a tragedien ... cride and saise ... (III P6, 2)

Curiously enough, the last example becomes in Queen Elizabeth's text:

— Wherefore the Tragik poet wrongfully exclaimes *not* ... (III P6, 2)

which is once again ambiguous, and where the Latin text has a more logical order:

— Unde *non* iniuria tragicus exclamat ...

In some examples, *nothing* and *noght* seem to be equivalent to *not at all, in no way*, but sometimes correspond to Latin *nihil*, for example:

— myne ententes weren *nothyng* endamaged (I P1, 63)

Latin: nihil

— ... affections, whiche that *ne* bien *nothyng* fructifyenge ... (I P1, 56)

Latin: infructuosis

— al hadde *noght* Fortune nen aschamed that innocence was accused ... (I P4, 136)

Latin: nihil

— ... ne yet ne doute I it *naught* ... (III P12, 25)

Latin: ne nunc quidem arbitror

As a last example in which the two types of ambiguity are possible, consider the following occurrence: the problem can be more complicated with *noght*:

— Feare *nought* therfore

which is translated from the Latin clause:

— *nihil* igitur perimtscas

In the first analysis proposed by Klima (1964:263), the *neither*-tag should have a different subject nominal and a predicate identical to that of the base sentence (p. 262). Such a derivation is not feasible when the subject nominal is *nought* or *nothing*, so that Klima himself changes the formula in his example:

'No one was pushed, and nobody was hit either' (p. 274).

This last example is found in Queen Elizabeth's text, thus two hundred years later than Chaucer, at a time when *noght* had generally developed into a general negative particle already written *not.*

In conclusion, two types of ambiguity occur in Chaucerian English. The first type is morphological: it is particularly met with in English of that period. It is a product of gradual development in the language. The second type of ambiguity is syntactic: it is not restricted to this particular period of the language. On the contrary, it can occur in other periods as well, as is witnessed by the comparison with similar cases of ambiguity in Queen Elizabeth's English, that is, some two hundred years later.

References

Chaucer: Boece in *The Complete Works of Geoffrey Chaucer*, ed. F.N. Robinson, (1st edn, 1933, London; 2nd edn, 1957, London)

Klima, E.S. 'Negation in English' in *The Structure of Language*, J.A. Fodor and J.J. Katz (eds) (1964) Englewood Cliffs, pp. 246–323

Queen Elizabeth's Englishing of 'Boethius' De Consolatione Philosophiae', AD 1593, ed. Miss C. Pemberton, published 1899 for the Early English Text Society, London

5
Goodbye to All 'That'? The History and Present Behaviour of Optional 'That'

Joan Beal
University of Newcastle-upon-Tyne

Introduction

In extant writings from the Early Modern English period (henceforth ENE), there are many instances of a linguistic phenomenon which, until recently, has attracted little attention from scholars of diachronic linguistics: the apparently random appearance of 'that' after conjunctions and other subordinators.

Examples from the Shakespearean canon are:

Though that the queen on special cause is here
Her army is moved on.
(Lear, IV, vi, 218)

For that our kingdom's hearth should not be soil'd
With that dear blood which it hath fostered;
And for our eyes do hate the dire aspect
Of civil wounds plough'd up with neighbours' sword ...
... Therefore, we banish you our territories.
(Rich. II, I, iii, 125)

Such writers as have dealt with this issue in recent years, (Klima (1964), Keyser (1975) and Lightfoot (1979)) have tended to treat it parenthetically, their main concern being with the development of relative clauses in English. The older writers such as Curme (1931), Jespersen (1927) and Poutsma (1929), on the other hand deal with the history of 'that' + conjunctive sequences in a purely descriptive but thorough and informative manner. Since all the above-mentioned writers are more or less agreed as to the basic historical sequence of appearance and disappearance of 'that', the account which follows is largely culled from these sources, and will be modified later in the paper, in the light of further evidence.

A historical account of the functions and distribution of 'that'

In Old English (henceforth OE), the uninflected particle 'the' could be found in the following functions and positions:

1. Introducing a relative clause, for example:
His sio hea goodnes the he full is. (888. Boethius)

2. Following an inflected form of 'se' introducing a relative clause, for example:
Seo ilce burg ... seo the maest waes. (893. Orosius)

3. Following certain complex conjunctions, for example:
For tham the hit waes strang wind. (1000. Anglo-Saxon Gospel)

4. Following certain simple conjunctions — at this stage a fairly small number, for example:
Theah the ealle dagas aelce geare habban heora concurrentes. (c. 1050. Byrhtferth)

In later OE 'the' was replaced by 'that' in all the above functions and positions. In fact, even in earlier OE 'that' could be found following certain conjunctives, for example:

He gehet Romanum his freondscipe, swa thaet hi mostan heora ealdrihta wyrthe beon. (888. Boethius)

Ne maeg (thaet sealt) to nahte, buton thaet hit sy utaworpen. (1000. Anglo-Saxon Gospel)

The complex conjunctions referred to above also evolved into simple conjunctions, optionally followed by 'that', for example:

Tha wakemenn to frofrenn Forr thatt hi wisste wel thatt tegg off himm fordraedde waerenn. (c.1200. *Ormulum*)

Efter thet ure drihten hefde thet folc adreint ... (formerly 'after tham the' was used) (1175. *Lamb. Hom.*)

In the Middle English (henceforth ME) period, 'that' is found in the following functions and positions:

1. Introducing a relative clause:
The peple that dwelte in derknessis say grete ligt. (1382. Wyclif)

2. Following a 'wh- relative' introducing a relative clause:
Every wyght weche that to rome went. (c.1374. Ch. *Troilus*)

In whos handes that ever they were found. (1450. Rolls of Parl.)

3. After all conjunctions:
Bifore that Abraham was made, I am. (1382. Wyclif)

If that thou me tellest skill
I shall don after thi wil (c.1300. *Dame Sirith*)

Bithat hit was middai hig
Floriz was the brigge nig (1300. *Floriz & Bl.*)

4. After a 'wh- interrogative' introducing an indirect question:
Wotest thou wherefor that he hath sente me. (1470–85. Malory)

In the Early Modern English period, the following restrictions on the functions and distribution of 'that' come into play:

1. 'That' ceases to occur after a 'wh-relatives' introducing a relative clause. The exact date at which this ceased is difficult to determine, but a late example is:

Spite of his spite, which that in vain
Doth seek to force my fantasy. (c.1570. Ingelend, *The Disobedient Child*, The Song, 1–2)

2. 'That' ceases to occur after a 'wh- interrogative' introducing an indirect question. A late example of this is:

If I demand ...
Why that the naked, poor and mangled Peace

... Should not ... put up her lovely visage? (1599. *Hen. V*, 5, ii, 32-7)

3. 'That' ceases to occur after conjunctions. Here, my findings contradict the received opinion that sequences of 'that' + conjunction only survived 'down to the Stuart Period' (Poutsma, 1929:672). From the extensive exemplification of such sequences in the Oxford English Dictionary (OED) and in Poutsma (1929), it appears that the only conjunctions which cease to be found with 'that' before the end of the 18th century are, in order of disappearance:

(i) 'lest' for which the latest example found is:

Hence
Least that th'infection of his fortune take
Like hold on thee. (1605. *Lear*, 4, vi, 234-6)

(ii) 'ere', for which the latest example found is:

And sick of welfare found a kind of meetnesse
To be diseas'd ere that there was true needing (1609. Sh., Sonn. 118)

(iii) 'before', for which the latest example found is:

Before that Philip called thee, I saw thee. (1611. KJV John, I, 48)

(iv) 'by', for which the latest example found is:

By that these pilgrims had been at this place a week, Mercy had a visitor. (1684. Bunyan, *Pilgrim's Progress* 2)

(v) 'since', for which the latest example found is:[1]

Since that your worships have made me a rogue, I hope I shall have my money again. (1706. Farqhuar, *Rec. Off.* 5, vi, 342)

(vi) 'though', for which the latest example found is:

It appears to be a mock-siege, tho' that Ginckle gained the town in earnest. (1711. 16th Rep. His.)

This evidence suggests that the disappearance of 'that' after conjunctions has been a gradual process, which was certainly not completed by the end of the ENE period. Indeed, there are sequences of conjunction + 'that' in Present-Day English (PDE), but Keyser (1975:28), and Quirk *et al.* (1972:727) describe these sequences as 'compound conjunctions' and 'compound subordinators' respectively. Keyser cites as examples of this phenomenon:

now that, but that, so that, in order that, in that

Although this list is not meant to be exhaustive, Keyser implies that conjunctions followed by 'that' are a rarity in PDE by referring to them as constituting a 'small residue' (1975:28) Quirk *et al.* add to this list:

such that, except that, for all that, save that

as well as a number of conjunctives which are formally participial and adverbial, and which are optionally followed by 'that' in PDE. These are:

providing, provided, supposing,[2] considering, given, granting, granted, admitting, assuming, presuming, seeing, immediately, directly

Once such forms are placed in the class of subordinators along with established conjunctives such as 'now that' etc., Keyser's 'small residue' begins to grow out of all proportion to the 'exception' status accorded it hitherto, and any explanation of the history of 'that' and its functions must take into account its continuing presence after conjunctives in PDE.

Table 5.1 below shows the various contexts in which 'that' could follow a subordinator at successive stages in the history of English, from OE to PDE. It is evident from this tabulation that 'that', as it were, reaches a peak during the ME period and goes into a decline from ENE onwards, in terms of the number of contexts in which it can appear. The increase in the use of 'that' after subordinators from late OE to late ME is explained by Curme (1931) as follows: in EME, certain adverbs and prepositions, in combination with the demonstrative 'thaet', came to function as conjunctives: 'till that'; 'by that'; for instance, are

Table 5.1

	After relative	After conjunction (1)	After conjunction (2)	After interrog.
OE	+	+	–	–
ME	+	+	+	+
EME	–	–	+	–
LME	–	–	–	–

Conjunction (1) = Earlier conjunctions
Conjunction (2) = Later conjunctions

recorded from 1200 onwards and, in face 'swa thaet'; 'buton thaet' appear earlier still, right back in the OE period. As more and more of these combinations are used, the situation develops into that described by Curme:

> In ME, the determinative 'that' was so often associated with a preceding word ... linking this word to the following subordinate clause that it was construed as a sign of subordination and was attached to other words, which originally were not followed by a determinative, such as interrogatives.

To translate this into a more familiar jargon, we could say that, for the generation acquiring English at this stage in its history, i.e. the 14th century, there would be so many instances of 'that' following subordinators in the sentences output by the parents that the optimal grammar constructed by the child must be one in which 'that' was present as an independent constituent occurring in all subordinate clauses, and could be deleted by the operation of an optional rule. This 'translation' of Curme's argument in fact corresponds very closely to the view put forward by Klima (1964). In Klima's opinion, there is further evidence for the status of 'that' as an independent constituent in all subordinate clauses from ME onwards, in the existence of sentences like the following:

> But that it was high noon, and that no circumstance of ghostliness accompanied the curious cachinnation; but that neither scene nor season favoured fear, I should have been superstitiously afraid. (1847. C. Bronte, *Jane Eyre*, Chapter XI)

In such sentences, there are two subordinate clauses joined by a co-ordinating conjunction ('and'): the first is introduced by a sequence of conjunction + 'that', whilst the second is introduced by 'that' alone. In the second clause, 'that', as it were, 'stands for' the whole sequence 'but that'. According to Klima, this sequence is generated by the application of an optional rule for the reduction of repeated conjunctions. Furthermore, there exist in ENE sentences such as the following:

I love and hate her, for she is fair and royal
And that she hath all worthy parts more exquisite. (1609. *Cymbeline* 3, v, 71-2)

Here, 'that' in the second of two clauses joined by a co-ordinator is preceded by a conjunction alone in the first. This would suggest that the rule for reduction of repeated conjunctions applies before that for the simplification of subordinate conjunctions, the former generating in this case 'but that ... and that'; and the latter reducing this sequence further to 'but ... and that'. (Figure 5.1, below, shows the derivation of such a sentence.)

Altogether, the evidence from such sentences as those above, from the large range of contexts in which 'that' can appear after a subordinator in late ME, and from the appearance of 'that' alone in declarative and relative clauses, does strongly suggest the existence of 'that' as an independent conjunctive element present in all subordinate clauses up to ENE. The restrictions on the contexts in which 'that' appears from ENE onwards would suggest that the function of 'that' changes during this period, and, indeed, Klima views the changes in the occurrence of conjunctive 'that' as 'one of the main points of syntactic divergence between, on the one hand, Middle English and Early Modern English, and, on the other hand, the later stages of Modern English' (1964:266).

Klima suggests that this 'syntactic divergence' can be accounted for by positing two innovations, both involving 'only the valencies of rules' (1964:282): firstly, the rule for simplification of subordinate conjunctions, classed as optional in ENE, is rendered obligatory except after a few items like 'so', 'once', 'now'; secondly, the rule for the reduction of repeated conjunctions becomes inoperative. The combined result of these two changes is 'to remove the motivation for considering the

Figure 5.1

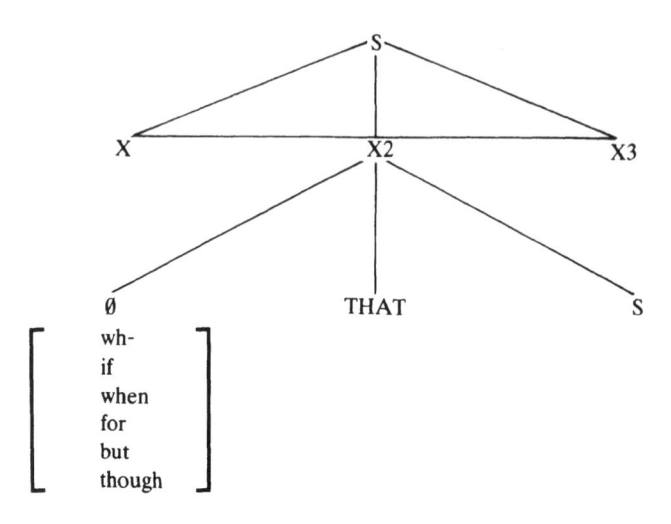

```
              S
        /     |     \
       X      X2      X3
            / | \
           Ø  THAT  S
         ┌────┐
         │wh- │
         │if  │
         │when│
         │for │
         │but │
         │though│
         └────┘
```

1. *Reduction of Repeated Conjunctions*

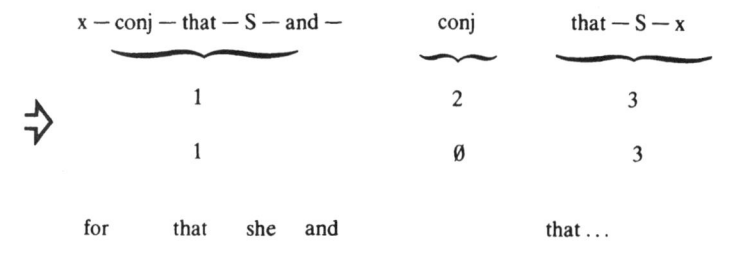

$$x - \text{conj} - \text{that} - S - \text{and} - \quad \text{conj} \quad \text{that} - S - x$$

$$\Rightarrow \quad \underbrace{\qquad 1 \qquad} \quad \underbrace{2} \quad \underbrace{3}$$

$$\qquad\qquad 1 \qquad\qquad\qquad\qquad \emptyset \qquad\qquad 3$$

for   that   she   and   that . . .

2. *Simplification of Subordinate Conjunctions*

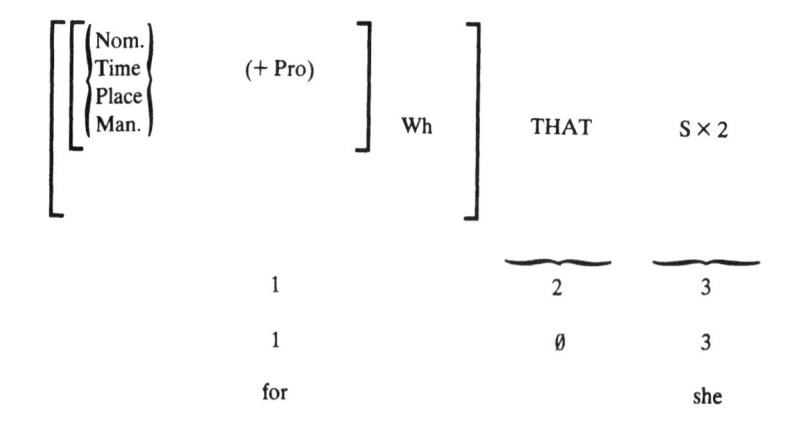

$$\left[\left[\begin{Bmatrix}\text{Nom.}\\\text{Time}\\\text{Place}\\\text{Man.}\end{Bmatrix} \quad (+\text{Pro})\right] \text{Wh} \quad \text{THAT} \quad S \times 2 \right]$$

$$\qquad\qquad\qquad 1 \qquad\qquad\qquad 2 \qquad 3$$

$$\qquad\qquad\qquad 1 \qquad\qquad\qquad \emptyset \qquad 3$$

$$\qquad\qquad\qquad \text{for} \qquad\qquad\qquad\qquad \text{she}$$

=   for   she   and   that   she

conjunctions as a class to be associated with a following optional "that"' (1964:283). In other words, the optimal grammar constructed after these innovations had taken place would no longer include 'that' in the expansion of the clausal adjuncts introduced by subordinate conjunctions. The rule for simplification of subordinate conjunctions would then be much more limited in its domain, applying only to subordinate clauses introduced by relatives and interrogatives.

Klima has little to say about the timing of these innovations and subsequent changes, except to suggest:
(i) that the changes in valency take place gradually, progressing from item to item or class of items to class of items;
(ii) that these innovations are being introduced from the Elizabethan period onwards. It is during this period that relatives, interrogatives and some conjunctions cease to occur with following 'that', but the crucial factor in dating the innovations is, according to Klima, the non-occurrence of relative 'who' with 'that' at this or any other time. Since 'who' as a relative begins to appear in restricted contexts only in the late 15th century and more freely not until the 16th century, Klima concluded that the change in valency of the rule of simplification of subordinate conjunctions had taken place, at least with regard to relative pronouns, before 'who' is established as a relative in ENE. Therefore, the new relative 'who' never appears in the output with a following 'that'.
(iii) that the change in the valency of the rule for simplification of subordinate conjunctions is completed by the time we reach PDE.

Of the intervening period, i.e. Later Modern English (LNE), Klima has little to say, except that the conjunctions or prepositions followed by 'that' are still common in Shakespeare, that at least up to Defoe the optional rule for deletion of repeated conjunctions is operative, and that in the case of 'for' and 'but', the loss of 'that' may be very recent. Here, of course, Klima is contradicting his previous statement that 'that' is no longer found after conjunctions in PDE. He explained these apparent 'exceptions' as involving rather a change from compound conjunctions ('for that'; 'but that') to single ones ('for', 'but'). This, I feel is a serious flaw in Klima's argument: if, as Klima suggests, the change in valency of this rule was gradual, and if even as few as two of the group of conjunctions cited as constituting a 'residue' are becoming subject to a change identical to that resulting from the change in valency which earlier affected the other conjunctions, there are already grounds for us to suspect that the rule change is not complete at all in PDE, but is still progressing item by item or class by class through the range of subordinate conjunctions. The fact that, as we noted above, the number of conjunctives in PDE followed, either optionally or compulsorily, by 'that' is far too large to be called a 'residue', provides further evidence that this change in valency is not yet complete: a closer examination of evidence from LNE should show even more clearly just how gradual this change has been.

Table 5.2, below, shows the earliest and latest examples found of certain conjunctions followed by 'that': the horizontal line drawn between the 'first' and 'last' dates for each conjunction represents, then, the period in the history of English during which this particular conjunction could be followed by 'that'. Where the line extends to the extreme right-hand side of the table, the conjunction may still be followed by 'that' today; where the line begins at the extreme left of the table, it was already found with following 'that' in OE; in all other cases, exact 'first' and 'last' dates are given. Looking at the table as a whole, two points are immediately obvious:

(i) That combinations of conjunctive + 'that' are acquired in English just as gradually as they are dropped from it. Some combinations are first encountered in the very period in which, according to Klima and Keyser, 'that' is ceasing to be associated with conjunctives in English: 'saving that'; 'since that'; 'besides that'; 'such ... as that'; are all first found in the course of the 16th century. Moreover, some of the participial forms acting as conjunctives and optionally followed by 'that' in PDE are not found in this combination until much more recently: 'barring that', for instance, is cited by Poutsma (1929) with the following sentence as an example:

> Barring that he's a Protestant, of course, he's a very good match for her. (c.1847. Trollope, *Macadam*, Chapter 15)

However, the OED does not even mention this function of 'barring' or the combination 'barring that', suggesting that this conjunctive use of the participial form is fairly recent. Of the other participial forms mentioned by Quirk *et al.*, the following

Table 5.2

	1100	1200	1300	1400	1500	1600	1700	1800	1900
So	←――――――――――――――――――――――――→
After	←――――――――――――――――――――――┤
For	←――――――――――――――――――――――┤
Unless	←――――――――――――――――――――――┤
Though	←―――――――――――――――――┤
If	├―――――――――――――――――――――┤
Without	├―――――――――――――――――――┤
By	├―――――――――――――――┤
Before	├――――――――――――┤
Until	├―――――――――――――――――――┤
Ere	├――――――――――┤
Lest	├――――――――┤
Because	├―――――――――――――――――┤
How	├―――――――――――――――――┤
Notwithstanding	├――――――――――――――――――→
Now	├――――――――――――――――――→
Save	├――――――――――――――――――→
In	├――――――――――――――――→
Except	├――――――――――――――――→
Providing	├―――――――――――――――――→
Provided	├――――――――――――――――→
Considering	├――――――――――――――――→
Seeing	├―――――――――――――→
Saving	├―――――――――――――→
Since	├―――――┤ ― ― ― ― →
Besides	├―――――――――――→
Such ... as that	├――――――→

are not cited as having this conjunctive function by the OED:

'Given', 'granting', 'granted',
'admitting', 'assuming', 'presuming'

On the other hand, the OED entry for 'seeing' reads as follows:

Quasi-conj. (orig. the present participle of SEE v. The use in concord with the subject developed into the conjunctional use as in considering, excepting, providing, supposing etc.

Of these latter, only 'considering, provided, providing' and 'seeing' have entries in the OED in this use. All of these are first used conjunctively during the 15th and early 16th centuries, and the first examples of them in conjunctive use are in combinations with 'that': examples of the participles used conjunctively without 'that' are not found until the 16th or 17th centuries. Examples which illustrate these points are:

> Cosetheryng that your doutyr is desendyde of hym be the modyr side. (1454. Past. Lett. 223, 1. 311)

> Considering the diverss knychtis fere
> Ar of uncouth and strang landis here. (1500. *Lance.* 1, 2165)

> Provided alwey that no man be harmyd. (1460. Fortescue. *Abs. and Lim. Alon.* xiv, 143)

> Now or whensoever, provided I be so able as now. (1604. *Ham.* 5, ii, 210)

> Providing evir more that thei ... may have ... (1423. Rolls Parl., IV, 256)

> The Wooll ... is nothing inferior to that ... of Spaine providing they had skill to fine ... (1632. Lithgow, Trav., X, 495)

> I wol ... exhorte you to take it as ... paciently as ye can, seeing that we al be mortal. (1503. Past. Lett., III, 401)

> I pray ... that it may be turned into a better use (seeing it is in the face of the world). (1537. Cranmer, Orig. Lett., I, ii, 77)

The dates of these examples suggest that the presence of 'that' is a signal of subordination, particularly when the form preceding 'that' is not yet fully established in the language as a subordinating conjunction: association with 'that' will arise when a form is beginning to be used as a conjunctive, but when that form is established as a conjunctive in its own right, 'that' may be dropped. Curme's analysis of LME 'that' as 'a sign of subordination' (1931) would, then, appear still to be relevant in PDE, and this functional explanation of its presence after 'new' conjunctives may go a long way towards accounting for the gradualness of its adoption and loss as shown on Table 5.2.

(ii) A different feature of Table 5.2, but one which suggests the same explanation of the presence/absence of 'that' as (i) is that, apart from 'so', which occurred in OE in collocations with 'thaet' rather than the usual predecessor 'the', those conjunctions which may or must be followed by 'that' today tend to have been introduced as conjunctives followed by 'that' no earlier than LME. Conversely, of those combinations introduced later than the 14th century, only 'since' and 'such ... as' may no longer be followed by 'that' in PDE. This would suggest that, the more recently a form has become used as a conjunctive, the more likely it is to be followed by 'that' in PDE.

It would appear from the above evidence that the appearance and disappearance of 'that' after conjunctives has indeed been a gradual process throughout the history at least of NE. How far, then are Keyser's and Klima's explanations of the linguistic changes involved in need of modification in the light of these findings?

Keyser's explanation of the restrictions imposed on the occurrence of 'that' after subordinators in ENE is that an output condition was introduced into the grammar at this stage, barring the appearance of anything before 'that' at the beginning of a clause. Such combinations with 'that' as persist into PDE, he describes as constituting a 'small residue'. Given the evidence above, that some combinations with 'that' only begin to appear at the very stage of English for which Keyser is proposing such an output condition, and given the number of conjunctives which still take a following 'that' today, such an 'output condition' can never have existed at any time in NE.

Klima's account, on the other hand, does allow for the gradualness of syntactic change, and so need not be totally dismissed in the light of the evidence presented above. What this new evidence suggests, is that the change in valency of the rule for simplification of subordinate conjunctions is still going on, and therefore that there must still be an underlying 'that' in the expansion of clausal adjuncts introducing subordinate clauses. With regard to relatives, the rule became obligatory in ENE, before the new relative pronoun 'who' was fully established as a relative: hence, 'who' never appears with a following 'that', this collocation having been preempted by the change in valency happening prior to the adoption of 'who'. For one 'class of items', then, the change in valency is complete, and can be dated as having occurred before the establishment of 'who' as a relative, i.e. some time in the 16th century. However, for another 'class of items', i.e. conjunctives, the change in valency is not yet complete, but is still progressing, item by item, through this class, for there are still many conjunctives followed by 'that' in PDE, and some of these have in fact only been adopted as conjunctives in LNE. If the change in valency was complete with regard to conjunctives, then 'new' conjunctives, like the 'new' relative 'who' would never be found with following 'that'. It would appear, rather, that when a change is progressing through a class of lexical items, new additions to that class have to 'go to the back of the queue' and will not be subject to the change until much later, whereas items added after the change is complete will 'miss the bus' altogether and never be subject to the earlier rules. This 'queueing' metaphor can be useful in explaining why some changes take so long to complete: if a class, like the conjunctives, can be expanded a great deal, through borrowing ('except' from French 'excepté' being an example) or transference from another class (such as prepositions, adverbs, participles), then, before the change has applied to all items in the class, more will be joining, so that the 'end' is perhaps never reached. Moreover, as we saw in the case of 'who', completed changes can be dated quite accurately if new items do 'miss the bus', for in this case the change in valency must have been completed more or less before the first records of the new item being unequivocally used as a member of this class are found. The metaphor is, however, more than just the product of an Englishwoman's obsession with queueing: there is a functional explanation for this tendency for new items to 'go to the back of the queue', at least in the case of conjunctives.

The motivation for 'going to the back of the queue' in this case lies in the continuing association of 'that' with subordination: the presence of 'that' in the surface structure emphasises to the hearer that a new clause is beginning and that it is subordinate. Where a lexical item has not long been assigned to the class of conjunctives, there is all the more need for 'that' to appear after it, as a signal of subordination: later, when the item is established as a conjunctive, 'that' may be dropped altogether. Where a conjunction, like 'but' or 'for', develops both subordinating and co-ordinating functions, 'that' continues to appear after the conjunction when it is used as a subordinator, thus keeping the two senses distinct. This tendency again points to 'that' being used after conjunctions as an extra signal of subordination where such a signal is needed: in this case, the need arises not because the conjunction is 'new', but because it has another, non-subordinating function. In PDE 'but that' only occurs when the 'but' means something like 'except', and is therefore a subordinator. Furthermore, 'that' is more likely to follow when the subordinate clause introduced by 'but' appears first in the sentence — a marked order in English. Examples which illustrate these points are:

> But that I fear to give you offence, I should say that Herr Hauzel is not very amiable. (Buchan, *That Winter's Night*, Chapter 7. Quoted in Poutsma, 1929 p. 698)
>
> *I'd love to come to your party, but that I can't get a baby-sitter.

The history of the construction 'for that' lends further support to the idea that 'that' in such collocations is a signal of subordination. The last example I have found of 'for that' is:

> Dick showed Bessie the letter, and she abused him for that he had ever sent Torpenhow away and ruined her life. (1890. Kipling, *The Light that Failed*, Chapter 8)

In PDE, 'for' is a co-ordinating conjunction. Unlike subordinating conjunctions, it never appears at the beginning of a sentence: thus the following sentence is ungrammatical:

> *For he is a Christian, I hate him

and even if the two clauses were transposed, there would still have to be a comma or pause before 'for', indicating its co-ordinating function. Compare the ENE use of 'for' with underlying 'that' in the following quotation:

> I hate him for he is a Christian
> But more for that in low simplicity
> He lends out money gratis. (1597. *Merch. Ven.*, 1, iii, 43-5)

In this case, when the conjunction ceases to be used as a subordinator, it ceases to be found with 'that' following: 'that' is only needed as long as the subordinating function continues to exist. In PDE, 'but' is almost exclusively used as a co-ordinator, so that 'but that' except in set phrases associated with negation like 'not but that', 'I don't doubt but that', hardly occurs today. It is not strictly ungrammatical, but rather 'marked' or unusual.

Another factor conditioning the likelihood of 'that' appearing after conjunctives in PDE is the intercalation of a phrase after the conjunctive. Of the example below, Poutsma (1929:711) notes: 'the intercalary phrase makes the use of "that" necessary':

> Notwithstanding — I confess — that appearances are against me. (1777. Sheridan, *School for Scandal*, 4, iii, 419)

The same point could be made about this sentence:

> Now, however, that the representative of the Foreign Office is pressing. (*The Times*. Quoted in Poutsma, 1929 p. 658)

Here, after the interruption of 'however', 'that' acts as a link, reminding the hearer of the subordinate nature of the clause previously signalled by 'now'.

Such examples, indicating as they do certain conditions under which 'that' is more likely to occur after conjunctives in PDE, point to the desirability of variable rules for the description of subordinate structures introduced by conjunctives in PDE. Indeed, Warner (1982), suggests that the information concerning presence or absence of 'that' after relatives in the writings of Wyclif can best be summarised in the form of a variable rule. Unlike Warner, though, I have not yet been able to undertake the kind of detailed, corpus-based study of NE from which variable rules could be constructed. Such a study would, of course, be essential for the discovery of the conditions which favoured loss or retention of 'that' in ENE and LNE and which determine the retention of 'that' after certain conjunctives in PDE. The 'queue' theory proposed above may well account for the presence of 'that' after 'new conjunctives' like the participial forms, but does nothing to explain the continuance of, for example 'now that': in such cases, synchronic variable rules might prove helpful. A more detailed synchronic study might also solve the mystery of the persistence of compulsory 'that' after certain conjunctives in PDE, as listed in Quirk *et al.* (1972:727-8). From this list, 'so' and 'for all' no longer take 'that' compulsorily, at least in my dialect, as the following examples illustrate:

I quite like Geoff, for all he's a transformationalist.
For all he's a transformationalist, I quite like Geoff.
I'll draw you a map so you don't get lost.
So you don't get lost, I'll draw you a map.

Unless my dialect is totally outlandish, it would appear that gradual changes in valency are in operation again with regard to these structures: deletion of 'that' is becoming optional where it was previously not possible, and may eventually become obligatory, as it has done after 'unless' etc. Meanwhile, yet more items may be added at the 'back of the queue', to the stock of conjunctives in the lexicon, and may, for a time, need a following 'that' as a signal of subordination. What is certain is that conjunctives followed by 'that' do not constitute a 'small residue' at all, but continually appear in the language as items make the transition from other word classes to that of subordinating conjunction.

Notes

1. This was the latest example found in the OED. However, I have recently discovered a children's song, in which the following line appears:

Ever since that he was given
As a tiny little kitten ('Jess The Cat': Post Music Ltd 1982)

Obviously, considerations of metre and rhyme make the insertion of 'that' desirable here, but the same could be said of many of my examples taken from verse. What is of interest here is that, contrary to the received opinion of linguists, the songwriter has the option of inserting 'that' open to him at this late stage!

2. The status of these participial forms as conjunctives is a matter of some controversy. Quirk *et al.* (1972) list them as such without comment, whilst the OED classifies only some of them as conjunctions, or in the case of 'seeing', as 'quasi-conjunctions'. The arguments in favour of this classification are as follows:

(i) These forms, like other subordinating conjunctions, can appear at the beginning of a sentence, for example:

Providing (that) he comes home early, you can see him tonight.
If he comes home early, you can see him tonight.

(ii) Unlike the formally identical participles, these conjunctives do not have a subject identical to that of the second clause. Compare:

Seeing (that) she's asleep, John has to leave quietly.

where two interpretations are possible: either John sees and then has to leave, or the 'seeing' has no deep structure subject and so is conjunctive, with:

Seeing (that) she's asleep, there's nothing to do but leave quietly.

where no corresponding subject can be found, and 'seeing' is unambiguously conjunctive, and more or less synonymous with 'since'.

There is no space here for a full rehearsal of the arguments for and against treating these forms as conjunctives. However, it is interesting to view them in the context of other conjunctives, formerly adverbs or participles, for which 'that' served as a crutch to help them over the transition to full status as subordinating conjunctions. The reluctance of some speakers to accept participial forms as conjunctives, may, like the optional presence of 'that', be a pointer to the fact that these forms are at present in transition.

References

Abbott, E.A. (1872) *A Shakespearean Grammar*, 3rd edn, Macmillan and Co., London

Curme, G.O. (1931) *A Grammar of the English Language in Three Volumes*, Volume II, *Parts of Speech, Accidence*; Volume III, *Syntax*; D.C. Heath and Co., Boston, New York

Jespersen, O. (1927) *A Modern English Grammar on Historical Principles*, Part III. *Syntax*, Second Volume, George Allen and Unwin Ltd., London

Keyser, S.J. (1975) 'A Partial History of the Relative Clause in English', in *Papers in the History and Structure of English*, University of Massachusetts, Occasional Papers in Linguistics, 1, Boston, Massachusetts

Klima, E.S. (1964) 'Studies in Diachronic Transformational Syntax', Harvard University Ph.D. Thesis, Cambridge, Massachusetts

Lightfoot, D.W. (1979) *Principles of Diachronic Syntax*, Cambridge University Press, Cambridge

Poutsma, H. (1929) *A Grammar of Late Modern English.* Part 1, Second Half, 2nd edn, P. Noordhof, Groningen

Quirk, R. *et al.* (1972) *A Grammar of Contemporary English*, Longman, London

Warner, A. (1982) *Complementation in Middle English and the Methodology of Historical Syntax*, Croom Helm, London

6

The Rise of the *For NP to V* Construction: An Explanation

Olga Fischer
University of Amsterdam

1. Introduction

Recently there has been renewed interest in the origin of the *for NP to V* construction as in (1):

(1) it is time for you to go
     it is intolerable for John to get away with this

This construction did not exist in Old English (OE); it slowly developed in the course of the Middle English (ME) period, gaining more and more ground in Modern English. Various attempts have been made in the past (Stoffel, 1894; Zeitlin, 1908; Jespersen, 1940; Zandvoort, 1949) and more recently (Visser, 1963-73; Lightfoot, 1979, 1981a) to explain the appearance of this new construction. Briefly, some of the following suggestions have been made concerning its emergence. Stoffel and Lightfoot (1981a) have suggested that the construction arose under the influence of so-called accusative and infinitive constructions. This would indeed help to explain *one* of the interpretations of this construction, in which the NP following *for* is the subject of the infinitive, but the use of *for* itself remains a mystery.[1] Visser (1963-73:968) states that the shift from *for you* as benefactive-to-the-matrix-predicate to subject-of-the-infinitive can be explained by 'the frequent occurrence in other kinds of context of "inorganic" *for*'.[2] He does not notice that 'inorganic' *for* is itself a new development which needs to be explained in turn.

There are also differences from a methodological point of view. Stoffel's, Zeitlin's (etc.) and also Visser's main interest is in the description of the data, on the basis of which they hint at possible causes of the change. Lightfoot, on the other hand, is specifically interested in providing an explanation for the change within a restrictive and therefore falsifiable theory of grammar. According to Lightfoot, a historical change will only be explained

> if one demonstrates two things: (a) that the linguistic environment has changed in such a way that some parameter of U[niversal] G[rammar] is fixed differently ...; and (b) that the new phenomenon ... must be the way that it is given some general principle(s) of grammar and the new property of the particular grammar. (Lightfoot, 1981a:90)

The advantage of this approach over the others is that it does not only provide an explanation for the change within the theory of grammar, but the historical changes themselves give new insight into the properties of the theory of grammar.[3] In this respect Lightfoot's approach, working as he does within the restrictive framework of the Extended Standard Theory,[4] is more fruitful, provided one does not fall into the trap of misinterpreting data to suit one's theory, as I will show Lightfoot has done in this particular case.

The first part of this paper (section 2) will be mainly concerned with Lightfoot's treatment of the data. In section 3, I will take a fresh look at the data relevant for the *for NP to V* construction. There I will pay essential attention to an older construction without *for*, as in (2):

(2) now were it tyme a lady to gon henne (Chaucer, *T&C* Robinson (1957: 427))

which provides an indispensable link in the explanation of the new development. Finally, an explanation for the new development that follows from the theory of grammar will be offered in section 4, which is concluded by a brief discussion about the type of change this case represents.

2. Lightfoot's presentation of the *for NP to V* construction

2.1 Lightfoot (1979, 1981a) postulates a direct link between the disappearance of the *for to* infinitives (as in *no wys man nedeth for to wedde*) and the emergence of the construction where the infinitive has a lexical subject NP (*for NP to V*). This approach is unfortunate, because one-sided: in this way the development of the new construction depends entirely on the disappearance of the *for to* infinitives so that an explanation for this development is only sought in this direction, while other interesting facts are left unexplored. Thus, in 1979, Lightfoot believed that the *to*-infinitive developed from a nominal into a verbal category in ME, which would explain the earlier impossibility of a NP appearing in front of the infinitive. In Fischer and van der Leek (1981) it was shown that there is no evidence that in ME the infinitive was still nominal (see the arguments presented there) and that consequently there was no category change to explain the new development. In his 1981 article, Lightfoot has also abandoned the idea of a category change, presumably because he no longer needs it. He still believes, however, that the two changes are linked. In his later article, the disappearance of the one and the emergence of the other are linked up with the introduction of a new rule of Š-deletion into the ME grammar.

There are several weaknesses in this second 'solution', some of which were already apparent in the earlier one. The time scheme is not correct. Lightfoot asserts that the new constructions appear consistently about two hundred years later than the old *for to* infinitives. This is essential for his idea of a necessary change to work.[5] But some of Lightfoot's own examples (1979:187, examples 29(c) and 29(i)) show that the two constructions may appear more or less simultaneously. (Interestingly enough, these same examples are left out in his 1981a account.) This would argue against a direct link between the emergence of the new and the disappearance of the old construction.

It is also difficult to see what Lightfoot means when he says that the disappearance of the *for to* infinitives is related to the introduction of the new rule of Š-deletion; in his own words (1981a:112): 'As infinitive subjects became governable, (35) [i.e. constructions like *(for) to go is necessary*; *it is good (for) to go* p. 111] became obsolete and (36) ... [i.e. constructions like *for us to go is necessary* etc.] started to appear.' There are various objections to this. First of all, it is obvious that constructions like Lightfoot's (35) with a lexically empty NP (PRO) before the infinitive as such did *not* become obsolete. What did happen was that the infinitive marker *for* began to disappear. It is unclear how this disappearance of *for* is related to the introduction of S̃-deletion. Lightfoot seems to have argued as follows:

(i) A new rule of S̃-deletion is introduced into the language as a result of the Latin accusative and infinitive construction being adopted (Lightfoot, 1981a:113).
(ii) As a result of this rule, it now became possible for infinitives to have a *lexical* NP as subject, i.e. infinitive subjects became governable (110).
(iii) On the analogy of this, the subject NPs in *for to* constructions became 'governable' too. These NPs, which had always been PRO — because the position was ungoverned — will now take a lexical form since they *are* governed.
(iv) *For* becomes a governor and has to disappear when, instead of a lexical NP, PRO appears, with the result that *for to* infinitives disappear (112).

(iii) is the weak link. It is obvious that the new rule of S̃-deletion does not *necessitate* the appearance of a lexical subject before the infinitive in the *for to* construction. Presumably, all one can say is that this *may* have happened. Lightfoot also seems to think that the structure underlying the *for to* infinitive construction is (a) rather than (b):

(a) [for PRO to go]
(b) [PRO for to go]

because in Lightfoot's view the *for to* infinitive can no longer be generated when *for* becomes a governor. This conclusion only follows if the underlying structure is (a).

It can be shown, however, that the only possible structure in ME is in fact (b), because of the occurrence of clauses like (3) and (4) in ME:

(3) But he semede for to be/A man of gret auctorite (Chaucer, *HF*, Robinson (1957:302))

(4) And wel a lord he semede for to be (Chaucer, *LGW*, Robinson 1957:501))

Kayne (1981) shows, with reference to the French complementiser *de*, that true complementisers (like French *de* and Modern English *for*) are incompatible with raising because of the well-known restriction that subjects cannot be extracted across an adjacent complementiser. It follows that *for* in (3, 4) cannot be a complementiser. It is likely therefore that *for* is an infinitive marker in the *for to* constructions.[6] This means that PRO must precede *for* in the *for to* infinitive constructions (as shown in (b)). Thus the fact that the complementiser *for* becomes a governor cannot explain the disappearance of *for* in *for to* infinitives.[7]

Something else pleads against Lightfoot's explanation. In his account, the new rule of S̄-deletion, which causes *for NP to V* to emerge, is due to the fact that Latin accusative and infinitive constructions were adopted in ME. If it is true that ME accusative and infinitive constructions are due to Latin influence (as seems very plausible, cf. Warner, 1982:134ff),[8] it seems strange that these constructions did not catch on in OE, which was as heavily influenced by Latin as ME was. The question arises, why was ME ready to accept these constructions, while OE on the whole was not? Lightfoot does not address this question, thereby ignoring any changes in the grammar of English between the OE and ME periods that made the adoption possible. His disregard of this is all the more remarkable since Lightfoot himself objects to attributing new constructions in a language to foreign influence in certain cases: 'where a productive new construction type appears, ... it will be hard to attribute this to foreign borrowing or stylistic novelty; rather a change in the grammar is likely to be involved' (1981b:357). If one accepts that the rise of the accusative and infinitive construction and the *for NP to V* construction are somehow linked (i.e. via the re-analysis of the older *NP to V* construction, see section 3) — as many linguists do — it is more probable that these two new constructions are caused by *one* change in the grammar, rather than that one is caused by the other.

2.2 These are already considerable objections. Even more important, however, is the fact that many of the examples Lightfoot gives of the so-called *new* construction are not necessarily examples of what he calls 'governed subject infinitive constructions'. This means that these new *for NP to V* constructions are not necessarily related to the introduction of S̃-deletion. Thus, Lightfoot gives as an example of the new construction the sentence type *it is necessary for a man to go* (1979:188), which first appears in 1385. This is in itself correct, but it appears almost certainly with the structure given in (5a) and not with the one given in (5b):

(5) a NP V for NP [s [s PRO to V]] ('benefactive construction', organic *for*)
    b NP V [s for [s NP to V]] ('subject construction', inorganic *for*)

(5)a is not an example of a 'governed subject' construction because the *for NP* receives its thematic (θ) role from the matrix verb and not from the infinitive.[9] The first unambiguous examples of the (b) construction are found very late (for this type, according to Visser, only in the eighteenth century, other types appear from the sixteenth century onwards, cf. also Jespersen (1940)).

It is true that the construction with *for* is a new construction in ME, but what is new about it is not the position of the NP before the infinitive, as Lightfoot asserts, but the introduction of the preposition *for* before the NP. In ME the preposition *for* starts to take over the old benefactive dative function used in OE. With the loss of the morphological case system, prepositions begin to take over the roles played by the case endings in OE. The dative case is replaced by the prepositions *for, to, at,* or *on* depending on its function. Examples from OE make clear that the 'newness' of the *for NP to V* construction consists in the introduction of *for*, not in the introduction of a NP before the infinitive:

(6) Hit is swiðe earfoðe æniʒum (DAT) to ðeowienne (INF) twam hlafordum
     (It is very difficult for anyone to serve two lords)
     (*Hexameron St Basil,* Visser (1963–73:963))

(7) sceamu hyt is menn (DAT) nellan wesan (INF) þæt þæt he ys
     (it is shameful for (in) a man not to want to be what he is)
     (*Æl. Coll.*, Garmonsway (1939:42))

That the introduction of *for* is not restricted to datives before infinitives is clear from the following examples from OE and ME respectively:

(8) bettre him (DAT) wære þæt he on læssan hade ond on eorðlicum weorcum his lif geendode.
(it would be better for him that he would end his life in a lesser order performing the works of this world) (*Past. Care*, Bright (1895:34))

(9) Light is nought good for sike folkes yën! (Chaucer *T&C*, Robinson (1957:433))

In ME the plain dative[10] is also still found beside the newer *for NP*:

(10) þanne is ðe (DAT) swiðe holsum ðat ðu þis ofri ðine louerde god. (*Vices and Virtues*, Holthausen (1888: 111))

Very often too, *to* is found instead of *for* (especially in the earlier texts):

(11) ... it schulde not be to thee hoolsum (Pecock, MED vol. IV:880)

2.3 The introduction of *for* before the infinitive is also a new development in ME, but, in my view, it is in no way related to the introduction of *for* discussed in the previous section (just as there is no direct relation between the rise of *for NP to V* and the disappearance of infinitival *for*). To account for this introduction of *for*, the traditional notion still provides the best explanation: namely that it was introduced in ME in order to emphasise the idea of purpose, earlier (in OE) expressed by the *to*-infinitive (in contrast to the plain infinitive). All the earliest instances of the *for to* infinitive clearly express purpose (cf. Mustanoja, 1960:514). In the course of the ME period the meaning of *for* weakened (just as *to* had weakened and needed strengthening by *for*) and the result was that the *to*- and the *for to* infinitives came to be used almost indiscriminately and finally became interchangeable.[11] Now *for* no longer served any real function, and the language presumably was in need of a new expression to convey purpose. It is therefore no surprise to see new expressions of purpose appear where *for* had lost force and was slowly disappearing. The last instances of the *for to* infinitive are found in the early part of the seventeenth century (cf. Visser, 1963–73; Lightfoot, 1979), the earliest examples of (*so*) *as to* + infinitive, according to the *Oxford English Dictionary*, date from the second half of the sixteenth century; *in order to* + infinitive makes its entrance at the end of the seventeenth century. It is possible that the disappearance of *for* was stimulated by the use of *for* in its other function. Constructions like:

(12) Hit by-comeþ for clerkus crist for to seruen (*Piers Pl.*, Skeat (1886:85))

sound rather clumsy and are fairly rare, but this is pure conjecture.

3. The *NP to V* construction in OE and ME

As I have already indicated above, it is crucial for an explanation of the rise of the *for NP to V* construction to distinguish two underlying structures, as I have done in (5). It follows from the discussion in section 2.3 that what must be explained is not the occurrence of *for NP to V* constructions as such (because that is a straightforward matter) but the occurrence of these constructions with structure 5(b), which is essentially the new development. It is wrong to collapse the two constructions into one, as Lightfoot has done, and explain the emergence of both in one move.

Now that the two underlying structures of the *for NP to V* construction are separated out, it would be interesting to see whether the predecessor of the (5a) *for NP to V* construction, i.e. the construction without *for* (examples of which are found in OE and in ME after semi-impersonal predicates, cf. (6) and (7)) also have two underlying structures similar to (5a) and (b) above.[12] If these older constructions already appeared with the (b) structure, then it is clear that the development of *for NP to V*, with the NP given its θ-role by the infinitive, is not in any way related to a change in the status of *for*, and consequently also not related to the disappearance of the *for to* infinitives due to this change in *for*.

In order to decide that the older *for*-less construction could have underlying structure (5a) as well as (b), we need unambiguous examples of (b) structures. In the past linguists (Stoffel (1894), Jespersen (1940), Zandvoort (1949), Stockwell (1976)) have developed syntactic and lexico-semantic criteria to distinguish between the (a) ('benefactive') and (b) ('subject') analyses of the *for NP to V* construction. Two well-known syntactic criteria are the 'double *for*' construction (13) and front-placement (14):

(13) it is pleasant for$_1$ the rich for$_2$ poor immigrants to do the hard work (Chomsky (1981:239))

(14) for man to tell how human life began is hard (Stoffel (1894:65))

In (13) the second *for NP* cannot express a benefactive function since that is already carried by the first *for NP*. According to the θ-criterion (cf. Chomsky (1981:36)) 'each thematic role is assigned to one and only one argument'. Thus in this example *for*$_2$ can only be a complementiser. Front-placement is also a clear indication that we are dealing with a 'subject' construction. In (14) the whole infinitival clause *for man to tell* is moved to the front. If *for man* expressed a benefactive function, it would follow the predicate *is hard* which governs it and would not have been moved together with the infinitive.

These same criteria can also be applied to the older *for*-less construction in order to find out whether these older constructions were also amenable to two different analyses. It did not prove difficult to find examples of both the 'double *for*' construction and of front-placement:

(15) *Me, here to leue, & þe, hennys þus go, hit is to me gret care & endeles wo* (*Rel. Lyrics*, Brown (1924:228))

(16) for hyt ys the custom *of my contrey a knyght* all weyes to kepe his wepyn with him (Malory, Vinaver (1947:83))

The examples are not as tidy as the invented one given in (13), but it is clear that in (15) the NP *me* (and also *þe*) cannot be governed by the predicate *is ... care* because its possible thematic role is already taken by the NP contained in *to me*. The same is true for (16). (15) at the same time provides an example of front-placement. Other examples of front-placement are:

(17) But a man to lyue pesibly with harde & ouerthwart men ... is a gret grace & a commendable & a manly dede. (*Imit.Chr.*, Ingram (1893:43))

(18) A kynges sone to ben in swich prysoun,/And ben devoured, thoughte hem gret pite. (Chaucer, *LGW*, Robinson (1957:510-11))

Stoffel (1894) provides another criterion. He indicates that the *for NP to V* construction can only be analysed as a 'subject' construction when it is preceded by *as*, *but*, or *than*. His examples are:

(19) there is nothing more common than for gentlemen of this cast to be involved in what is called a love-match.

I know well that nothing is so unfashionable as for a husband and wife to be often together.

In these examples the words *as* and *than* introduce a new clause so that the *for NP* can no longer receive its θ-role from the matrix predicate, which is necessary for the 'benefactive' analysis to be possible. The following instances were found with the *for*-less construction in ME:

(20) No thing ... so bitter is .../ As man for God & heuen blis to suffre deth with gode wille. (*Stanzaic Life of Chr.*, Forster (1926:206))

(21) No thyng ... is so muchel agayns nature as a man to encressen his owene profit to the harm of another man (Chaucer, *Melibee*, Robinson (1957:182))

(22) Better is it thy kinne to ben by thee gentyled than thou to glorifye of thy kinnes gentilesse. (Usk, *Test. of Love*, Skeat (1897:76))

Zandvoort (1949:267) draws attention to examples where *for NP to V* is nominal part of the predicate as in:

(23) the rule was for women and men to sit apart.

For the older construction I also found examples of this type (see (24), (25)). For these clauses to make sense, it is clear that the NP must be given its thematic role by the embedded infinitive and not by the verb in the main clause.

(24) The thridde grevance is a man to have harm in his body. (Chaucer, *Pars. T.*, Robinson (1957:249))

(25) ther is a manere garnysoun that no man may venquysshe ne disconfite, and that is a lord to be biloved of his citezeins and of his peple. (Chaucer, *Melibee*, Robinson (1957:177))

Stockwell (1976) mentions two types of constructions where it is evident 're-analysis has taken place', i.e. where the only possible analysis is according to (5b). He calls these 'weather' (26) and 'existential' (27)

(26) It is essential for it to rain soon.

(27) It is vital for there to be a conference on syntactic change soon.

I prefer to class these under one heading. Within the EST framework, both *there* and *it* are non-arguments, i.e. they bear no thematic role.[13] This means that they cannot have a benefactive function, which leaves only the (b) possibility open. These examples (which are very recent, cf. Visser 1963–73:967–9) are in fact the final stage of a development in which *for* NPs can no longer have a benefactive function because they are non-animate. Typically, only animate NPs can bear benefactive θ-roles. There are quite a few examples in ME with the old (*for*-less) construction, where only the (b) analysis is possible because the NPs (*heuene and erthe* in (28) and *wallis* in (29)) are non-animate:

(28) it is liȝter heuene and erthe to passe than o titil falle fro the lawe. (Wyclif, *N.T.*, Forshall & Madden (1879:158))

(29) What profite is it wallis to schyne wiþ preciose stonys and crist to die for hunger in þe pore man (Pecock, Visser (1963–73:966))

Another criterion which establishes that re-analysis has taken place is connected with the subcategorisation frame of the matrix predicate. The *NP to V* construction is found in ME after predicates whose subcategorisation does not provide for a benefactive θ-role. A modern example of this is (30):

(30) It is wicked for you to smoke.

I found the following instances in ME:

(31) it is a woodnesse a man to stryve with a strenger or a moore myghty man than he is hymself. (Chaucer, *Melibee*, Robinson (1957:180))

(32) we wolde wite ... wheþer it be þi wille, lord, hem falle into vs or no. (Pecock, Visser (1963–73:966))

(33) no wonder is a lewed man to ruste (Chaucer, *GP*, Robinson (1957:22))

In neither OE nor ME have I found examples of these predicates (*is woodnesse, be þi wil, is wonder*) with a dative or accusative (objective) case. When the (b) interpretation has to be expressed, one invariably finds a subclause in OE (introduced by *þæt, hu, if*); in ME subclauses are also far more common than the re-analysed *NP to V* construction.

In some instances, in which it is clear that re-interpretation has taken place according to one or more of the criteria mentioned above, this re-interpretation is further confirmed by the fact that the dative (objective) personal pronoun has been replaced by a nominative.[14]

(34) and thou (NOM) to love that lovyth nat the is but gret foly. (Malory, Vinaver (1947:322-3))

(35) and thou (NOM) to ly by oure modir is to muche shame for us to suffir. (Malory, Vinaver (1947:612))

It also happens that different manuscript versions make clear that re-interpretation has taken place (cf. (36)); similarly, in one text, two parallel phrases may be found in different syntactic configurations. (37) shows that the predicate *it be a foul thing* is first followed by the structurally ambiguous *NP + infini-*

tive phrase and the second time by a finite clause. It is highly likely that the *NP + infinitive* must be interpreted as a 'subject' construction parallel with the clause.

(36) 'Hit shall nat nede', seyde Merlion, 'thes two kynges to com agayne in the wey of warre' (Malory, Vinaver (1947:39))
other ms.: '... nat' saide Merlyn 'nede that these ...'

(37) if it be a foul thing a man to waste his catel on wommen, yet is it a fouler thing whan that ... wommen dispenden upon men hir catel and substaunce. (Chaucer, *Pars.T.*, Robinson (1957:256))

4. An explanation for the re-analysis of *(for) NP to V*

It has been shown that the older construction without *for* was re-analysed in ME, in many cases already before the newer construction with *for* (still only in the (a) interpretation) became current. It is clear that the new *for* construction ultimately becomes amenable to re-analysis as well, but unambiguous instances of this are found much later. The first unambiguous examples given in Visser (1963–73: §914) and Jespersen (1940) date from the sixteenth century. (In examples which do not contain semi-impersonal constructions, *for NP* is found slightly earlier as subject of the infinitive, cf. Visser (1963–73: §952).)

We are now left with two questions. One, why was the *NP to V* construction re-analysed in ME? And two, why did the re-interpretation take place earlier in the *NP to V* construction than in its parallel with *for*? I assume that the 'subject' analysis was not possible in OE since I have found no unambiguous examples of re-analysis in OE. That means that the new analysis only became available in ME. What occasioned the new interpretation?

In order to answer this question, it is important to look at other changes the syntax underwent between the OE and the early ME period. The most noticeable changes are:

(i) the gradual loss of inflexions
(ii) the rigidification in word order
(iii) the change in basic word order from S(ubject) O(bject) V(erb) to SVO (cf. Canale (1978))

The Rise of the For NP to V Construction

I do not wish to go into the cause of these changes, but I hope to show that these earlier changes made the new interpretation possible, perhaps even likely. How changes (ii) and (iii) affected the *NP to V* construction can best be shown with an example. Compare the following OE (38) and ME (39) clause structures:

(38) genoh bið munece (DAT) twa tunecan habban, (*Ben. Rule*, Visser (1963-73:951))

(39) if it be a foul thing a man to waste his catel on wommen (cf. (37))

The basic word order for OE was SOV,[15] thus (38) would have the following underlying structure:

(40)

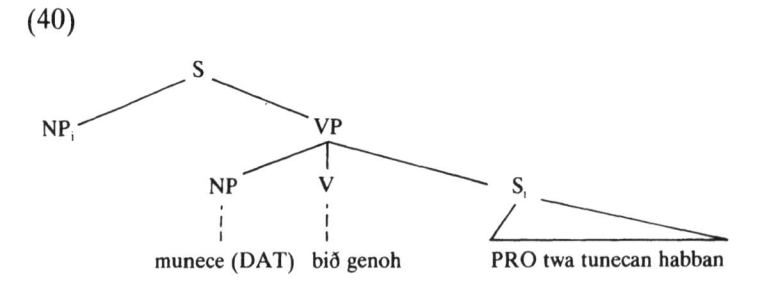

```
             S
           /   \
        NP_i    VP
               /|\
              NP V  S_1
              |  |   \
         munece(DAT) bið genoh   PRO twa tunecan habban
```

ME, with basic word order SVO, would have (41) as the underlying structure:

(41)

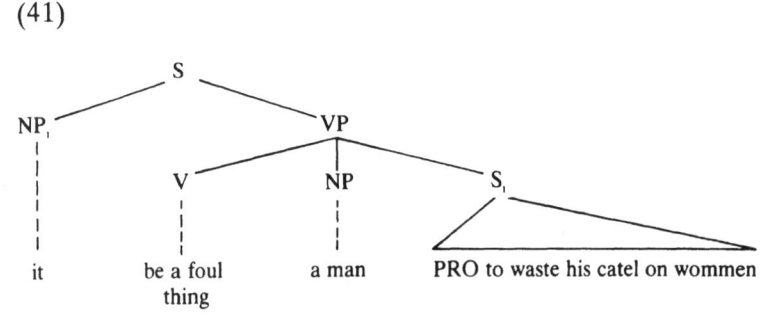

```
             S
           /   \
        NP_i    VP
         |     /|\
         |    V NP  S_1
         |    |  |    \
         it  be a foul  a man  PRO to waste his catel on wommen
                thing
```

These structures show that in OE the benefactive NP (*munece*) and the infinitive (*habban*) were not adjacent in underlying structure, whereas in ME, the NP *a man* and the infinitive *to waste* are adjacent in underlying structure, and — due to the rigidification in word order — also almost always in surface structure. It is my contention that, because of this adjacency, re-analysis became possible.

It will be clear from the discussion given above that I consider the change to be an optional one and not a necessary one, as Lightfoot believes. It cannot be a necessary change because the old (a) interpretation went on to exist side by side with the new one, (b) (just as 'organic' and 'inorganic' *for* constructions still exist). Even though the change is not necessary, it can still be explained within the theory of grammar given the word order change (step (a) in Lightfoot's scheme, given in section 1) and the presence of adjacency, which is related to Lightfoot's step (b), but with a difference. Under (b) Lightfoot has stated that the change must be the way it is given some general principle of *grammar*. In my scheme, this would not necessarily have to be a principle of grammar; it can also be another general principle, in this case the principle of perceptual strategy. The adjacency of NP and infinitive made it possible, given the basic SVO word order in ME, to interpret this structure as representing Subject Verb rather than Object Verb.[16]

One question still remains, why did re-analysis take place earlier in the *NP to V* constructions than in the corresponding *for NP to V* forms? There are a number of reasons for this. The first one is fairly obvious: the *NP to V* construction is much older and therefore likely to be subject to re-analysis, made possible by adjacency, earlier than the new *for* construction. Secondly, it is important to consider the reason for the introduction of *for*. In the constructions in question, the preposition *for* was used to indicate the recipient of the action, since the old dative case endings no longer clearly expressed a benefactive function. Thus, with the introduction of *for* the (benefactive) NP became again closely linked to the matrix verb and not to the infinitive, in spite of adjacency. It is only because the old and the new constructions appeared side by side for a long time that the new constructions also came to be re-analysed.

The re-interpretation of *NP to V* was also helped by another factor, which could not have assisted the re-analysis of *for NP to V*. Because of the loss of inflexions in late OE, early ME, it was no longer possible to distinguish between dative and accusative case forms, either in NPs or in pronouns. This meant that the construction *NP to V* found after semi-impersonal predicates formally resembled the infinitive construction found after the so-called 'verba sentiendi' as in (42):

(42) ond ða wundra ðe ic ðē wyrcan geseah

(and the miracles which I saw you perform) (*Æl. Hom.*, Bright (1895:84))

where the accusative NP (*ðē*) also functions as the subject of the infinitive. This sort of construction becomes in ME reinforced by accusative and infinitive constructions adopted from Latin; but they appear roughly at the same time as the re-analysed *NP to V* constructions, which means that they cannot have been the cause of re-analysis. As I have already indicated, it is my opinion that the rise of the accusative and infinitive in ME was made possible by the same word order change that made re-analysis of *NP to V* possible (cf. Fischer, forthcoming).

It is possible that another construction found in ME has been influential in the re-analysis of *NP to V*. However, since this construction developed at about the same time as the re-interpreted *NP to V* construction, it may even be the case that it was itself a product of the re-analysis of *NP to V*. One frequently comes across examples like the following:

(43) Sche wold deliverly do þerto hire miȝt, Forto[17] saue hem fro sorwe, hirself for to deye (Will. of Pal., Visser (1963–73:1008))

(44) ... yn him desir noon other fownes bredde, But argumentes to this conclusioun, That she of him wolde han compassioun, And he to ben hire man, while he may dure. (Chaucer, *T&C*, Robinson (1957:394))

In (43) the infinitive construction *hirself for to deye* seems to replace a conditional/concessive clause, whereas in (44), as is clear from the parallel construction *that she ...*, the infinitive construction *he to ben* replaces an object clause. If these constructions are separate developments, not related to the *NP to V* constructions found after semi-impersonals, they may have influenced the re-analysis of the semi-impersonal constructions.

It is not at all unlikely, however, that these constructions, which are also new in ME, are in fact derivatives of the new construction (after so-called semi-impersonals) which is the subject of this paper. First of all, many of these constructions *implicitly* contain a semi-impersonal expression. Consider the following examples:

(45) Hym thought no worship to have a knyght at such availe,

he to be on horsebacke and hys adversary on foote (Malory, Vinaver (1947:50))

(46) I to take þe lesse when I may have þe more, my ffrendes wold þenke me not wyse (*Stonor Lett.*, Visser (1963-73: 1006))

In (45) we have a case of an impersonal verb followed by a noun which frequently occurs in semi-impersonal expressions: 'it is no worship ...'; similarly *my ffrendes wold þenke me not wyse* closely corresponds to the semi-impersonal expression 'it is not wyse ...' or 'it is gret folly ...' etc.

Likewise in (43) and (44) it is not difficult to add a semi-impersonal expression like 'it is nede', 'it is good' etc. A second reason is that the kind of subclause which one could substitute for the infinitive constructions in (43) and (44) (introduced by (*even*) *if* and *that* respectively) is also frequently encountered after semi-impersonal predicates (cf. also (31)-(33)):

(47) (i) it is ful *fair a man to bere* hym evene ... (Chaucer, *Kn. T.*, Robinson (1957:32))
 (ii) Yet were it *fairer that we toke* our leve (Chaucer, *T&C*, Robinson: 464)
(48) (i) no *wonder* is *a lewèd man to ruste* (Chaucer, *GP*, Robinson: 22)
 (ii) no *wonder* is, *if that* drede have I (*R. Rose*, Robinson: 601)
 (iii) no *wonder* is *thogh that* I swelte and swete (Chaucer, *Mi. T.*, Robinson: 53)

A final remark with reference to the factors that may have facilitated the re-analysis of *NP to V* concerns the use of object clauses occurring after semi-impersonal predicates. In ME the complementiser *that* can be deleted from object clauses, as in Modern English. As a result of the loss of inflexions — not only in the nominal but also in the verbal system — it became increasingly difficult to distinguish object clauses from infinitive constructions, as the examples show:

(49) 'Bet is', quod he, 'thyn habitacioun Be with a leon or a foul dragoun, Than with a womman usynge for to chyde' (Chaucer, *W. of B.P.*, Robinson (1957:83))

(50) my wyl is outrely, This mayden ... Received be tomorwe (Chaucer, *Cl. T.*, Robinson: 111)

(51) Therefore is good ye (NOM) for hir sende (*R. Rose*, Robinson: 620)

In the examples the verb *be/sende* can be interpreted as a subjunctive (the normal mood after semi-impersonals) as well as an infinitive (in ME the plain infinitive and the *to*-infinitive could be used here[18]) so that these sentences are ambiguous.

5. Conclusion

In this paper I have given an explanation for the rise of the *for NP to V* construction both as a 'benefactive' and as a 'subject' construction. It has been shown that the more recent 'subject' construction was made possible by the re-analysis of the older *NP to V* construction, the predecessor of *for NP to V*. The re-analysis of the *NP to V* construction, in turn, was shown to be an optional change explainable within the theory of grammar: it was the result of the change in word order from SOV to SVO and the subsequent adjacency of NP and embedded infinitive.

I would like to finish with one last note, thereby linking the 'history of English' and 'Modern English structure'. The explanation of the change as presented here has in another respect an advantage over the explanation given by Lightfoot. Kiparski and Kiparski (1970) and Bresnan (1979) have noted that *for* complement constructions only appear after certain predicate types, which Kiparski and Kiparski characterise as 'emotive' and Bresnan as 'emotive' and 'desiderative'.[19] Bresnan further notes that the reason why these predicate types occur with *for* complements has to be found in the meaning of the preposition *for* (for the arguments, which are very persuasive, see Bresnan (1979)). In the explanation for the change given here, it is emphasised that *for* in the *for* complement construction developed from the *preposition for*, whereas in Lightfoot's account *for* is already a complementiser before the *for NP to V* construction develops. Thus, the explanation offered here neatly captures and gives insight into the position of the *for* complements in Present-Day English.

Notes

A slightly shorter version of this paper was given at the Third International Conference on English Historical Linguistics, in March 1983, at the University of Sheffield, England.

1. For this reason, Lightfoot has linked the appearance of the *for NP to V* construction to the disappearance of the ME *for to* infinitives, which would account for the use of *for* (see section 2.1).

2. In the older literature, a distinction is made between 'organic' and 'inorganic' *for*. *For* is organic when used purely as a dative marker; it is inorganic when used as a complementiser.

3. For the interaction between the theory of grammar and the history of syntactic change, see Lightfoot (1979).

4. The explanation provided in this paper is also given in terms of the EST. For a detailed outline see Chomsky (1981).

5. It is essential because in Lightfoot's framework the old construction can no longer be generated by the grammar which generates the new one.

6. Cf. also Warner (1982:25), and note 17.

7. In this respect, it is interesting to note that there are still dialects of English where the *for to* infinitive is used next to the *for NP to V* construction. This seems to argue against the idea that *because for* became a governor, the *for to* infinitive *had to* disappear. Cf. also Carroll (1983) on some of these dialects. To account for this 'double' use of *for*, she suggests (contra Chomsky (1981) and other EST grammarians) that *for* in the dialects under discussion (i.e. Ozark English and Ottawa Valley English) should be analysed as a preposition before infinitives and as a complementiser before *NP to V* constructions.

8. Nagucka (1985) disagrees with Warner in this respect. Although her paper is mainly concerned with the methodology used by Warner, with which she finds fault, it also suggests that the use of the accusative and infinitive construction could well be a native development. It is my belief that a closer look at the accusative and infinitive constructions she discusses will show that these do not form a homogeneous group, and that Latin influence cannot be discounted once one has differentiated the group of verbs that allow accusative and infinitive constructions into different types (cf. Fischer forthcoming).

9. For the notion of θ-role assignment, see Chomsky (1981:35ff).

10. More accurately the objective case. In ME dative and accusative cases were no longer distinguishable.

11. Cf. the following pairs found in Chaucer (Robinson, 1957):

This prison *caused* me nat *for to* crye (28)
That *caused* hym *to* sette hymself afyre (83)

God *bad* us *for to* wexe and multiplye (76)
And *bad* hym *to* be glad and have no fere (86)

The goute *lette* hire nothyng *for to* daunce (199)
But I am sorry that I have yow *let To* herken of youre book (402)

12. The older construction without *for* is largely ignored by Lightfoot (1979:187) and completely left out in Lightfoot (1981a:111). This is of course not surprising since they fall outside the scope of his explanation, which is strictly dependent on the change of *for* from non-governor to governor. For the re-analysis of the older construction, see Fischer and van der Leek (1981) and also Warner (1982:32ff).

13. For non-arguments, see Chomsky (1981:101).

14. Unlike Zeitlin (1908), I believe that the construction with nominative case marking is a later development of the construction that shows objective case. This development in the semi-impersonal construction would then parallel that of the impersonal verbs, where in many cases the original dative or accusative was also replaced by a nominative at this time. (Support for this argument is given in Warner (1982:43ff).)

15. This is the normal word order. When the object was a sentential object, it would follow the verb for perceptual reasons (cf. Kuno (1974)).

16. For the view that not only necessary (or radical) changes can be explained within the theory of grammar, but also optional ones, see Fischer and van der Leek (1981:340–1).

17. Notice that *for to* is spelled as one word, not at all unusual in ME manuscripts. It corroborates the conclusion reached in section *2.1* that *for* like *to* is an infinitive marker and not a complementiser.

18. This is clear from the following example where *be* can only be an infinitive (because of the infinitival -*n* ending),

But it is good a man *been* at his large (Chaucer, Robinson (1957:39))

19. For this reason, they do not equate *for* infinitive complements with *for*-less complements as e.g. Rosenbaum (1970) has done, who always generates *for* in the base, irrespective of whether it surfaces or not. Chomsky (1981:69) also ignores the semantic differences between *for* and *for*-less constructions.

References

Andersen, H. (1973) 'Abductive and Deductive Change', *Language* 49, 765–93

Bresnan, J.W. (1979) *Theory of Complementation in English Syntax*, Garland Publishing Inc., New York

Bright, J.W. (1895) *An Anglo-Saxon Reader and Grammar*, Allen and Unwin, London

Brown, C. (1924) *Religious Lyrics of the XIVth Century*, Clarendon Press, Oxford

Canale, M. (1978). 'Word Order Change in OE: Base Re-analysis in Generative Grammar' (unpubl. PhD diss.) McGill University, Montreal

Carroll, S. (1983) 'Remarks on FOR-TO Infinitives', *Linguistic Analysis 12*, 415–51
Chomsky, N. (1981) *Lectures on Government and Binding*, Foris, Dordrecht
Fischer, O.C.M. (forthcoming) 'The Origin and Spread of the Accusative and Infinitive Construction in English', *Folia Linguistica Historica 8*
—— and van der Leek, F.C. (1981) Review Article of Lightfoot, D.W. (1979), 'Optional vs. Radical Re-analysis: Mechanisms of Syntactic Change', *Lingua 55*, 301–50
Forshall, J. and Madden, F. (1879) *The New Testament in English, According to the Version by John Wycliffe and Revised by John Purvey*, Clarendon Press, Oxford
Forster, F.A. (1926) *A Stanzaic Life of Christ* (Early English Text Society, 166), Oxford University Press, London
Garmonsway, G.N. (1939) *Ælfric's Colloquy*, Methuen, London
Holthausen, F. (1888) *Vices and Virtues* (Early English Text Society, 89) Trübner, London
Ingram, J.K. (1893) *De Imitatione Christi* (Early English Text Society, e.s. 63) Trübner, London
Jespersen, O. (1940) *A Modern English Grammar on Historical Principles*, vol. V, Allen and Unwin, London
Kato, T. (1974) *A Concordance to the Works of Sir Thomas Malory*, University of Tokyo Press, Tokyo
Kayne, R.S. (1981) 'On Certain Differences between French and English', *Linguistic Inquiry 12*, 349–71
Kiparski, P. and Kiparski, C. (1970) 'Fact', in Bierwisch, M. and Heidolph, K.E. (eds) *Progress in Linguistics* (Janua Linguarum Ser. Major 43) Mouton, The Hague, pp. 143–73
Kuno, S. (1974) 'The Position of Relative Clauses and Conjunctions', *Linguistic Inquiry 5*, 117–36
Kurath, H. and Kuhn, S.M. (eds) (1954–) *Middle English Dictionary*, University of Michigan Press, Ann Arbor
Lightfoot, D.W. (1979) *Principles of Diachronic Syntax*, Cambridge University Press, Cambridge
—— (1981a) 'The History of Noun Phrase Movement' in Baker, C.L. and McCarthy, J.J. (eds) *The Logical Problem of Language Acquisition*, MIT Press, Cambridge, Mass., pp. 86–119
—— (1981b) 'A Reply to Some Critics', *Lingua 55*, 351–68
Mustanoja, T. (1960) *A Middle English Syntax*, vol. I, Mémoires de la Société Néophilologique de Helsinki, Helsinki
Nagucka, R. (1985). 'Some Remarks on Complementation in Old English', in R. Eaton, O. Fischer, W. Koopman, F.v.d. Leek (eds) *Papers from the 4th International Conference on English Historical Linguistics*, John Benjamins, Amsterdam, 195–204
Robinson, F.N. (1957) *The Complete Works of Geoffrey Chaucer*, 2nd edn, Oxford University Press, London
Rosenbaum, P.S. (1967) *The Grammar of English Predicate Complement Constructions*, MIT Press, Cambridge, Mass.
Skeat, W.W. (1886) *The Vision of William Concerning Piers the*

Plowman, vol. III, Oxford University Press, Oxford
—— (1897) *The Complete Works of Geoffrey Chaucer*, vol. VII: *Chaucerian and Other Pieces*, Clarendon Press, Oxford
Stockwell, R.P. (1976) 'A Note on "The Base Component as a Locus of Syntactic Change", by D.W. Lightfoot' in Christie, W. (ed.) *Current Progress in Historical Linguistics*, North Holland, Amsterdam
Stoffel, C. (1894) *Studies in Written and Spoken English*, Thieme, Zutphen
Tatlock, J.S.P. and Kennedy, A.G. (1927) *A Concordance to the Complete Works of Geoffrey Chaucer and to the Romaunt of the Rose*, The Carnegie Institution of Washington, Washington
Vinaver, E. (1947) *The Works of Sir Thomas Malory*, vols I–III, Clarendon Press, Oxford
Visser, F.Th. (1963–73) *An Historical Syntax of the English Language*, Vol. I–IIIb, Brill, Leiden
Warner, A. (1982) *Complementation in Middle English and the Methodology of Historical Syntax*, Croom Helm, London
Zandvoort, R.W. (1949) 'A Note on "Inorganic *for*"', *English Studies* 30, 265–9
Zeitlin, J. (1908) *The Accusative with Infinitive and Some Kindred Constructions in English*, Columbia University Press, New York

7
Negation in Shakespeare

N.F. Blake
University of Sheffield

Although there have been several grammars of Shakespeare's language, they have not contained detailed surveys of his use of methods of negation. At best they have included incidental and unrelated comments on particular negative clauses, among which the so-called double negative has attracted most discussion.[1] The same holds true of more general studies of the language of the Elizabethan and Jacobean periods such as those by Partridge and Barber.[2] Often the comments have amounted to nothing more than a description of those features of negation which are different in Shakespeare's and Modern English. On the other hand, the historical development of negation in several languages was investigated by Jespersen some time ago, and more recently studies of negation in Middle English have appeared, though these have not taken their investigations beyond 1500.[3] Modern grammarians have approached negation with a view to establishing rules for its use, usually from a transformational standpoint.[4] Although such studies have considerable interest in their own right, they tend to be theoretical and because they are based on modern data they offer little help to understanding negation at earlier periods of the language. It therefore seemed appropriate to me, in a volume which honours the memory of Barbara Strang, who made so many contributions to our knowledge of the historical development of English, to offer a fuller investigation of negation in Shakespeare than has hitherto been attempted. The first task is necessarily to review the various means of expressing negation in his works, and so this essay will be descriptive rather than evaluative. The results are not based on a comprehensive listing of all examples, but they represent a study of a few plays supplemented by more cursory investigation of all of them.

As Jespersen made clear, all languages have a tendency to place the negative element early in the sentence, though it will not necessarily, or even usually, carry the principal stress. The absence of stress can result in this element becoming weak. When that occurs, the negation may be strengthened by the addition of a further negative element later in the sentence, and this later element may in time completely replace the original one. The process of weakening and strengthening can then commence again. In Old English negation was expressed through the particle *ne*, which was placed before the verb and thus had an early position in the clause. It was not stressed and as it weakened it was reinforced by various negative adverbs after the verb, the principal one being *noht/naht*, formed from *nawiht* 'nothing'. By the Middle English period the normal pattern of negation had become *I ne seye not*, though forms without either the first or the last negative were frequently found. The *ne* particle gradually fell out leaving *not* in the post-verb position as the only element of negation. This stage had been reached by the Early Modern English period. Certainly *ne* is no longer a living form. It occurs archaically in *Pericles* where Gower as the Chorus can say 'Ne aught escapen but himself' (II.Prol.36).[5] Gower uses various older forms and his use of *ne* helps to confirm its archaic status. Only one other example of *ne* occurs elsewhere in Shakespeare, where it has the sense of 'nor'. This example, in *All's Well that Ends Well* II.i.172, was felt to be unacceptable by earlier editors and was often emended out of the text. It is now more usually admitted to the text and may be taken as an exception to the general pattern of negation.

The standard negative adverb in Shakespeare is *not*. As Jespersen has reminded us, we would expect certain developments in its pattern of use to occur. The first is a tendency for it to move earlier in the sentence because the negative particle traditionally came early in the clause. This movement forward may be merely formal, though it may be related to the similar movement of the negative to the main clause from a subordinate clause as when 'I think he will not come' becomes 'I do not think he will come'. The movement of *not* to an earlier position in the sentence does not occur regularly so that its position in the clause becomes erratic. Even in those examples where it occurs after the verb, it need not necessarily come immediately after it. The negative had achieved a certain amount of freedom in its positioning. Naturally as the plays are mostly in blank verse, the demands of the metre may have affected the position of the negative, though in many cases emphasis and metre work together. The placing of the negative further forward in the sentence was assisted by the use of modals and auxiliaries such as *do*; this applies equally to past tense forms other than the simple preterite. Nevertheless, the use of auxiliaries had not developed as far as in Modern English, and verb forms like the progressive tenses and compound past tenses were not used as often then as now. Many of the forms like *do* and the auxiliaries had a stylistic rather than a grammatical function.[6] Often they were employed for a heightened style or to create additional emphasis. Thus verbs of believing and assertion are often found with a *do* when they are used to convey a sense of absolute belief or affirmation. In *The Winter's Tale* Polixenes says 'I do believe thee' (I.ii.446) when he wishes to reassure Camillo that there is no shadow of doubt in his mind. The use of *do* with negatives was well established in Shakespeare's plays, and one might almost say it was the more usual form in declarative sentences. Thus 'The grief that does not speak' (*Macb.* IV.iii.209) represents a regular pattern. But it must be admitted that in the plays negatives are more often introduced in some highly charged situation so that they are likely to be found in imperatives, interrogatives or with some emphasis. So declarative sentences, which we are at the moment concerned with, contain fewer negative forms. The verbs of knowing and affirming when they occur are emphatic; and in the negative they more frequently appear without *do*. When Paulina says 'We do not know How he may soften at the sight o'th'child (*WT* II.ii.39-40), this is a statement of fact and the *know* is not emotionally charged. Elsewhere this verb and others like it are used forcefully, and in this sense they are usually found without *do*. The negative *not* may be placed either before or after the verb, though the position after it seems more emphatic often because it comes at the end of a line or sentence. In *The Winter's Tale* Camillo can say emphatically to Polixenes 'I know not' (I.ii.432) and Hermione can equally firmly claim to Leontes 'You speak a language that I understand not' (III.ii.77). When *not* occurs before the verb without *do* there is also some emphasis, though it seems not to be as marked as when Francisco says in *The Tempest* 'I not doubt He came alive to land' (II.i.115-16). However, one must always keep in mind that the position of *not* and the presence or absence of *do* may be determined by metrical considerations. When in *Antony and Cleopatra* Menecrates says 'That what they do delay they not deny' (II.i.3), there is no doubt that *not* in the latter clause balances *do* in the first one and is so placed in order to allow the two clauses to parallel each other structurally. It would not be wise to probe this example for any deeper reason in the ordering of the negative.

The tendency for *not* to be placed before the verb is paralleled by its position before nouns, particularly those formed from a verb; in these cases *not* fulfils almost the same function as prefixes like *un-*. Consequently some editors introduce a hyphen after the *not*, though hyphens are not usually found here in the quartos or First Folio. In *Troilus and Cressida* III.iii.266 Thersites says 'he professes not answering'. In most glossaries and grammars the group *not answering* is understood to be a nominal group with the *not* dependent on the *answering*; it would, however, be equally possible to interpret it as a negative postposed after the verb meaning 'he does not profess answering'. The first interpretation may be justified by such examples as 'for not appearance' (*H8* IV.i.30) and 'in our not-fearing Britain' (*Cymb.* II.iv.19). When there is an adjective, whether formed from a verb or not, it is usual to place *not* before it, though in many cases the clauses in which these examples occur are elliptical. From *The Winter's Tale* we may note:

>   if industriously
> I play'd the fool, it was my negligence,
> Not weighing well the end. (I.ii.256-8)

and

> But this most cruel usage of your Queen —
> Not able to produce more accusation
> Than your own weak-hing'd fancy (II.iii.116-18).

The adverbial *not* may follow the verb, and when it does so it is possible to have the order verb–complement–negative particularly when the complement is a pronoun. Examples from *The Winter's Tale* include 'Though you perceive me not how I give line' (I.ii.181), 'and feel't not' (I.ii.207) and 'I love thee not a jar o'th'clock behind' (I.ii.43). In these cases there may be special

Negation in Shakespeare

reasons for the position of *not*. In the first there is the problem of focus which I will return to later. In the second it is the pronoun which has been weakened and amalgamated with the verb so that the negative has been put into the end position. In the third the negative has been strengthened by the addition of 'a jar o'th'clock' and so it has attracted the *not* further away from the verb. In all examples the *not* may need to be interpreted as having greater emphasis than would be the case if it had occurred before the complement.

A second aspect that one might expect from the historical development of negatives is that the *not* should be weakened and need some form of strengthening. This might take the form of being moved further forward in the sentence which we have already discussed, becoming unstressed in pronunciation and being represented as *n't*, or being strengthened by the addition of further negatives or even through replacement. As far as weakening of *not* is concerned the most interesting feature is that there are no examples in Shakespeare's works of the contracted form *n't*. Although there are many contracted verbal and pronominal forms and although one might have expected the development of an unstressed *not* in pronunciation, there is no evidence for such a form in the plays. Similarly *not* has not been amalgamated to preceding auxiliaries as in modern *won't* and *shan't*. In Modern English it is possible to have two shortened forms of some utterances, as in 'They're not going' and 'They aren't going'. The second of these is not found in Shakespeare. Although *not* is found in proximity to many abbreviated forms, it is not itself abbreviated. Since the abbreviated form is not found in other writings of the period, it seems probable that the orthographic convention for representing this kind of shortening had not yet been developed, rather than that the shortened form was not used in speech. Examples of *not* linked with other abbreviations include the following from *The Winter's Tale*: 'and feel't not' (I.ii.207), 'Ha' not you seen, Camillo?' (I.ii.267); 'But that's not to the point' (III.iii.88); and 'I'll not remember' (III.ii.227). Naturally abbreviations are readily expanded or eliminated from one text to another so there is considerable variety between quartos and First Folio and among modern editions. Where the Second Quarto of *Hamlet* has 'Looks 'a not like the King?' (I.i.43), other versions and many modern editions read *it* for *a*. Yet despite this variety, the negative form *not* is not abbreviated at all, although *never* may be represented as monosyllabic.

That *not* was felt to be weakened is suggested by its replacement by other words such as *never* and *nothing*. Although these two words can have a different meaning from *not*, in many instances it is reasonably certain that they are simply more emphatic forms of the negative. Thus in *Macbeth* when the captain describes the battle at the beginning of the play he reports the killing of Macdonwald by Macbeth as:

Which ne'er shook hands, nor bade farewell to him,
Till he unseam'd him from the nave to th' chaps. (I.ii.21-2)

Here the *ne'er* is a more emphatic form of the negative as is suggested not only by the context but also by its association with *nor* in the following clause. Similarly when Hecate is upbraiding the other witches for acting without her, she says:

And I, the mistress of your charms,
The close contriver of all harms,
Was never call'd to bear my part. (III.v.6-8)

When Macbeth claims somewhat later that he 'shall never vanquish'd be until Great Birnam wood to high Dunsinane Hill Shall come' (IV.i.91-3), he uses *never* where we today would certainly use *not*. *Never* like *not* can be placed in front of participles acting as nouns or adjectives, particularly the latter. In this function it has the force of a negative prefix like *un-*, and it is often hyphenated with the following word in modern editions. Examples include 'never-withering banks' (*Cymb.* V.iv.98) and 'never-quenching fire' (*R2* V.v.108). *Never* can also appear as part of a nominal group even when its head is not formed from a verb, in which case it acts as an emphatic form of *no*. Thus we find examples like 'ne'er a tongue' (*Merch.* II.ii.143) and 'ne'er a fantastical knave' (*AYL* III.iii.94). When there are expanded forms of verbs with an auxiliary or *do*, it is usual for the *never* to precede the auxiliary rather than to come between it and the verb, though the latter position can also be found. But an order such as 'I never may believe These antique fables' (*MND* V.i.2-3) seems to be rather more usual than that in 'I can never cut off a woman's head' (*Meas.* IV.ii.4), though naturally when the auxiliary is abbreviated the negative must necessarily follow it as in 'I'll ne'er put my finger in the fire' (*MWW* I.iv.78). This positioning of the *never* before the auxiliary may be intended to increase its emphatic nature. It may also be explained simply by the fact that *never* regularly comes before the verb in declarative clauses while *not* does not. Its early placing in the sentence may well reflect its emphatic nature. *Nothing* has the same range of use as *never* and *not*. It can be used in the same positions as *never* and in most cases may be considered a somewhat more emphatic negation than *not*. It does not seem necessary to include examples of its use here. It can be placed before or after the verb.

A different way of strengthening the negation was to add some words to turn the negative word into a negative phrase, to add a tag question at the end of the negative clause, or to add some other adverbial including other negatives to strengthen the sense of negation. The turning of a single negative word into a phrase occurs most often with *not*, which naturally seemed to be a word which needed strengthening most. We have already quoted 'I love thee not a jar o'th'clock behind' (*WT* I.ii.43) in which the 'not a jar o'th'clock' may be considered a phrasal addition to strengthen the negation in the sentence. The modern 'not a whit' and 'not a bit' were already well established, and the former could be used with *never* which in its turn could appear as 'ne'er a whit at all' as in *Titus Andronicus* IV.ii.53. Examples with *not* are found in *Taming of the Shrew* at II.i.235, and with *never* at I.i.229. Other additions can be more colourful, though many are likely to be fairly standard usages: 'not a word' (*Lear* II.i.12); 'not altogether so' (*Lear* II.iv.230); 'not a jot' (*Haml.* V.i.109); 'not for the world' (*Temp.* V.i.173); 'never a King's son in Christendom' (*1H4* I.ii.94–5); 'not a straw' (*WT* III.ii.108).

The normal procedure for tag questions is that negative polarity is followed by a positive tag, and conversely that positive polarity is followed by a negative tag. There are, however, very few apparent tags in Shakespeare's writings and some that might seem to be tags are excluded by the above definition. It is also characteristic of modern tags that they include abbreviated forms of the negative or even of other words. In Shakespeare this abbreviation is not found, since *not* is never abbreviated; but there are examples of elliptical forms which might be interpreted as tags. The absence of abbreviation leads to a ponderousness in some instances which tends to hide the nature of the tag itself. Thus when Polonius says to Reynaldo 'You have me, have you not?' (*Haml.* II.i.68), this represents a typical situation where you would expect a tag, although the full 'have you not' tends to destroy its nature. For the most part tags are not found in declarative sentences in Shakespeare, though one or two examples might be interpreted in that way except that the tag tends to indicate that the declarative is to be interpreted as an interrogative. When Hamlet says to Horatio 'His beard was grizzl'd — no?' (*Haml.* I.ii.239), the utterance is in the form of a statement which is seeking affirmation although the punctuation in the Alexander edition destroys the role of *no* as a tag. In this case the sentence is in the affirmative and the tag is negative. In an instance in *The Winter's Tale* the tag is placed immediately after the verb so that some editors have been uncertain how to handle it:

> Not noted, is't,
> But of the finer natures, by some severals
> Of head-piece extraordinary? (I.ii.225–7)

Here the sentence is negative and the tag is positive, but the tag helps to reinforce the negative by its position.

The addition of another adverb, particularly a further negative, is one of the best documented aspects of Shakespeare's methods of negation. The most frequent word used as a second negative is *neither*, as in *Two Gentlemen of Verona*: 'that cannot be so neither' (II.iii.18) and 'I care not for that neither' (III.i.332). This word may also be used to strengthen other negatives such as *nothing* or *no*, especially when these have been used in clauses where *not* could as easily have been employed. Hence there occur examples like 'you'll lie like dogs, and yet say nothing neither' (*Temp.* III.ii.19) and 'and yet give no thousand crowns neither' (*AYL* I.i.79). Other words can also be used to add the second negation, especially after *nor* which as we shall see often has a linking function in which the sense of negation is not very strong. Thus we find 'it is no addition to her wit, nor no great argument of her folly' (*Ado* II.iii.214), where the *nor* has a simple co-ordinate sense and the *no* in the second clause is used to echo that in the first. It is not surprising, therefore, that three negatives can sometimes be found together as in 'nor never none Shall mistress be of it' (*TN* III.i.156–7), where again the *nor* has a straightforward co-ordinate function. It is always possible to put another emphatic adverb in the clause to strengthen its negation, but such adverbs are not necessarily focused upon the actual negative word found. When they do occur, they are found mostly with *no* to reinforce a direct negative answer, as in 'No truly' (*Lear* IV.vi.4).

It was naturally possible to strengthen the negative by repeating it one or more times or to combine several of the methods which have been outlined already. Repetition makes for emphasis, but it may often result from the demands of the poetry and metre. The most famous example of repetition is Lear's 'never, never, never, never, never' (V.iii.308), but it must be admitted that this kind of repetition whether positive or negative is typical of Lear when he is under emotional stress. Examples from *The Winter's Tale* include 'my heart dances, But not for joy, not joy' (I.ii.110–11) and 'There is no tongue that moves, none, none i'th'world' (I.ii.20). In the latter example there is the addition of *none* which is then repeated and reinforced by *i'th'world* so that this negation has been strengthened through several means. This example shows how negation could be increased in emphasis and poetic effect. Another example from the same play worth considering is when Paulina says 'This is not, no, Laid to thy answer' (III.ii.195–6). Here the *no* may be taken as an added negative to strengthen the *not*. But it occurs in the same position as the tag *is't* in the same play which was quoted above (I.ii.225–7). It might almost be possible to interpret *no* here as a kind of tag as well, though the normal punctuation assumes an emphatic *no* simply strengthening the sense of negation expressed by *not*.

It is possible to replace the adverbial *not* by the determiner *no* so that 'I haven't any books' corresponds to 'I have no books'. In Modern English the former sentence demands the use of non-assertive forms like *any*, but in Shakespeare's English these words still had a rather different function to which we shall return. Hence Shakespearian English prefers the sentence type with *no* rather than that with *not*, for not only does this avoid the introduction of what would have been non-assertive forms, but it also allows the focus of the negation to be transferred to the noun from the verb, which means that the sentence appears to be more dynamic and forceful. There are therefore many examples of sentences like 'I know no answer' (*Lear* I.i.201), 'It is no vicious blot' (*Lear* I.i.227), and 'I am no honest man' (*Lear* I.ii.164). This *no* can be used ironically to suggest that there is a great deal, as when Falstaff says 'Here's no vanity' (*1H4* V.iii.31). When the noun is followed by *but*, the sense is 'only' as in the sentence 'Here's no scoring but upon the pate' (*1H4* V.iii.29). Naturally there is little typographic difference between *no* and *not*, and it is possible that some examples have been altered in the printing process. For in many cases *no* and *not* would each make perfect sense. In *Hamlet* Polonius twice says 'I use no art' (II.ii.96, 99), whereas Hamlet writes 'I have not art' (II.ii.120); and in either example the other negative would make just as good sense and syntax. *No* also appears before comparatives, among which *no more* is particularly common. Some examples of this form allow Shakespeare to create elliptical sentences as in

> and provide me presently
> A riding suit, no costlier than would fit
> A franklin's huswife. (*Cymb*. III.ii.74–6)

This group of *no* and a comparative can be used as a pre-determiner when it is followed by *a* as is still possible in more restricted examples today. Thus an example like 'whose beauty claims No worse a husband than the best of men' (*Ant*. II.ii.132-3) would be still possible, whereas 'with no greater a run' (*Shrew*. IV.i.13) is decidedly archaic now. When *no* is used before *other* the sense implied is usually positive. When the Duke in *Measure for Measure* says 'as I believe no other' (V.i.60), he means simply 'as I believe to be the case'. When used with *or* in conjunction with an affirmation *no* is used to mean 'not', though in many cases the use of *no* may be explained as elliptical because the following noun has been eliminated. Hence in *The Tempest* the clause 'If you be maid or no' (I.ii.427) the *no* may be assumed to stand for *no maid.* In other instances the *no* is parallel with a verbal rather than a nominal group and can only be interpreted as a variant of *not*. Hence we have 'Whether you will or no' (*Temp*. III.i.86). In some instances *no* appears as a variant of *not* before a verb which answers to a similar verb in a preceding sentence. In *King John* the following exchange occurs:

John   I had a mighty cause
To wish him dead, but thou hadst none to kill him.

Hub.   No had, my lord! (IV.ii.205-7)

The grammatical interpretation of the expression is difficult, though it may be possible to understand the *had* as a noun functionally shifted from the verb. It would also be possible to take the clause as interrogative rather than declarative.

None has a close relationship with *no* since it acts as its predicative form. When a question has a *no* nominal group, the answer will be *none* without the rest of the nominal group. This can be seen in:

Edm.   Found you no displeasure in him by word nor countenance?
Edg.   None at all. (*Lear* I.ii.148-50)

This *none* can take a qualifying adjective as in 'None rare' (*WT* I.ii.367) which means 'No news which is unusual'. If necessary the *no* and the noun may be repeated for emphasis, as in

Leon.   What noise there, ho?
Paul.   No noise, my lord. (*WT* II.iii.39-40)

Such examples may often have an ironic or satirical implication. *None* is also used pronominally in the sense 'not any, no body'. In some of these cases we may assume that it is acting again as a kind of predicative form of *no*. When Valentine says 'She gave me none except an angry word' (*TGV* II.i.146), the *none* refers back to *earnest* of the previous sentence. The same is true when Silvia says 'Better have none Than plural faith' (*TGV* V.iv.51-2), where the *none* looks forward to *faith*. On occasions the *none* will refer to a part of a nominal group. When Antigonus says 'I am none' (*WT* II.iii.82), he refers back to Leontes's 'nest of traitors' to mean that he is not a traitor. In many instances *none* is preferred where we would today use *not*. When Reagan calls Gloucester a traitor, he replies 'I'm none' (*Lear* III.vii.32) rather than 'I'm not'. It replaces *no* when the noun comes first, either immediately or with several intervening words. The variety of the various types of negation can be seen from the following passage from *The Tempest*:

>   for no kind of traffic
> Would I admit; no name of magistrate;

> Letters should not be known; riches, poverty,
> And use of service, none; contract, succession,
> Bourn, bound of land, tilth, vineyard, none;
> No use of metal, corn, or wine, or oil;
> No occupation. (II.i.142–8)

Here *none* after the nominal group interchanges with *no* before the nominal group as well as with *not* as part of a verbal group. In some expressions *none* seems closer to modern *not* than to *no*, particularly when followed by *of*, but in many cases the noun to which it refers may be considered to have been suppressed. When the Clown in *The Winter's Tale* says 'He must know 'tis none of your daughter nor my sister' (IV.iv.807), the *none* refers back to the 'strange sights' which they intend to show the king. Although grammatically elliptical, the sense must be 'He will recognise that they are not the sort of things which would belong to a daughter of yours or a sister of mine'.

So far in this essay I have mainly concentrated on declarative sentences, though naturally tags have to be taken in relation to interrogatives. The word order patterns which have been mentioned are those which occur in sentences with the normal pattern of subject–verb–complement. When this order is disturbed then the negator may occur in a different position. For example, when there is an adverb as headword of a sentence, this may cause the verb or auxiliary to be placed before the subject. In such cases the subject will then precede the negator which will remain in front of the verb. Hence 'I cannot come' will become 'Then can I not come' rather than 'Then cannot I come' or 'Then can I come not'. The latter two patterns are found, but they may be regarded as rare. Similarly *never*, which usually comes before the verb and auxiliary will be pushed further back in the clause if there is inversion of subject and verb. In *King Lear* the normal pattern of 'I never gave you kingdom' (III.ii.17) may be changed through re-arrangement of word order to 'See't shalt thou never' (III.vii.66) and 'But better service have I never done you' (III.vii.73), in which the *never* comes later in the clause.

The concentration so far on declarative sentences has been deliberate since a distinction between various types of clause has not been made by previous investigators in Shakespeare's language. This may have caused some misunderstanding in the development and pattern of negation. As already indicated, declarative sentences in the negative are frequently formed with *do* or with an auxiliary unless they contain emphatic verbs of believing and others of similar import. On the other hand, interrogative and imperative sentences are much less likely to have a *do* or an auxiliary as part of their structure and this may well be because the majority of such sentences tend to be emphatic. In *Macbeth* one might consider the following examples of the imperative without *do*: 'Hear it not' (II.i.63); 'Be not lost' (II.ii.71); 'Fail not our feast' (III.i.27); 'regard him not' (III.iv.58); 'speak not' (III.iv.117; IV.i.89); 'Stand not' (III.iv.119); 'Be not found here' (IV.ii.68); 'But fear not yet' (IV.iii.69); and 'Keep it not from me' (iv.iii.200). This list is not exhaustive, but it shows the many examples of this type that are found. Examples with *do* can also be found, and it is clear that this form was known; but the examples are relatively few. They include 'Do not bid me speak' (II.iii.70) and 'Yet do not fear' (IV.iii.87). It is difficult to account for these examples since there is little to set them off from the others. It may be that the metre was responsible for them or it may be that they are simply gradually becoming more popular. At all events the brevity of the normal pattern of imperative contrasts with the more customary extended form of the declarative. This may be accentuated because there are naturally no imperative forms with auxiliaries like *shall* or *will*, and because imperatives formed from compound verb tenses are also few not only in Shakespeare but also more recently. Yet there is the alternative form in *let*, which may include the speaker in its focus but need not. Thus when Macbeth says 'Let not light see my black and deep desires' (I.iv.51), this could have been expressed more succinctly as 'Light, see not my ...' and might be what is a more typical expression in Shakespeare. In other examples the speaker is certainly involved in the focus, which may appear to make the resulting imperative less decisive than otherwise as when Malcolm says 'Let's not consort with them' (II.iii.134). In the positive this could have been expressed either as 'Let's consort' or as 'Consort we', though in the negative the latter pattern is unusual. The negator *not* may be replaced by *never* or *nothing*, though the former is much commoner than the latter. When *never* occurs it comes before the imperative and hence strengthens the sense of negation. Consider 'Never go home' (*Troil.* V.x.2) and 'Never crave him' (*Meas.* V.i.425). *Nothing* follows the verb as in 'say nothing' (*Meas.* V.i.436).

With interrogatives the pattern seems to fall between those for declarative and imperative. There are more examples without *do* or an auxiliary than is the case with declaratives, but since many interrogatives can take an auxiliary there are fewer examples of a simple verb plus negator than one finds with imperatives. In most cases it is difficult to understand any difference in emphasis in interrogatives with or without *do* or auxiliary: 'Do you not hope' (*Macb.* I.iii.118) and 'Know you not' (*Macb.* I.vii.30) do not seem to be far apart in emphasis or significance. So it is probable that the variations that exist in the interrogative are caused by the metre. Nevertheless, examples with *do* are not particularly frequent, though those with auxiliaries do occur commonly. With interrogatives there is inversion of subject and verb or auxiliary where one is found. The negator *not* may be placed before or after the subject, though with auxiliaries it is more usual to have the pattern auxiliary–subject–negator. Hence one may find both 'Dismay'd not this' (*Macb.* I.i.33) and 'see you not' (*Macb.* II.iv.21), and both 'Did not you speak' (*Macb.* II.ii.16) and 'Did he not straight ...' (*Macb.* III.vi.11). As with the other sentence types it is possible to replace *not* by either *never* or *nothing*, though both forms of replacement are less commonly met with in interrogative than in declarative sentences. When *never* is used, it tends to be taken out of the immediate verbal group to be linked with the complement. It occurs most often with the verb 'to have' as in 'hast thou never an eye in thy head?' (*1H4* II.i.227) and 'Hath your Grace ne'er a brother like you?' (*Ado* II.i.290).

A characteristic feature of Shakespeare's style is his fondness for ellipsis which allows him to compress more meaning in fewer words. When there is a negative in the elliptical expression, this will naturally not be omitted since the sentence would otherwise change its meaning. Verbs or nouns may be left out as easily as the more grammatical parts of speech. The result is that the negation is thrown into greater prominence, though it is hardly provable that this was Shakespeare's intention. Inevitably, the absence of any set patterns of clause differentiation in his language may make it difficult to interpret the elliptical sentence. In *The Winter's Tale* when Polixenes has just been made aware of Leontes's changed regard for him, he says 'Not speak?' (I.ii.365). The Alexander text which is reproduced has a question mark, though other editions do not. It is possible to interpret these words as declarative, imperative or interrogative. Those editors who interpret it as the last type do not reveal whether they think Polixenes is expressing wonder why Leontes did not speak or questioning whether he himself ought to mention it to anyone. If declarative, it could be a statement of fact that Leontes did not speak, and then an exclamation mark (for which the question mark in Elizabethan times did service) might be appropriate. If the sentence is interpreted as imperative, it would indicate that Polixenes is telling himself not to speak about the incident. This particular play contains many elliptical expressions which may be ambiguous in their grammatical elucidation. Others are not necessarily ambiguous, but the effect is still to cast the negation into prominence. When Paulina says

> lest she suspect, as he does,
> Her children not her husband's! (II.iii.106–7)

the *not* occupies the key position in the final line and so acts as a kind of pivot. The omission of the verb allows the two nominal groups to be balanced around the negative.

One may perhaps attribute to compression the frequency with which a negative phrase or clause is used in an adversative way, particularly to contradict what has just been stated. In such cases *not* is the negator most likely to be used. The negative phrase or clause will normally presuppose what has already been said and not repeat it, though it must often be understood. In *The Winter's Tale* the following exchange takes place:

Leon.   Hence with her, out o'door!
           A most intelligencing bawd!
Paul.   Not so. (II.iii.67–8)

Here the *not so* is elliptical for 'It's not true that I'm a bawd', which in Modern English might be expressed either 'I'm not' or 'That's a lie'. The negator in such adversative statements often comes first and so creates the sense of a firm rejection of what has just been proposed. Naturally as in Modern English two clauses of which the latter is a negative may form part of a sentence, and in this case the second clause will often omit those parts of the first which would otherwise need to be repeated. Thus Angus says to Macbeth:

Negation in Shakespeare

> We are sent
> To give thee, from our royal master, thanks;
> Only to herald thee into his sight,
> Not pay thee. (*Macb.* I.iii.100–3)

In these sentences *not* is the common negator used. Again it will usually come at the head of the second clause and so act as the pivot around which the contrast is expressed.

The negator used to link phrases or clauses is *nor*, which might be assumed to have the sense 'and not', though in fact it is much harder to pin down its full range of meaning. This is partly explained by the typical Elizabethan uncertainty regarding conjunctions which may be either co-ordinating or contrastive, and partly by the common practice at the time to strengthen negation by repeating negative elements. Hence *nor* can be equivalent in many instances to modern *and* or *or*. Consider, for example, the following lines from *Macbeth*:

> Speak then to me, who neither beg nor fear
> Your favours nor your hate. (I.iii.60–1)

In the first clause the traditional *neither ... nor* contrast occurs, but the negative sense from that has been carried over to the second line where the contrast is positive rather than negative. Macbeth does not look for their favours *or* their hate. The focus of negation has been carried forward to the nominal groups which do not need it, presumably to emphasise the negative expression of the clause as a whole. It is true that the typographic difference between *nor* and *or* is slight so that there may be cases which could be explained simply as misprints. In *King Lear* where the First Folio reads *or* at III.iii.5, the Quarto reads *nor*, which may be the correct reading though it is not normally found in modern editions. However, the use of *nor* in cases which demand no negative or in which a co-ordinate conjunction might be expected are so frequent that typographical error cannot be blamed for them. A further example from *Macbeth* where negatives are grouped together in a clause is:

> O horror, horror, horror! Tongue nor heart
> Cannot conceive nor name thee. (II.iii.62–3)

Here in the first line the *nor* does duty for the expected **neither**

... *nor* construction. In the second we have two further negatives, one negating the auxiliary and the other the two verbs; in both these cases it would be more common now to have the positive forms. When *nor* occurs at the head of a sentence it has a co-ordinate function rather than an adversative one, which as we saw in the last paragraph is performed by *not*. So later in the same scene we find:

Don. Our tears are not yet brew'd.
Mal.   Nor our strong sorrow
Upon the foot of motion. (II.iii.122–3)

Here *nor* has the sense 'and not', though in the second clause the verb also has to be understood from the earlier one. This again, as we saw with *not*, is a common feature with negative clauses, even though there is as here a change of person. The sense is 'And our strong sorrow is not yet upon the foot of motion'. When a second clause contains a separate negator in it and is also introduced by *nor*, the *nor* will then approximate to modern *and*, for it will act as a co-ordinating link between the two clauses and also reinforce the negation which is expressed through the other negator. When Lorenzo says in *The Merchant of Venice* 'He is not, nor we have not heard from him' (V.i.35), the *nor* can be understood to represent modern *and* though it does indicate how readily negation was emphasised in Shakespearian language.

We saw in the previous paragraph how *nor* could do duty for the *neither ... nor* construction. This can also be expressed through *nor ... nor*. Indeed *nor* can be introduced before a string of nouns or verbs which are to be negated, or it can appear before some of them only. In the latter case it is more usually the middle elements that are likely to be without the negator. The following example from *Macbeth* is typical of this usage:

Treason has done his worst; nor steel, nor poison,
Malice domestic, foreign levy, nothing,
Can touch him further. (III.ii.24–5)

Here of the four nominal groups the first two are introduced by *nor* and the latter two simply follow without negation in a list. But the negation is reinforced after the list is concluded by the insertion of *nothing*, which in this edition is made to go with the nominal groups rather than with the following verb. Some editions prefer to have no comma after *nothing* and so leave the latter interpretation open as a possibility. If *nothing* is taken with the nominal groups, the verb is not negated. *Nor* can appear with other negators in similar lists. With *never* one can get a sentence like 'I never spake with her, saw her, nor heard from her' (*Meas.* V.i.221). Naturally there are times when the *nor* seems logically misplaced as when Malvolio in *Twelfth Night* berates the revellers 'Is there no respect of place, persons, nor time, in you?' (II.iii.88-9). Here the *nor* links *time* to the other negated part of the sentence, namely *respect*, though it belongs in practice with *place* and *persons*. In some cases a list may have only a single negator included, and that will appear at the front. Lear says 'Nor rain, wind, thunder, fire, are my daughters' (*Lear* III.ii.15). A similar omission of *nor* when it introduces clauses can also occur:

> Mine eyes
> Were not in fault, for she was beautiful;
> Mine ears, that heard her flattery; nor my heart
> That thought her like her seeming. (*Cymb.* V.v.62-5)

The middle clause in this sentence is also negative, for the implication is that also Cymbeline's ears were not at fault. This is another example where the negator is dropped from the middle of a list.

Modern English has developed non-assertive forms which must be used in negative clauses. A sentence like 'We've had some' can be negated by either 'We've not had any' or 'We've had none', though the latter is much less common. In the former *any* replaces *some*. As Elizabethan English makes extensive use of the so-called double negative, it is hardly surprising that these non-assertive forms have not been developed. The Shakespearian equivalent of the negatives mentioned above would be 'We've not had none', though other possibilities existed. The ability to use two negative forms in this type of clause made it unnecessary to have non-assertive forms. Although *any* and *some* have a less restricted use in Shakespeare than today, they are not frequently employed with negatives because the equivalent negative *none* will be employed. The absence of non-assertive forms can be appreciated in this quotation from *Macbeth*:

>   and to be King
> Stands not within the prospect of belief,
> No more than to be Cawdor. (I.iii.73–5)

In this instance Modern English would have *any more* for Shakespeare's *no more*. In the same way there are certain words today which are associated with negative expressions. The phrase *at all* would occur only in a negative clause like 'I didn't say anything at all'. There are traces that this restriction is beginning to operate with some words and phrases in Shakespeare, but it has certainly not become rigid. The group *at all* is most commonly found with negatives, to which it acts as a kind of intensifier. Sometimes the negation may be included only in a negative preposition as in Hamlet's 'without more circumstance at all' (I.v.127). *Till* in the sense 'before' is also most often found within a negative context, as is true of Modern English, but by Shakespeare's time regularity had not been established.

There are a number of adverbs in Modern English like *scarcely* and *seldom* which are treated grammatically as negatives although they do not look like negators. They are considered negative because they take non-assertive forms and positive tag questions, and because as head of a sentence they can cause subject–verb inversion. Since non-assertive forms and tag questions had not been fully developed by Shakespeare's time and as many other adverbials when head caused subject–verb inversion, these words can be considered negative only from their meaning and not from their grammatical surroundings. Such words can be used with other negatives in the same clause and when that happens we must think in terms of a double negative, as in 'Cannot be quiet scarce a breathing while' (*R3* I.iii.60). There are also many verbs which imply negation, such as *deny*, and other words like prepositions such as *without* which have the same status as the adverbs mentioned above. These words have a different grammatical status from that found today. They do not need to take non-assertive forms and often the verbs like *deny* will have a negative in a dependent subordinate clause rather than the equivalent modern non-assertive form. In 'First he denied you had in him no right' (*Com.* IV.ii.7) the subordinate clause has *no right* where today we would have *any right*.

In addition to the negators which have already been discussed, Shakespeare used a variety of affixes to create negation. The most important of these are perhaps the prefix *un-* and the suffix *-less,* the former of which is the more flexible in its application. There can be little doubt that these words increase the poetic quality of the text partly because they imply negation through different means and partly because they lend variety. It is also possible to create echoes and word play through these words which are more marked than simple negatives precisely because many of the words so created are particular to Shakespeare. In *King Lear,* for example, the sense of deprivation can be created by the echoic effect of such phrases as 'you houseless poverty ... this pitiless storm ... your houseless heads and unfed sides' (III.iv.26-30). At the same time the scope of negation is not so extensive in these words because they are adjectives, and so the sentences can seem positive although there is a strong sense of deprivation indicated through the negative words. In some instances a particular word is used to create an immediate echo as in 'and all ruinous disorders, follow us disquietly to our graves' (*Lear* I.ii.110). The word *disquietly* is not used elsewhere by Shakespeare, who otherwise uses the form *unquietly* (e.g. *Lear* III.i.2). The prefix of *disquietly* echoes that in *disorders* and it is therefore implied that the two are linked in meaning. A similar use of *un-* is found in *Macbeth* 'Or else my sword with an unbattered edge I sheathe again undeeded' (V.vii.19-20). Shakespeare can often create verbal punning by inventing new words in *un-*. The Prince can joke with Falstaff 'thou art not colted, thou art uncolted' (*1H4* II.ii.39). Here *uncolted* stands in contrast with *not colted,* and the first form being otherwise unknown calls attention to itself and helps to create the joke. The prefix can also be used in other ways, often indeed in situations which have some emotional charge. Edmund says to his father that Edgar had called him 'thou unpossessing bastard!' (*Lear* II.i.67) where the prefix is designed to inject contempt and fear into the utterance. Generally, however, one may assume that the main reasons for using these forms were their contribution to stylistic variety and their restricted negative focus.

Many of these words are involved in double negatives which have a positive sense. Shakespeare himself suggested that 'your four negatives make your two affirmatives' (*TN* V.i.18), but this is not often the case in his writings as we have seen. The wish to strengthen negation led to the introduction of more than one negator in many sentences. However, there are instances where an affirmative is implied by two negatives. In most cases this is found when there is a negator and the prefix *un-*. In Modern English there is frequently the implication with examples of this type that the affirmative is only moderate. Thus to say someone is 'not unhappy' would suggest that he is moderately happy rather than very happy. This implication does not appear to be present in Shakespearian examples. When Camillo says to Polixenes:

> Be not uncertain,
> For, by the honour of my parents, I
> Have utt'red truth. (*WT* I.ii.441-3)

he is clearly using the double negative to suggest absolute, rather than moderate, certainty. The same holds true for Gloucester's assertion regarding the fugitive Edgar 'Not in this land shall he remain uncaught' (*Lear* II.i.57). An interesting example of this double negative occurs in *Macbeth*. On receipt of Macbeth's letter Lady Macbeth ruminates on his willingness to go forward with Duncan's murder and she says:

> Thou wouldst be great;
> Art not without ambition, but without
> The illness should attend it. (I.v.15-17)

In view of the other examples of double negatives and of the context in which the words are uttered, this example implies that Macbeth has enormous ambition rather than only a moderate amount. However, examples of these double negatives with affirmative meaning are not too common in Shakespeare's works presumably because the circumstances in which they could be used were restrictive.

It is difficult to be certain about the scope and focus of negation at this period because non-assertive forms were not used and because there is no definite method for deciding where the stress fell within a given sentence. In addition, as the negative element was often repeated, and as it could appear in a variety of different places in the clause, it is difficult to be certain how far the focus or scope extended. We have already noted the use of forms like *nor* where we might logically have expected either *and* or *or*. Conversely there are examples where the negator has not been repeated, although it is clear that negation extends beyond the immediate scope of the negator. Examples given above have been those of negative phrases, but the same applies equally to clauses. Lear says 'I never gave you kingdom, call'd you children' (III.ii.17), in which the second clause lies within the scope of the *never* in the first one. It is particularly with negators like *not* and *nothing* that the scope of the negation is difficult to determine, and as we have seen this is why affixes were used, because their scope is more restricted. However, the movement in Modern English of the negator from a subordinate clause to its main clause, particularly when its verb is one of thinking or believing, is not found so often in Shakespeare's works. In *The Winter's Tale* we find the following examples in which the negator has remained in the subordinate clause: 'I think there is not in the world either matter or malice to alter it' (I.i.31-2) and 'But I'd say he had not' (II.i.62). On the other hand, if there is a negative element in the main clause the negation can be carried over to the subordinate clause, even though to us the resulting sense may appear hard to disentangle. In some instances the resulting sense implied may well be positive. Edgar in *King Lear* says:

> No port is free; no place
> That guard and most unusual vigilance
> Does not attend my taking. (II.iii.3-5)

Here modern editors separate *no port* from *no place* so that the second half of the clause means that all places have set a guard to capture him. This punctuation breaks up the rhythm of the sentence and may not be what Shakespeare intended, but it does give a more logical shape to it.

Unfortunately, as so little has been done on negation either in the Elizabethan period or with other writers from any period, it is not easy to decide how idiosyncratic Shakespeare is in his use of it. Certainly there are many aspects of it which need further elucidation and this short essay may perhaps provide a spur. It has also become clear to me that certain plays such as *King Lear* acquire some of their tone from the rather high use of negation in the play. A comparative assessment of the amounts of negation across Shakespearian plays might well produce interesting results.

Notes

1. See particularly W. Franz (1939) *Die Sprache Shakespeares in Vers und Prosa*, 4th edition of *Shakespeare-Grammatik*, Niemeyer, Halle; G.L. Brook (1976) *The Language of Shakespeare*, Deutsch, London; and E.A. Abbott (1872) *A Shakespearian Grammar*, rev. edn Macmillan, London
2. A.C. Partridge (1969) *Tudor to Augustan English*, Deutsch, London; and C. Barber (1976) *Early Modern English*, Deutsch, London
3. O. Jespersen, 'Negation in English and Other Languages' in his *Selected Writings of Otto Jespersen* (n.d.) Allen and Unwin, London; Senjo, Tokyo, pp. 3–152; and George B. Jack (1978) 'Negation in Later Middle English Prose,' *Archivum Linguisticum* n.s.9, pp. 5–72
4. See for example Edward S. Klima, 'Negation in English' in *The Structure of Language*, Jerry A. Fodor and Jerrold J. Katz (eds) (1964) Prentice-Hall, Englewood Cliffs, N.J. pp. 246–323
5. The texts are quoted from the Alexander edition which is the best single volume edition available; the abbreviated titles follow the abbreviations in N.F. Blake (1983) *Shakespeare's Language: an Introduction*, Macmillan, London
6. See Blake (1983) pp. 82–4

8
Englishmen and Their Moods: Renaissance Grammar and the English Verb

John O. Reed
Kyushu University, Japan

If we look in the earliest grammars of English, published before the end of the sixteenth century, we find two analyses of the English verb which are startlingly different in their employment of the concept of mood.

The first (set out for convenience in our tabulating style rather than the cramped, paper-saving manner of the sixteenth and earlier centuries) runs like this:

> The Englishmen haue in the coniugation of their verbes six moodes, To know,
> > The Indicatiue
> > The Imperatiue
> > The Optatiue
> > The Subiunctiue
> > The Potentiall
> > and the Infinitiue:
>
> And haue also fiue Tences, That is to witte,
> > The presente,
> > The imperfect,
> > The perfect
> > The plusperfect,
> > and the future.

These moods and tenses are explained to have 'signes' and these appear to be what later grammarians have called auxiliary verbs. Thus the signs of the present indicative are 'Doe, Doest, Doeth in the singular number, and in their plurall, throughout all their persons ... Doe'. For the imperfect 'Did' etc., for the perfect 'Haue', for the plusperfect 'Had', and for the future

'Shall or Will'. 'The selfe same signes' as are used for the indicative are also used for the optative and subjunctive moods. The signs of the potential mood are however more complicated and may be set out as follows:

Present	May or Can
Imperfect	Might or Could
Perfect	Might, Would, Should or Ought to haue
Plusperfect	the same signes of the Perfect, and therein doe onely chaunge Haue into Hadde.
Future	the same signes of the Present in this same moode, there adding onely, Hereafter.

To complete the account of the signs for the remaining two moods, 'the imperative has Let him, Let us, Let they', and the infinitive has for sign, 'To'.

The other type of analysis of the English verb to be found in these early grammars makes no mention of signs or of moods. It uses only tenses, or rather since the grammar is written in Latin Tempora, 'times'. These times are present, past and future:

[p.15] Praesens — I hate
[p.16] Praeteritum primum — I hated
[p.21] Praeteritum secundum — I have hated
Praeteritum tertium — I had hated
Futurum primum idem est cum themate, postposita persona expressa, aut intellecta ut *Hate thou hate he.* plur. Hate vve, Hate ye, hate they
Futurum secundum circumscribitur syntaxi infiniti & praesentis verbi *Will* vel *Shal* vt *I shall* vel *will hate* etc.

The two models I have used are the earliest I can find of each kind of analysis in a book setting out to give a grammatical description of the English language. The first comes from a work by Jacques Bellot *Le Maistre d'Escole Anglois or The English Scholemaister*, published in 1580, and intended as a manual of instruction for 'the naturall borne french men, and other straungers that haue their French tongue to attayne the true pronouncing of the English tongue'. It is printed throughout in two columns with the French on the left (in Roman type) and the English translation on the right (in black letter) — so that the analysis from which I have quoted appears in French as well as English, though of course in both columns it is the English verb which is treated. The second example is taken from a short grammar of English written in Latin, published in 1594. The title is *Grammatica Anglicana* and the author is given as Paul Greaves.

It is in the use that they make of mood that the two analyses are most strongly contrasted. In one, mood takes precedence over tense in the order and there are six moods, three of them, the indicative, the optative and the subjunctive, without formal distinction. In the other, mood is completely absent. What is usually described as the imperative is associated with the combinations of *will* or *shall* as the first and second futures.

Neither Greaves nor Bellot appears to have written anything except these grammars which are certainly not works of originality or importance in the history of grammar. To find why two minor textbook writers come to treat the English verb in such different ways we must trace the grammatical traditions which they found to hand. Bellot's immediate source is not hard to identify. Assuming he went to school in England, we may say he is merely applying to the English language the only grammar he knows, that of his school Latin. This would have been Lily's grammar, the school textbook first published in 1548-9 as *A Short Introduction of Grammar* and used in all English schools until the seventeenth century. From Lily he takes the 'signs', the words in an English text which give a helpful signal to the schoolboy which conjugational or declensional form he should put in his Latin version; from Lily also come the six moods or modes. Any Englishman who had studied long enough at school to have covered his Latin grammar would hardly have questioned that the verb had six moods — though what the natural born Frenchmen made of it, if any there were who tried to learn English from Bellot's book, without the benefit of a schooling in Lily, leaves room for wonder.

Lily's *Grammar* was not Lily's unaided work. As the anonymous authour of *Reflections upon Learning* in 1700 remarks:

> In our times the Common Grammar that goes under the name of Mr. *Lily* was done by some of the most considerable men of the Age. The English Rudiments by *Dr Colet Dean of St Pauls*, with a Preface to the first Editions, directing its use by no less Man than *Cardinal Wolsey*; The most Rational

part, the Syntax, was writ or corrected by *Erasmus*, and the other parts by other hands: so that tho' Mr. *Lily* now bears the name, which while living, he always modestly refus'd; yet it was carri'd on by the joynt endeavours of several Learned men, and he perhaps had not the largest share in the work. (pp. 19–20)

However the most important name in the search for the origin of Lily's analysis of the moods of the Latin verb as the indicative, the imperative, the optative, the potential, the subjunctive and the infinitive is missing from this account. That name, even if it could be overlooked in 1700, would certainly in the sixteenth century have been placed among the most considerable of his age. The name is Thomas Linacre.

Linacre in the early years of the sixteenth century wrote a short introductory grammar of Latin in English. This appeared in two versions, one entitled *Progymnasmata Grammatices Vulgaria*, the other *Rudimenta Grammatices*, neither volume with a date. In the *Progymnasmata* there is the following account of the moods of the Latin verb.

> Modys be. vi, the indicatyf, the imperatyf; the optatyf: the potential: the subiunctyf: and the infinytyfe.
> The indicatyf signifieth a dede, as told as amo I loue.
> some tyme as axyd, as amo ego? Loue I.
> The imperatyf betokenyth a thing as bodyn or commaundyd. as ama loue thow.
> The optatyfe signifieth a dede as wysshyd. symtyme with an aduerbe of wysshyng. and sum tyme with out. as vtinam amer God graunt I be louyd.
> The potential mode signyfyeth a thyng as mayying or owyng to be doone. And his sygnes in englysshe be these. may might. wold. or shuld. and hit hath v. tens in euery verbe of lyke voyce to the subiunctyve mode, as amem I may loue. amarem. I myght wolde. or shold loue. Amauerim I may haue louyd. Amauissem I myght had louyd amauero: I shall may loue. sumtyme I shall haue louyd. And this mode also may be takyn in axyng or dowtyng, as amem ne ego inimicum.
> The subiunctyfe mode signyfieth like the indicatyf mode but hyt commyth neuer with out a nother verbe sett out or vnderstond. as rogo vt facias.

> The infinytyfe signyfieth doyng beyng or sufferyng with out nombre and parson as amare. [XXVIII]

In the *Rudimenta Grammatices*, the declensions and conjugations are given in the first part and here we find

> The uerbe is declined with modes, tenses, persons and nombres.
> Modes. Modes be. v. the indicatyue, the imperatyue, the optatyue, the subiunctyue, the infinityue. [B 2v]

In the second part where the various parts of speech are explained, the moods are given as six, and are described as in the *Progymnasmata* with a few differences. Thus in the account of the potential, 'amauero: I shall may loue' becomes 'I shall or may loue' and 'sumtyme I shall haue louyd' (which in the *Progymnasmata* is not given in its place but has to be supplied from the list headed 'Errores' at the end of the volume) is omitted.

Thus to an original list of five moods, a sixth, the potential mood is added and receives a more detailed description than any of the other moods.

Linacre's care to explain the potential mood is understandable, since this is the first time such a mood has ever been proposed. The other five moods come to Linacre from a tradition going back to the earliest grammar of Greek, and applied to Latin in almost all grammars until his time. The potential mood is a personal contribution made by Linacre himself. It had already been set out and justified in his detailed treatise on Latin grammar, *De emendata structura Latini sermonis libri sex*, which was not published until 1524, the year of Linacre's death.

In this work, after listing the five traditional moods, Linacre continues:

> Nobis alium his adjicere visum est. In quo est Latini sermonis non solum lepos, sed etiam compendium, cum quod alias per debeo, vel possum, est interpretandum, una voce dixisse liceat, ut mox ostendemus.[1] (Fol. 11v)

He goes on to show that in Latin the subjunctive is sometimes used where the sense is equivalent to *possum* or *volo* followed by an infinitive. Thus from Quintilian.

Non expectes, ut statim gratias agat, qui sanatur invitus

to which Linacre adds '*pro debes expectare*'.

Linacre also sees this potential mood as an equivalent in Latin to the use of the conditional particle ἄν in Greek conditional clauses, sometimes with a past indicative tense, sometimes when fulfilment is possible with the optative. Since two formally distinct moods are involved this cannot constitute a mood of its own in Greek. But in Latin this conditional possibility is expressed always with the subjunctive, or rather as Linacre takes it, with the optative. Since the subjunctive and the optative are already two separate moods employing the same forms, there is no reason why a third mood should not be constituted, since this meaning clearly does not coincide with that proper to the optative.

> Nec est (ut arbitror) quod aliquem torqueat, quo minus hic duos esse modos concedat, propterea quod una sit utriusque vox, non magis quam ubi optativum et subiunctivum duos facit, quorum non minus, ut clare liquet, una est vox. Haec vero nostra sententia cui placebit, potest, si volet, hunc, quem novamus modum, potentialem appellare.[2]

'*Quem novamus modum*' — the Latin could cover the meaning of reviving something from the past, but there can be no doubt that Linacre thinks that the potential mood is his own invention and that he means 'this new mood which I have introduced'. There is no trace of this mood in any earlier writers, and Linacre, who discusses for example, Grocinus's new division of the tenses very favourably, though he does not adopt it, would surely mention earlier authorities in favour of a potential mood, if these existed. From Linacre the potential mood, a radical innovation in the traditional grammatical analysis of Latin, passes directly to Lily, who is to be the official and authorised version of Latin grammar in England for two centuries, and therefore, since Latin was during this period the only language widely learned grammatically by Englishmen, the authorised version of grammar itself. The potential mood which Linacre himself excluded from Greek eventually finds its way there for in Liddell and Scott's Greek Lexicon under ἄν we read 'hence the Indicative with ἄν represents a potential mood' and further on in the same article 'hence the optative with ἄν becomes a potential mood'. The potential mood is in Lindley Murray, and as late as 1893 the OED article on *can* has the following acerb comment at the beginning of its treatment of the word as 'an auxiliary of predication'.

> (Many manuals of English Grammar have ineptly treated *can* so construed as an auxiliary of the subjunctive or 'Potential' mood!)

But Linacre himself takes a rather more relaxed attitude towards his theoretical innovation

> Cui diversa sententia erit, siue optativum esse contendat, (nam subiunctivum esse (ut Priscianus non recte censet) nulla ratio efficit), sive voces quinque temporum, quae publice subiunctivo tribuuntur, triplici significato donet, optandi, potentiae, subiunctivi (hoc autem est indicandi, caeterum sub altero verbo subiecti, ut post dicetur) dummodo significationis ipsius et usus admonitus Latinius loqui incipiat, me certe non offendet.[3] [Fol. 13v]

Though to some extent Linacre's arguments are theoretical, as the final phrases in the quotation above show, his real concern as a linguist is practical — directly related to teaching, to improving the standard of Latin in his day. Certainly his hope, that the student of his book 'Latinius loqui incipiat' appears to belong to applied rather than theoretical linguistics, however different we may feel the intellectual atmosphere in the great humanists is from that found in today's TESL. The disfavour with which the humanists are regarded by literary medievalists as having destroyed the living language of medieval Latin and replaced it by a sterile simulacrum of classical literary Latin, and the fact that Chomsky has directed admiration at a later Renaissance grammarian like Sanctius, who tended to dismiss the works of the humanists, has made it easy to ignore the particular value of their achievement. No one would wish to defend the excesses of Ciceronianism or indeed most aspects of the classical education system which was founded in the sixteenth century. But what is often forgotten is that the best work of the humanists, in attempting to write and encouraging others to write in what they called better Latin, drew attention to the individuality of the Latin language, its genius and distinction from, on the one hand, Greek, and on the other the European vernaculars. Because many of the humanists were also Hellenists they were able to some extent, for the first time since Latin ceased to be a genuine first language, to deal with the unsuitable framework of Greek grammar clamped down upon Latin by the derivative grammarians of earlier centuries. At the same time their concern for the purity of Latin was an awareness of the profound differences of idiom and syntactical structure between Latin and the various European vernaculars, even, or perhaps particularly, those actually deriving from Latin. It is this work — against the grain of general or philosophical grammar — which I find exemplified in Linacre's thought by the proposal of the potential mood.

In this suggestion Linacre is, as he makes explicit, proposing for Latin a system of moods distinct from that in Greek. It is true of course that the proposal is shaped by the very situation of the pattern of Greek moods imposed unsuitably on Latin — it is because the subjunctive forms in Latin already express two moods, subjunctive and optative, in order to bring Latin into line with Greek, that Linacre claims there can be no objection to his adding a third. But he perceives clearly that the Greek system of moods does not, as he shows in the case of conditionals, provide a satisfactory way of describing Latin usage. In fact, Linacre also puts forward a tentative mood system for Latin based on formal distinctions:

> Modi, si vocum discrimen spectes, quatuor tantum sunt.[4]
> [Fol.15v]

He then gives the characteristic endings of the indicative, imperative, subjunctive and infinitive, and describes the use of the third of these:

> Tertius alias rebus optandis convenit, qua ratione optativus dicitur ...
> Alias posse, vel debere fieri aliquid ostendit ... Alias velle aliquid.[5] [Fol.16r]

On the other side, Linacre in proposing the potential mood is drawing attention to what he calls '*latini sermonis lepos*'; he is attempting to show that Latin frequently uses the subjunctive where modern vernaculars use an auxiliary verb — the equivalent of *volo, possum* or *debeo*. Latin after all has to be written by men who speak modern vernaculars, and there would be a natural tendency to carry over this segmentation of the subjunctive into Latin. When Linacre cites Quintilian's

Non expectes, ut statim gratias agat, qui sanatur invitus

and says '*pro debes expectare*' it is surely because anyone thinking in a modern European vernacular might be tempted to translate the idiom of his own language into Latin in this way.

The five moods of Latin grammar to which Linacre adds his sixth are found in the earlier humanist grammarians like Perottus (1473) and Sulpicius (1495). This was itself a modification of the usual medieval tradition deriving from Donatus, which had six moods. Donatus added a mood, the impersonal. Latin verbs used impersonally were said to be in this mood (Keil IV p. 359, 1.9.). So the humanists had restored to Latin the five mood system of Priscian, who carried over to Latin the five '*enkliseis*' of the Greek verb in the grammar of Dionysius Thrax.

horistike	(indicativus)
prostaktike	(imperativus)
euktike	(optativus)
hypotaktike	(subjunctivus)
aparemphatos	(infinitivus)

In this analysis the optative and subjunctive in Latin have identical forms, and as we have seen it was this discrepancy between form and meaning in the system of Latin moods that gave Linacre the opportunity to remodel Latin moods so that they no longer corresponded exactly with those of Greek — though not by the expedient of dismissing the optative from Latin as later grammarians have done, but by adding yet another mood. The importance of this new treatment of mood in Latin to the early analysis of the English verb is due to the accident that Linacre's speculation was almost immediately incorporated into the elementary Latin grammar appointed for use in all English schools. Linacre's *De emendata* where the potential mood is treated in detail however does not appear to have been much studied in England and all the later editions of the book are from continental presses.

The other grammarian who figures largely in the story of mood also concerned himself with school grammars. Though not an Englishman he was to have a powerful but short-lived influence on early English grammar. Greaves's *Grammatica Anglicana*, from which the moodless analysis of the English verb was quoted, is characterised on its title page as '*ad unicam P. Rami methodum concinnata*', 'arranged after the matchless method of Peter Ramus'. It was Pierre de la Ramée, latinised as Petrus Ramus, who solved the problem of finding a way to deal with the confusion over moods in Latin by abandoning the concept of mood altogether. Ramus published his Latin grammar in 1559 and an English translation of this appeared in 1585. In this Ramus employs three tenses, past, present and future, and a distinction between perfect and imperfect (not made use of by Greaves for English). The tenses which cannot be distinguished by these are simply given numbers. Thus the first present tense is 'amo' (present indicative by more recent Latin grammar), the second, 'amem' (present subjunctive), the third, 'amarem' (imperfect subjunctive). The first preterite or past tense is 'amabam' (imperfect indicative), and the second preterite is 'amarem', also the third present. The first future tense is 'amabo' (future indicative) and the second future 'ama' (imperative mood). This of course is the source of Greaves's association of the English imperative with *shall* and *will* combinations as first and second future. I suppose Greaves reverses the order and makes the imperative the first future because it is so obviously simpler and more primary. The grammars of Ramus contain no discussion of grammatical questions or any justification of the analyses adopted. To discover his arguments for discarding mood we must look at Book 14 of his *Scolae in Liberales Artes*, on the moods and tenses of the verb.

The word used in Greek grammar for mood is '*enklisis*'. The meaning of this word is usually expressed in Latin by '*inclinatio*' though the Latin grammarians preferred to translate it by '*modus*', a much wider term (equivalent to the Greek word '*tropos*', Linacre observes in *De emendata* (Fol. 11) that because they used the broader term the Latins sometimes included participles as a separate '*modus*' or manner of the verb. This did not happen in Greek grammar because it was part of the usual definition of the verb that it was without case. Since participles were declined like adjectives they could not really be considered as verbs at all. Linacre makes it clear that his intention is to use '*modus*' in a more restricted manner, corresponding to '*enklisis*' in Greek. Latin grammar though translating '*enklisis*' by '*modus*' preserved the narrower meaning of the Greek word in the definition of mood which appears in Priscian (Keil II p. 421)

> Modi sunt diversae inclinationes animi, varios eius affectus demonstrantes.[6]

This definition works well enough for the imperative and the optative but not for the subjunctive, which in Latin is usually no more than a mark of subordination. The definition also works against the inclusion of the infinitive as a mood. Ramus quotes it derisively in his *Scolae* (p. 131) and says

> Haec definitio nihil definit et voluntatis humanae definitio potius fuerit, quam ullius verbalis proprietatis.[7]

However Ramus notes that grammarians have sometimes distinguished in the moods a '*prima partitio*' between the finite and the non-finite moods and then have made special distinctions within each category — between the indicative, imperative, optative and subjunctive (or conjunctive as Ramus calls it here) as the finite moods, and among the non-finite moods have given the infinitive, the gerund and the supine. It is only the separation of the various finite moods which Ramus rejects;

> Dico enim, per species istas finiti modi, nihil verborum naturam distingui, nil dividi sed omnes istos modos inter se penitus confundi.[8]

He has little difficulty in demonstrating how deeply confused these moods are, largely by drawing on the examples cited by Priscian himself to illustrate the use of one Latin mood in the meaning of another. There is indeed very great confusion, not only because of the imposition of the five moods of Greek grammar upon the Latin language, but also because Priscian has a different assignment of the formal tenses between the indicative and the subjunctive-optative from that now accepted as correct, making '*amavero*' the future of the subjunctive instead of an indicative, now called the future-perfect. In this way Priscian has five indicative tenses and a subjunctive (and optative) corresponding to each. Ramus can see that for all its symmetry this does not work and he prefers the treatment of the verb in the much earlier Latin grammarian Varro whose division of the tenses into an imperfect and perfect sequence of past, present and future is adopted by Ramus into his own grammar. By general argument about the vagueness of the concept and particular arguments about Latin usage Ramus justifies his rejection of the finite moods

> Tempus est prima differentia verbi, quam Aristotles in logica & poetica observavit. Tempus igitur est differentia verborum ut genus nominum.[9]

Ramus made his reputation as a philosopher by undertaking to defend the proposition: Whatever has been said by Aristotle is false. But in this case the later Greek grammatical tradition had been in agreement with Aristotle. Dionysius Thrax includes tense but not *enklisis* in his definition of a verb. *Enklisis* or mood is only mentioned in the list of no less than eight ways in which the verb is affected (Uhlig Vol I. 1, p. 46). It is Priscian who promotes mood into the definition of the verb as a word without case, showing tense and mood, signifying something done or suffered. This definition is followed by the humanist grammarians. The tendency to ignore mood and see the verb entirely in terms of tense conforms more with Greek than Latin views of the verb. Yet when Ramus wrote a Greek grammar he retained the finite moods

> Tempora plura sunt, & distinctior quam Latinis: Itaque modos hactenus retinebimus, dum melius occurrerit.[10]

In 1562 Ramus published a grammar of the French language in French. In this he uses the moodless analysis of the verb found in his Latin grammar. But although he always gives the Latin equivalent for each French tense, his analysis of the French verb is not closely modelled on that of the Latin because he considers as tenses only those formed entirely by inflexion of the verb. All the perfect tenses formed by *avoir* with the past participle he says '*s'expriment par Syntaxe*' and these he treats quite separately. The distinction could of course be usefully applied in English, but it is ignored by Greaves who treats *shall*

Englishmen and Their Moods

and *will* as forming a future tense and not a *syntaxe* of a tense. Yet there is one grammar of English of the earlier seventeenth century that draws on Ramus not only for the moodless analysis of the verb but also for the strict separation of simple from compound tenses. This is Ben Jonson's *English Grammar*, first published in the 1640 Folio of his works, though probably written in his middle rather than later life.

In Chapter XVI, *Of a Verbe*, Jonson sets out the tenses, using Latin to illustrate, like Ramus in his French grammar.

> A *Verbe finite* therefore hath three only *Tymes*, and those alwayes *imperfect.*
> The first is the *present*: as
> *Amo*, Love
> The second is the *tyme past*: as
> *Amabam*, Loved
> The third is the *Future*: as
> Ama, amato: Love, love. [p. 61]

Here, as in Greaves we find that the imperative is considered to be the primary future tense. Jonson continues:

> The other *Tymes* both imperfect: as
> *Amem, amarem, amabo.*
> And also *perfect*: as
> *Amavi, amaverim, amaveram*
> *Amavissem, amavero*
> Wee use to expresse by a *Syntaxe*, as shall be seene in the proper place.

Jonson's *Grammar* is divided into the two parts:

> *Etymologie* which is the true notation of words. *Syntaxe* which is the right ordering of them. [p. 35]

We must turn to the 'Second Booke, of the English Grammar, *Of Syntaxe*' and to the sixth chapter, 'Of the *Syntaxe* of a *Verbe*, with a *Verbe*', to find these compound tenses described.

> And here those Times, which in *Etymologie* we remembered to be wanting, are set forth by the *Syntaxe* of the Verbes joyned together. The *Syntaxe* of *imperfect* Times in this manner:

124

> The Presents by the *infinite*, and the Verbe, *may* or *can*, as for, ***Amem, Amarem***: *I may loue : I might loue.*
> And againe, *I* can *loue,*: *I could loue.*
> The *futures* are declared by the *infinite*, and the Verbe, *shall*, or *will*: as ***Amabo***: I shall, or, will *loue.*
> ***Amavero*** addeth thereunto, *haue*, taking the nature of two divers Times; that is, of the *future*, and the Time *past*:
>   I *shall* have *loued*: or,
>   I *will* have *loued.* [p. 79]

Here then *can* and *may*, *will* and *shall* are classed together as syntaxes of tenses and this is surely an improvement on Linacre–Lily which treats the first as a mood and the second as a tense, and on Ramus–Greaves which does not recognise the first but also treats the second as a tense.

Judged by Jonson's *English Grammar*, the Ramist approach looks much more promising as an account of the verb in English than the other tradition taken over from Linacre and Lily's Latin grammar — but it was Linacre–Lily that held the field, and Ramist grammar seems to wither away more rapidly than Ramism generally. Milton's *Artis Logicae Plenior Institutio* published in 1672 is like Greaves's grammar '*ad Petri Rami methodum concinnata*' but his Latin grammar certainly is not. Supported by the continued use of Lily in the schools, the grammar of English showed the English verb with an array of moods. Certain words like *can*, *may* and *ought* could be used in forming a mood, often called the potential mood, in the same way as *will* and *shall* were used to form a future tense. Ramism repudiated mood entirely but in Jonson's adaptation to English suggested that *can* and *may* could be used to form a special syntactical tense of the verb. Between these two, no one perceived the inflected subjunctive in English until towards the end of the eighteenth century. An account of the late eighteenth century uncertainties about whether the inflected subjunctive existed in English can be found in Michael (1970). The use of *be* as an indicative form and the frequent failure to observe agreement in number between subject and verb all helped to obscure the formal marks of the subjunctive in English. The subjunctive form *be* in the present tense is noticed though not of course identified by Greaves in his final chapter *De Syntaxi coniunctionis cum verbo.*

> *Be* in presenti raro utimur, & fere semper post coniunctionem *That*, expressam, aut intellectam, ut, *If that perfect constancie be the childe of chance, let wisdome be counted the root of wickedness.* Huiusmodi vero loquutiones non videntur praecepto quadrare, ut *Suppose all men be honest, Imagine pleasure be a companion of vertue*: veritas tamen semper & ubique eadem est, nam in his & huiusmodi exemplis elipsis est coniunctionis *That*, aut praepositionis *to*, si *that*, tunc *be* est praesentis iuxta regulam, si *To*, tum infiniti, & sic explenda est oratio. *Suppose that all men be honest, Imagine that pleasure be a companion of vertue.* Alias *Suppose all men to be honest, and pleasure to be a companion of vertue*. Nam inerti, at vulgari solaecismo laborat haec oratio, *I be negligent, thou be honest.*
> Idem de *were* imperfecto singulari, verbi *Am*, dicendum est.[11]
> [p. 35]

In fact Greaves's 'clumsy, vulgar solecism' of *be* in the present where there is no possibility of a subjunctive use is common in the literary prose of the sixteenth and seventeenth centuries, though not of course in the first and second persons. In spite of the evident existence of a variant of the indicative with *be* a study of the prose of the period shows that the writers employed the subjunctive forms of which they were unaware with great consistency. Ironically, later Latin grammars often show the verb with four moods. Milton's Latin grammar gives the indicative, the imperative, the potential or subjunctive, alternative names for the same mood, and the infinitive. But by this time it seems, English grammar was being influenced less by Latin grammar than by traditions of English grammar already established.

Curiously, there was a way of treating mood in Latin which if it had been applied to English would not only have given a very satisfactory analysis of the verb into moods (six, as it happens like Linacre's, but not the same ones) but also would have provided an explanation for the peculiarities of the development of the 'syntactical moods' by means of the modal verbs which still seem rather puzzling, even with all the advanced technology of today's grammar.

As we have seen Ramus accepted the '*prima partitio*' between finite and non-finite moods. The finite moods he refused to accept. The distinctions between the '*modi infiniti*', the non-finite moods, he accepts, it seems, provided they are not called moods. In the *Scolae* these are given as the infinitive, the gerund and the supine. Participles are excluded as has been noted because in traditional classical grammar they are not considered to belong to the verb at all. When he comes to treat the non-finite parts of the French verb, Ramus finds there are three forms and he avoids using the term participle in describing them. (I quote from the edition of the *Grammaire* of 1587 as the *Gramere* of 1562 employs a confusing reformed spelling.)

Le verbe infini est perpetuel ou gerondif.
Le perpetuel present est comme aymer, voir.
Le perpetuel preterit est semblable au preterit fini parfaict, comme ayme, ayme, veu, veu.
L'infini gerondif est comme aymant, voyant.

Had Ramus not come down against the finite moods but adopted the three formally distinct finite moods to be found in Latin, the indicative, the subjunctive and the imperative, he would surely have had little difficulty in matching these with the moods in French; the French subjunctive being by no means as elusive as the English. A French grammar on these lines, with three *modi infiniti* and three *modi finiti* might have enabled some English grammarian to have guessed at the secret of the subjunctive in English and to have produced these six moods

love   loves, loved
loved   love, loved
loving love!

Six moods in all, three finite, of which two display tense. Now the syntax of a verb with a verb in English uses *be* in the way that French uses *être* to form a passive voice, and early Modern English uses *be* and *have* in a similar way to the French use of *être* and *avoir* to form perfect tenses. These auxiliary verbs in their combination can appear in any of the six moods except one — the mood which translating Ramus we may call the preterit perpetual. We cannot say 'been killed' or 'had loved' as complete verbal phrases, but apart from this each of the six moods can be expanded in this way. We can speak of being loved and of having loved, to be loved and to have loved may be the subjects of our sentences. We can say 'Be gone!' or 'Have done!' 'Be hanged!' or 'Have regained your composure before you venture again into my presence'. And of course 'if he have seen it' is as possible as 'if he see it'.

But in English — and here in sharp contrast with French — the syntax of a verb with a verb can be employed to make what are in effect compound moods, parallel to the compound tenses made with *be* and *have*.

> *will* and *shall* to make a mood of expectation
> *can* and *may* a mood of permission and possibility
> *need* and *must* and *ought* a mood of obligation and necessity

perhaps sharing out between them the same semantic area covered by the subjunctive, the optative and the desiderative in ancient Indo-European.

These verbs have to combine with the infinitive or the present perpetual in Ramus's terminology. However, because they form moods they have themselves no modal variation. Since they are able to show tense we may conclude that they must be either indicative or subjunctive, but they do not display any of the formal marks by which we can distinguish these two moods. They appear in none of the non-finite moods nor in the imperative. This is not in all cases for semantic reasons since *be able* which replaces *can* in those moods can certainly be used as an imperative. We can then describe the modal verbs as verbs that have come to lose mood.

Every verb and verbal phrase in English can then be assigned to one of the moods of the verb, either one of the primary moods or one of the three additional syntactic moods. Those that come in one of the primary non-finite moods we can probably say do not show tense. But our conclusion must be that the English language confirms the strong consensus from Aristotle onwards that it is tense and not mood which is the defining characteristic of a verb. For there are a handful of verbs in English which do not show mood at all, whereas all English verbs show tense. On the other hand these moodless verbs can only be used together with other verbs and then they themselves provide the mood. Thus whenever a verb is used a mood can be assigned to that use. The Englishmen in the conjugation of their verbs turn out to need even more than the six moods that Bellot proposed, and Ramus's idea that grammar would be better off without moods, like many radical solutions, gave useful leads in demonstrating how necessary they were.

Notes

1. I have thought fit to add to these moods one more. In it there is not only an elegancy but also a compendiousness of the Latin language, for it enables us to say in one word what would otherwise have to be expressed by putting in '*possum*' or '*debeo*', as I shall now show.

2. Nor is it (I think) a thing to deter anyone from granting that there are here two different moods, because they have the same form, any more than that the subjunctive and the optative are two different moods, the forms of which are manifestly identical. Anyone who finds this opinion of mine acceptable, can if he wishes call the new mood which I have introduced the Potential Mood.

3. If anyone holds a different opinion, either maintaining that this mood is the optative (for by no reckoning can it be made out to be the subjunctive as Priscian incorrectly accounts it), or else will bestow on the forms of those five tenses which are generally classified as the subjunctive, the threefold significance of optative, potential and subjunctive (the subjunctive being merely the indicative when subordinated to another verb, as is pointed out below), so long as he bears the meaning itself and the use of it in mind and so comes to speak with better latinity, he will certainly not displease me.

4. If you regard difference of forms there are only four moods.

5. The third mood is sometimes applied to things wished for and so is called the optative ... sometimes it shows what can or ought to be done ... sometimes what is willed.

6. Moods are the different tendencies of the mind, showing its various dispositions.

7. This definition defines nothing and might better have been a definition of the human will than of any property of verbs.

8. I say then, by these species of the finite mood no distinction or division in the nature of verbs is made, but all these moods are thoroughly mixed up among themselves.

9. Tense constitutes the first distinction of a verb, as Aristotle observes in the Logic and the Poetics. Tense is therefore the distinction in verbs which corresponds to gender in nouns.

10. There are more tenses than in Latin and they are more distinct. Therefore moods have been retained until something better is found.

11. *Be* in the present we rarely use and almost always after the conjunction *that* either expressed or understood, as 'if that perfect constancie be the childe of chance, let wisdome be counted the root of wickedness'. Sentences of the following kind seem not to agree with this rule, 'Suppose all men be honest', 'Imagine pleasure be a companion of vertue'. Truth is however always and everywhere the same, for in these and examples of this kind there is elipsis of the conjunction *that* or of the preposition *to*. If of *that* then *be* is present tense according to the

rule, if of *to* then *be* is infinitive and the sentence can be expanded 'Suppose that all men be honest', 'Imagine that pleasure be a companion of vertue' or 'Suppose all men to be honest', 'Imagine pleasure to be a companion of vertue'. Sentences like 'I be negligent' or 'Thou be honest' are spoilt by a clumsy and vulgar solecism.

The same may be said of *were* in the singular of the imperfect of the verb *to be*.

References

Anon. (1700) *Reflections upon Learning.* rpt Scolar Press, Menston, England
Bellot, J. (1580) *Le Maistre d'Escole Anglois — The Englishe Scholemaister.* rpt. 1967 Scolar Press, Menston, England
Greaves, P. (1594) *Grammatica Anglicana praecipue quatenus a Latina differt ad unicam P. Rami methodum concinnata.* rpt. 1969, Scolar Press, Menston, England
Jonson, B. (1640) *English Grammar* (from *The Works*). rpt. 1972, Scolar Press, Menston, England
Keil, H. (1857 etc.) *Grammatici Latini*, 7 vols, Leipzig
La Ramée, P de. (1562) *Gramere*, Paris
—— (1562) *Grammatica Graeca, quatenus a Latina differt*, Paris
—— (1578) *Scolae in Liberales Artes*, Basel
—— (1585) *The Latine Grammar of P. Ramus, Translated into English.* London. rpt. 1971, Scolar Press, Menston, England
—— (1587) *Grammaire*, Paris
Lily, W. and Colet, J. (1549) *A Short Introduction of Grammar.* rpt. 1970, Scolar Press, Menston, England
Linacre, T. (1523?) *Rudimenta Grammatices.* rpt. 1971, Scolar Press, Menston, England
—— (1524) *De emendata structura Latini sermonis libri sex.* London. rpt. 1968, Scolar Press, Menston, England
—— (1525?) *Progymnasmata Grammatices Vulgaria*, London
Michael, I. (1970) *English Grammatical Categories and the Tradition to 1800*, Cambridge University Press, London
Milton, J. (1672) *Artis Logicae Plenior Institutio*, London
Perottus, N. (1473) *Rudimenta Grammatices*, Rome
Sulpicius J. (1495) *Grammatica*, Paris
Uhlig, G. (1878–1910) *Grammatici Graeci*, Leipzig

PART II
Middle to Modern English Period

9
The Great Vowel-Shift and Other Vowel-Shifts

John Frankis
University of Newcastle-upon-Tyne

A comparison between the English Great Vowel-Shift and similar phenomena in other Germanic languages has been made by Samuels (1972:145) and Bynon (1977:192), but the fullest and most systematic recent consideration is by Lass (1976:Chapter 2), who cites evidence from German, Swedish and Norwegian in support of views of the Great Vowel-Shift that are primarily based on the evidence of modern English dialects. In so far as Lass is concerned with criticising the theories of Chomsky and Halle (1968), I am in general agreement with his position, but there is room for further discussion of some details of his argument, and the present paper is no more than an extended footnote to Lass's Chapter 2.

My concern is with that part of Lass's discussion that deals with the rival theories of the 'drag-chain' and 'push-chain' (respectively, Jespersen's belief that diphthongisation of high vowels caused the raising of others, and Luick's view that the raising of mid vowels led to the diphthongisation of high vowels); Lass concludes in favour of the latter and sums up his conclusion in the statement, 'High vowels will not diphthongise unless the vowel immediately below in the same series (front, back) raises' (p. 67). He then goes on to consider evidence from German and Swedish that leads to the modification of this statement in certain details, but his final 'metarule' (p. 82), 'an overall characterisation of Germanic vowel shifts', asserts the same basic push-chain principle. The evidence seems to me, however, not necessarily to exclude the alternative hypothesis of the drag-chain, even though it could not be so economically formulated. Although in German the diphthongisation of the Germanic mid vowels[1] /e:/ and /o:/ to <ie> and <uo> (modern dialects /iə/ and /uə/) is very early, long before the diphthongisation of the high vowels, one could still argue that the latter occurrence (i.e.

the diphthongisation of MHG /iː/ and /uː/ to Modern German /ai/ and /au/) opened up the way for the monophthongisation of MGH <ie> and <uo> to Modern German /iː/ and /uː/. The argument in these terms seems to me to be insoluble. One may note, however, two particular cases where Lass's preference for the push-chain effect may be questioned.

First, although in Swedish the raising of ON <á> /ɑː/ to a mid-back vowel <å> is clearly very early, one cannot insist that it 'pushed' the raising of /oː/ to /uː/ any more than one can insist that the fronting of original /uː/ to /ɯː/ 'dragged' the raising of /oː/ to /uː/. That the push-chain effect need not apply is in fact demonstrated by the closely related evidence of Danish, for Danish shared with Swedish (and other Scandinavian languages) the early raising of /ɑː/ to <å>, but there was no consequential raising of /oː/ in Danish: the push-chain did not operate. Modern Danish retains the original ON back vowels /oː/ and /uː/ substantially unchanged, and generally distinguishes the original /oː/ from the sounds represented by <å> in a way that is approximately comparable to the Middle English distinction between /oː/ and /ɔː/ (though in Modern Danish the point of articulation is in both cases somewhat higher than that postulated for the ME vowels). The evidence of Danish may thus lead one to question the operation of a push-chain effect in Swedish.

Secondly, the arguments concerning German may be reconsidered in the light of the closely related evidence of Dutch. The Dutch front vowels have a history similar to that of the German front vowels: i.e. Germanic /aː/ is retained, /eː/ is diphthongised to <ie> (presumably /iə/) and later monophthongised to /iː/ <ie>, and /iː/ is diphthongised, in German to /ai/, in Dutch to the intermediate stage of /ɛi/ <ij>. The development of the back vowels in Dutch, however, differs in one crucial respect from that in German. At an apparently early stage (certainly by the twelfth century) Germanic /uː/ was fronted in Dutch to /yː/, so that there was no need for diphthongisation of this vowel to take place as a push-chain effect when Germanic /oː/ was raised to Dutch /uː/ <oe>. Nevertheless, diphthongisation still occurred, and occurred in the same way as it did in German and English, namely, by the insertion of a mid-vowel on-glide.[2] Thus, where modern standard German and English have a diphthong of the general type /au/ from Germanic (OE, OGH) /uː/ (arrived at, on the evidence of modern dialects, through intermediate stages of the type /əu/ and /ou/), Dutch shows the development of Germanic

/uː/ first to /yː/, then by diphthongisation to Modern Dutch /œy/ <ui>.³ This, of course, contravenes Lass's rule that 'high vowels will not diphthongise unless the vowel immediately below in the same series raises'. Whatever motivated the Dutch diphthongisation of /yː/ to /œy/, it was not any push-chain or pressure from below; and whatever motivated it could equally well have motivated the diphthongisation of Dutch /iː/ to /ɛi/ <ij>, and presumably the general diphthongisation of high vowels in German and English too. One may acknowledge that the diphthongisation of high front vowels in English, German and Dutch is systematically related to that of high back vowels in the same languages, and perhaps to other vowel-changes too, but the relationship cannot be formulated in terms of any single push-chain or drag-chain theory.

Furthermore, although the Germanic languages show numerous common features as regards vowel-shifting, it should be noted that neat tables summarising this (as for example in Lass 1976, pp. 73–81) conceal good deal of chronological disparity. The conventional (but admittedly not unchallenged) view of the English Great Vowel-Shift as a phenomenon that occurred within a relatively short period of time, c.1500 to 1700, contrasts sharply with the chronology of the corresponding developments in German, which involve a time-span of six or seven hundred years. The OHG spellings <ie> and <uo>, showing diphthongisation of Germanic /eː/ and /oː/, begin to appear in the early ninth century and are regular by c.900, while the other changes, including the diphthongisation of high vowels, were not complete in standard German before the end of the Middle Ages or even the Early Modern period. This does not invalidate Lass's comments, but it raises questions about the degree of interdependence in sound-changes that may have been separated by long periods of time. If we argue for a unitary system in any of these patterns of development, we must ask whether our criterion of unitariness is purely linguistic or whether time factors should also be taken into account.

Finally, one might also consider whether the vowel-shifts of the various Germanic languages might have had a sociolinguistic aspect. Lass does well to remind us that discussion based solely on standard forms of English and German needs to be supplemented by consideration of regional variations, and his account of vowel-shifts in modern English and German dialects throws great light on the whole process. It also suggests some modification of the statement by Samuels (1972:145) that there is a North–South distinction in some Germanic language areas with regard to the diphthongisation of high vowels, for this view is based in each case on a national standard language (English, German, Dutch) that happens to be southern in relation to a northern form of somewhat different status (Scots, Low German, Frisian); but the fact that numerous South German dialects also have undiphthongised high vowels invalidates any simple North–South dichotomy; see for example the remarks on Swiss German by Lass (1976:77). What thus appears is that it is especially the standard forms of English and German that show consistent diphthongisation of high vowels, while various dialects modify the pattern in various ways. Since the rise of standard forms of language in the past five hundred years is at least in some degree an urban phenomenon, one might ask how far the systematic diphthongisation of high vowels is an aspect of urban speech, while rural dialects are less systematically affected (the case might be marginally stronger for English than for German). As Barbara Strang (1970:104–6, 156, 164) pointed out, the urbanisation of society plays a central role in language-development, but it is by no means clear that the diphthongisation of high vowels is a case in point. One notes, for example, that the evidence of Scandinavian languages points in the reverse direction, for there the diphthongisation of high vowels is found only in the dialects of rural areas and remote islands (e.g. in some Norwegian dialects and partly in Faroese),[4] whereas standard modern Danish, essentially the dialect of Copenhagen, the largest single Scandinavian conurbation, retains the original ON /i:/ and /u:/ substantially unchanged.

The foregoing notes may appear disappointingly inconclusive, but my concern is to point out some of the difficulties in the way of systematic generalisations about vowel-shifting (and by implication about language development in general), so that the inconclusiveness is in fact my conclusion: language, like other aspects of human behaviour, is partly systematic, and attempts to make it appear wholly so are liable to involve some omissions.

Notes and References

1. In the present paper I use phonetic symbols between oblique strokes to indicate a phonemic transcription both of current spoken forms and of conjectural reconstructions of pronunciations of the past, though I realise that the latter have a somewhat different status from the former. Where it seems helpful I have indicated conventional spellings between angle-brackets.

2. Lass (1976:14-26) shows that the Chomsky-Halle hypothesis of diphthongisation by an off-glide has no support in the phonetics of British English. The transition from /i:,u:/ to /ai,au/ by way of /əi,əu/ is evidenced in current English speech by (*inter alia*) the occurrence of /əi,əu/ both as derivatives of ME /i:,u:/ in some conservative dialects and as counterparts of RP /i:,u:/ in some advanced dialects.

3. On the history of Dutch see M.J. van der Meer (1927) and A. van Loey (1949). Some grammars of modern Dutch allege that the phoneme /œy/ may have an unrounded allophone [œi]: see for example E. Blancquaert (1964:88, 91-3); and some allege the spread of this unrounded form to all positions: e.g. E. Rijpmaa and F.G. Schuringa (1961:23), and R.H.B. de Koninck (1970:viii, xiv and under separate words); most recently, I. Mees and B. Collins (1983:64-75) seem to discount the alleged unrounding of the second element of the diphthong (see p. 70): I am indebted to Professor N.E. Osselton for this last reference. My point that an earlier /y:/ was diphthongised by the insertion of an on-glide to /œy/ is not affected by any subsequent unrounding in either element of this diphthong. The further fact that diphthongisation of /y:/ did not occur before /r/ supports my view that no kind of phonetic pressure was involved.

4. See Haugen (1976:74, 254-7); on Faroese see Lockwood (1955); for the diphthongisation of /u:/ in Danish dialects see Brøndum-Nielsen (1951:115, 120).

Blanquaert, E., *Praktische Uitspraakleer van der Nederlandse Taal* (7th edition, Antwerp, 1964)
Brøndum-Nielsen, Johannes, *Dialekter og Dialektforskning* (Copenhagen, 1951)
Bynon, Theodora, *Historical Linguistics* (Cambridge, 1977)
Chomsky, N. and Halle, M., *The Sound Patterns of English* (New York, 1968)
Haugen, Einar, *The Scandinavian Languages* (London, 1976)
de Koninck, R.H.B., *Groot Uitspraakwoordenboek van de Nederlandse Taal* (Antwerp, 1970)
Lass, Roger, *English Phonology and Phonological Theory* (Cambridge, 1976)
Lockwood, W.B., *An Introduction to Modern Faroese* (Copenhagen, 1955)
van Loey, A., *Middelnederlandse Spraakkunst*, II. Klankleer (Groningen, 1949)
van der Meer, M.J., *Historische Grammatik der niederländischen Sprache* (Heidelberg, 1927)
Mees, I. and Collins, B., 'A phonetic description of the vowel system of Standard Dutch (ABN)', *Journal of the International Phonetic Association* 13 (1983) 64-75
Rijpma, RE. and Schuringa, F.G., *Nederlandse Spraakkunst* (Groningen, 1961)
Samuels, M.L., *Linguistic Evolution* (Cambridge, 1972)
Strang, Barbara M.H., *A History of English* (London, 1970)

10
Thematic Genitives

Noel E. Osselton
University of Newcastle-upon-Tyne

Any attempt to sum up 'the meaning' of the genitive is doomed.[1]

The wisdom of this comment by the late Barbara Strang will be readily apparent to those who try to catch the elusive relationships which the genitive can convey. In particular, it has always seemed near impossible to provide comprehensive rules for the use of the genitive where it stands in rivalry with an *of-*construction. As Strang points out, the relationship of possession is in such cases probably the dominant factor: 'there is a tendency to avoid the genitive of nouns whose referents cannot possess (are not, or are not thought of as being, human or at least animal)'. So we may speak of *a student's book*, but not of **a book's student*; we may have *a ship's captain*, since some speakers like to think of a ship in human terms, but hardly **the typewriter's ribbon*.

Yet attentive readers of literary reviews must be aware that though you cannot have **a book's student*, you can certainly refer to

the book's form
the book's second paragraph
the novel's overwhelming archness

to take only three examples from a single review in the *Times Literary Supplement* on 3 May 1974. Since *book* is neither human nor animal, and cannot 'possess' as a student possesses, why has the reviewer preferred *book's form* to the more readily expected *form of the book*? To take another example from the same source, since cameras and typewriters may be thought of as roughly equivalent bits of private gadgetry, why *the camera's subjects* (14 November 1980) but not **the typewriter's ribbon*?

The object of this contribution to the memorial volume is to suggest that for any explanation of why the genitive should be preferred to the *of*-construction in such cases, we need to look beyond the bounds of the sentence in which the construction occurs, and even beyond the paragraph. It is the general topic upon which the writer of the piece is engaged which seems to be the determining factor in the selection of genitive-taking nouns. And it follows that each review or article will tend to have its own distinctive cluster of thematic genitives.

It will be useful first to set out some recent examples of such genitives:

(1) One could perhaps argue that *the book's* balance could have been different ... There are also perhaps too many minor factual errors and inconsistencies. But these are comparatively trivial blemishes, much outweighed by *the book's* virtues. John Miller, *Times Higher Education Supplement*, 1 September 1978

(2) It would seem that here is a sizeable rogue element which the mainstream of Christianity has been able neither to eliminate nor to assimilate in a wholly satisfactory fashion ... a popular feminist movement that exalted Mary was current at a very early stage in *Christianity's evolution*, possibly even within Mary's own lifetime. Gillian Tindall, *The New Statesman*, 21 May 1976

(3) *The ending's* contravention of the beginning can be explained, if you will, by the literary difficulty of effecting the scheme originally projected. R. Baldwin, 'The unity of the Canterbury Tales', in Richard J. Schoeck and Jerome Taylor (1960) *Chaucer Criticism*, Notre Dame, vol. I, p. 29

(4) In December 1945 an Egyptian peasant made, with his mattock, an archaeological find that has come to generate a substantial industry among students of early Christianity ...

The story of *the find's* zig-zag course towards eventual publication is a mixture of folly, selfishness, generosity and energy. Henry Chadwick, *Times Literary Supplement,* 21 March 1980

(5) The near miraculous switchabout in *boxing's* status can be made comprehensible by examining ... *Times Literary Supplement,* 28 March 1980

(6) I have a scholarly addendum to my paragraph last week about the hilarious ennoblement of Mr Wilson's one-time typist, Mrs Marcia Williams, to the House of Lords.
   At the time of *the peerage's* announcement, old political chestnuts were dragged out — most repeated of all was the one saying that the last time such a thing had been seen was when Caligula made his horse a senator. *Punch,* 12 June 1974

(7) With international soccer authorities already imposing penalties, it is *boxing's* turn to have its eye blackened. *Now!* 3 October 1980

(8) But as always with Larkin the cogitatory life of the poem is more absorbing and ambiguous than its rhetoric. Perhaps the young really are getting it, now? The poem knows the irony that deprivation and desire for oblivion can be held in an image, but not the unreflected and unreflecting existence envied in *the poem's* opening. John Bayley, reviewing Philip Larkin's 'High Windows' in the *Times Literary Supplement,* 21 June 1980

(9) ... along with two Norwegians wanted for questioning about *the painting's* disappearance. *The Times,* 22 April 1980

(10) As a window into the remoteness of Britain's recent past, the historian could hardly choose a better subject than the Victorian Sunday ... One suspects that much of *the Sunday question's* vitality originated in purely local issues and alignments. Brian Harrison, *Times Literary Supplement,* 26 December 1980

(11) Investment in the land was low, and *the soil's* productivity correspondingly meagre. G.E. Mingay, *Times Literary Supplement,* 19 March 1976

(12) ... are known as *the sound's* formants ... regardless of *the sound's* position in the word or its voiced or voiceless

quality. A.C. Gimson (1962) *An Introduction to the Pronunciation of English*, London, pp. 20 and 73

(13) Having thus become sensitized to *the text's* 'intonational structure' one can turn one's attention to the discourse ... Finally, one can judge *the text's* place in the social and cultural world. *Times Literary Supplement*, 14 April 1978

(14) More than 15,000 Ford workers were laid off last night ... duty free perks, although an incentive, were not *the dispute's* critical issue. *Daily Telegraph*, 3 February 1981

(15) As the quality of continuous supervision varies, so does the supervisor's effective interest in ensuring *a thesis's* acceptance ... staff will not support *a thesis's* submission until they are as sure as possible that it is adequate. John Freeman, *Times Higher Education Supplement*, 25 July 1980

In the analysis of genitives given by Quirk *et al.* in *A Grammar of Contemporary English*,[2] a number of seemingly similar examples are listed with the explanation that they involve 'nouns of special interest to human activity'; these include

the book's true importance
the novel's structure
a word's function
the wine's character
the poll's results

For the first three of these, the 'human activity' would presumably be 'reading', for *the wine's character* we may suppose it to be 'drinking', and for *the poll's results*, 'voting'. But what about *science's influence on our society*, or *the treaty's ratification* (other examples in Quirk *et al.*)? The definition of 'human activity' becomes vague here, and clearly with some of the genitives quoted above, such as *the ending's* (3) or *the soil's* (11), the notion of 'activity' can hardly apply at all. For these, other explanations must be sought.

The quotation from Richard Baldwin at (3) provides a useful starting point. Here, the rather unexpected genitive form *ending's* occurs in a section of a study of Chaucer's *Canterbury*

Tales where the central concern of the critic is with literary endings: he argues that whereas a great deal of critical attention has in the past been focused on the beginnings of Chaucer's *Tales*, very little has been devoted to the endings. 'Ending' is thus here a thematic word, one which is of special and immediate concern to the author and his readers, and I would argue that it is this special status which is marked by the use of the genitive. There is no formal reason why the author should not have written 'The contravention of the beginning by the ending can be explained ...'.

The text's in (13) provides an even more striking example of the same phenomenon. This sentence is taken from a review of a book in which Roger Fowler proposes the construction of a linguistically-based 'text grammar'. The reviewer explains at length the notion of 'text' that underlies Fowler's proposal:

> *Texts*, he says (with a most inappropriate disregard for genre), are not only made of sentences, but are also made like a sentence. *Text* and sentence have a common grammar which consists of a surface structure formed by transformations of a semantic deep structure consisting of a modality component, the latter based on a predicate attended by one or more nouns in different roles. Boiled down, the three main elements of this grammar of fiction are the surface structure of the *text*, the modality or discourse (i.e. the authorial stance) and the context. [Italics added]

It is from this point on in the review, when 'text' has been established in the reader's mind as a chief focus of critical attention, that the examples of the word with the genitive occur.

In the quotation under (4) Henry Chadwick is reviewing a book on the Gnostic gospels: but it is the *archaeological find* dramatically announced in the opening sentence which forms his main topic, and the genitive *find's* comes some 200 words later on. The linguistically striking *Sunday question's vitality* (10) is in a review of a book called *The Rise and Fall of the Victorian Sunday*, in which 'the Sunday question' naturally forms the central theme. In (2), in reviewing a book on the Blessed Virgin Mary, the writer produces *Christianity's evolution*, though for some reason she avoids **Christianity's mainstream* only a few lines before. *Boxing's* occurs in (5) in a discussion of a book on Jack Dempsey, and in (7), in an article under the heading 'Boxing: Britain in a tight corner'. *The soil's productivity* (11) is in a piece about the history of European farming systems. Whatever the immediate stylistic motives for the two examples in (12) — emphasis on *formant* in the first, avoidance of the double *of* in the second — there is no doubt about the centrality of *sounds* to Gimson's book. Even the triple sequence of sibilants in *thesis's* does not restrain John Freeman from using the genitive in (15) in an article on 'The thesis business'.

Examples could easily be multiplied, especially of *book's* as in (1) — also of *novel's*, and *poem's* — but journalistic items such as (9) and (14) will show, along with (6) and (7), that the use of such thematic genitives is not merely a scholarly affectation.

On the basis of genitive constructions such as those given above and from a study of their contexts we might then revise the Quirk formula 'nouns of special interest to human activity' to read 'nouns of central concern to the writer's immediate theme': that is, in a book on phonetics, *sound* will get its genitive, in one on farming, *soil* will do so, and in a book on economics you can expect to find *a fund's success, the pound's strength, inflation's consequences*, and so on.

Why should this be so? Why should the genitive construction thus occur with nouns which (to use Strang's phrase again) clearly 'cannot possess', seemingly as a marker of their special status in the context? One indication may be provided by John Bayley's review in (8). He is writing about a Larkin poem, and *poem* is here thematic in the way that *text* is thematic in (13). In this short passage the word *poem* enters both into an *of*-construction and into a genitive construction. Of the two, the *of*-construction might be thought to be the more likely one, since a poem (in Strang's terms) 'is not, or is not thought of as being, human'. But when we note that for John Bayley the poem (not the poet) 'has a cogitatory life', and may 'know' irony, it becomes clearer why he should opt to say *the poem's ending* rather than *the ending of the poem*: it is the objects which are of central interest to us in a particular context which we tend to institutionalise and to treat as though they have a life of their own, while yet stopping short of full personification.

An instructive parallel to this use of the genitive for themewords may be provided from the history of capitalisation in English. The initial capital has been used at least since the sixteenth century as a sign of personification, and it is of course still recognised as being that, thus occupying some part of the grey area between inanimate and human animate. But for a period during the seventeenth and eighteenth centuries, initial capitals began — for one reason or another — to be attached much more frequently to all kinds of common nouns in English, including contexts where there could be no question of personification. So frequently in fact, that writers of grammars and spelling books thought it necessary to instruct their public on the matter of when to use a capital, and when not to.[3] Various categories were proposed of nouns which merited this sub-personificatory initial capital, and most of these need not detain us here. But one of the formulations used was

Such Words as are the main Subject upon which you treat.[4]

It would be hard to find a neater description than this of the status of *boxing's*, *find's*, *thesis's* and all the other nouns taking the genitive which have been dealt with above.

The anonymous seventeenth century scholar thus clearly recognised a distinct category of thematic words, just as reviewers and other writers evidently do today. The only difference lies in the means by which such nouns were foregrounded: three hundred years ago there was an optional orthographical variant for doing so, but now we use a syntactical one.

Notes

1. B.M.H. Strang (1968) *Modern English Structure*, 2nd edn, p. 109.
2. R. Quirk, S. Greenbaum, G. Leech and J. Svartvik (1972) *A Grammar of Contemporary English*, London, section 4.98(h).
3. For an extended discussion of the phenomenon, see N.E. Osselton, 'Spelling-Book Rules and the Capitalization of Nouns in the Seventeenth and Eighteenth Centuries' in M.-J. Arn and H. Wirtjes (1985) *Historical and Editorial Studies in Medieval and Early Modern English*, Groningen.
4. Anon. (1689) *Thesaurium Trilingue Publicum*, p. 16.

11
The Discourse Properties of the Criminal Statute

Michael Hoey
University of Birmingham

A great deal has been written over the years on the subject of legal language, by experts in law, experts in language, and experts in neither. Relatively little, however, has been written about statutes as complete and unified communications. This paper attempts to plug that gap and is concerned with identifying the properties of one kind of statute, the criminal statute, as a complete and unified communication, i.e. as a discourse, a stretch of language felt to be complete in itself. In doing this, it passes through three quite distinct stages. The first stage of the paper is concerned with the unusual relationship of the reader to the criminal statute, and is really a restatement in linguistic terminology of what I suspect most lawyers already know, though not perhaps in so many words (using that phrase in both its figurative and literal sense). But it is needed in order to pave the way for the second stage, where the paper is concerned with the discourse properties of the criminal statute. These properties mean that the criminal statute cannot be described using normal methods of discourse analysis, so the third stage of the paper is concerned with presenting a tentatively offered alternative method of description.

The first point that has to be made about the criminal statute as discourse is that it is a very odd kind of discourse and conforms to very few of the neat generalisations that linguists have made about the way discourses are typically organised. Longacre (1983), for example, argues that the structure of discourses may be described in grammatical terms; it is hard to imagine what a grammatical statement that covered a statute would look like. Van Dijk (1972, 1977) talks of discourses (which he terms texts) as having a macrostructure derivable by well-defined means from the way propositions depend on each other; again, the dependencies present in a typical statute are such as to make any attempt to find a macrostructure fraught with difficulties. In case, however, it is assumed that I am engaging in the time-honoured device of knocking down the opposition before parading a favoured model as an exception to the general condemnation, let me candidly state that the discourse approach which I have been involved in developing is no better equipped to account for the special properties of the statute than any of the others (or not much better, anyway). The statute has defied description, except in terms of cohesion. It is worth considering why. To this end, I start by looking at how other kinds of discourse can be described using the last-named approach.

A number of linguists have found it fruitful to describe the organisation of a typical discourse in terms of the semantic relationships holding among its parts (e.g. Winter, 1968, 1974, 1979; Beekman, 1970; Beekman and Callow, 1974; Ballard *et al.*, 1971; Graustein and Thiele, 1979, 1981). The exact way in which this is done and the terms used to label the relations vary from linguist to linguist, but the agreed common ground is that a 'structure' is built up for a discourse by means of hierarchically organised semantic relations such as cause–effect and contrast. Winter (1974) notes that these relations fall into two fairly well-defined camps — the Sequence relations such as cause–effect, instrument–achievement, premise–deduction condition–fulfilment, and time sequence, and the Matching relations such as contrast, compatibility, hypothetical–real and general–particular. The characteristic feature of the Sequence relation is that one member of the relation is deemed to be prior in argument or time to the other, while for the Matching relations the characteristic feature is that they are all the result of viewing two (or more) pieces of information together to see how they shed light on each other. Hoey and Winter (1986) define the relation (which they term the *clause relation*) as follows, building on an earlier definition in Winter (1971):

> A clause relation is the cognitive process, and the product of that process, whereby the reader interprets the meaning of a clause, sentence, or group of sentences in the context of one or more preceding clauses, sentences, or groups of sentences in the same discourse. It is also the cognitive process, and the product of that process, whereby the choices the writer

makes from grammar, lexis and intonation in the creation of a clause, sentence or group of sentences are made in the context of the other clauses, sentences, or groups of sentences in the discourse.

Some unkind readers have felt that the complex wording of this definition has been coloured by an interest in legal language, but it does make several points relevant to the present discussion. It emphasises that semantic relations do not inhere in the discourse; they are made by a writer, who may or may not choose to mark them explicitly; they are then interpreted (or reinterpreted) by a reader, who uses whatever signals the writer has given but does not usually depend on them. The relations are the result of a reader's interpreting a sentence (or group of sentences) in the context of preceding sentences and writers compose on the presumption that readers will interpret in this way.

Assumptions are being made here about written discourses which are questionable when applied to the criminal statute. First, there is an assumption that whatever is written will be read linearly. This is not necessarily or even usually the case with statutes. There is also an assumption that a reader will cooperate with a writer in order to arrive at the same interpretation of the text as the writer had in mind. A criminal statute however is frequently read in a manner that is highly uncooperative. To show why this is the case, it is necessary to represent the way a reader treats a normal written discourse in terms we might use for the description of spoken discourse. Sinclair and Coulthard (1975) describe the structure of the spoken exchange in terms of actions performed. The most common exchanges, they argue, are made up in part of Opening and Answering moves, which are themselves structured. When a speaker opens an exchange they may perform either an informative, elicitation, or directive act, and the person they address may answer with an acknowledge, reply or react act. Applying these terms to the relationship of written discourse to the reader, we find we have, in the most common case, a written discourse serving as an 'informative' which readers need only silently acknowledge. Novels and textbooks are of this kind. Where appropriate, readers may add the information or argument conveyed to their current stock of knowledge, or simply reject it, but no action (verbal or otherwise) is required of them. Less frequently, a written discourse may take the form of an 'elicitation' to which the appropriate response on the part of a reader is a 'reply'. Many letters are instances of written discourse 'elicitations'; so invariably are examination papers. Least frequently, a written discourse may be a 'directive' to which the reader is expected to respond with a non-verbal 'react'. Instances are notices enjoining one not to spit on the underground or smoke in filling stations.

While it would be tempting to regard criminal statutes as special instances of 'directives', that is not their main function. Rather, they are (like most written discourses) 'informatives', listing what will count as offences.

However, the reader's reaction to the informatives in a criminal statute may be very different from that predicted by the simplified model just given. For in the courtroom, counsel are concerned to relate the informatives made in the statute to those they are making about a defendant. In so far as their desire to do so is for the purposes of protecting the interests of a client or of putting the strongest case for a prosecution, their reading is liable to be unco-operative with the writer in that they will not have as their only motive in interpretation the recovery of the writer's original meaning. Of course, this is not true of the judiciary, but it is, I would maintain, sometimes true of counsel. Counsel are concerned to match the specific statements that are being made about a defendant to the general ones present in the criminal statute. What they seek to show is that the specific statements exemplify the general statements or alternatively contrast with them.

The simplest and least interesting case is where both counsel agree that the statements made about the defendant exemplify those in the statute but disagree about their truth. This may be represented diagrammatically thus:

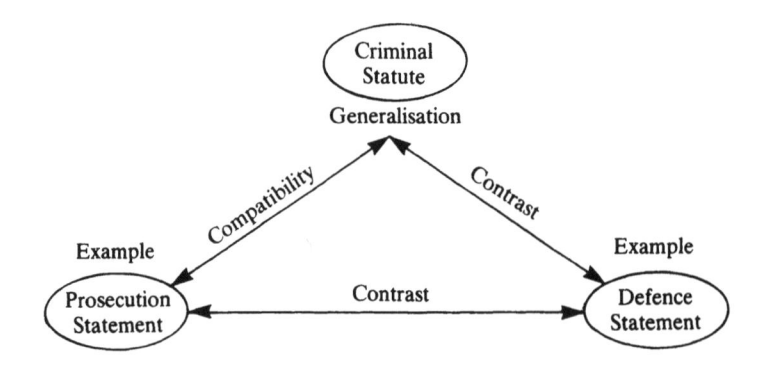

Such cases are disputes about fact not law.

More interesting is the situation where both counsel agree about the truth of statements made about a defendant, but disagree about the relationship they have with the general statements contained in the statute. Such cases are disputes about law. They can be represented diagrammatically as follows:

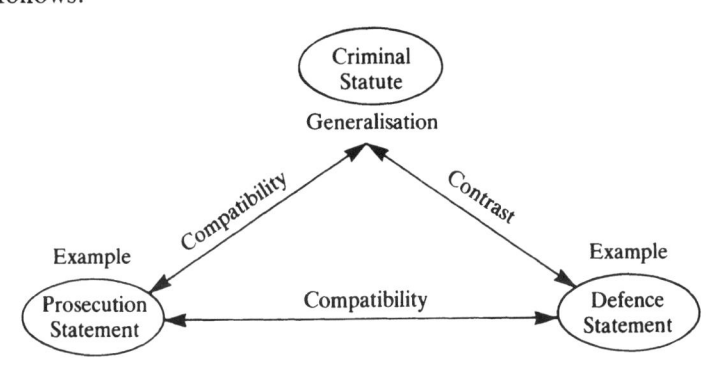

```
                    Criminal
                    Statute
                 Generalisation
                     ↑  ↑
           Compatibility  Contrast
              ↙              ↘
   Example                      Example
  Prosecution ←── Compatibility ──→  Defence
   Statement                       Statement
```

To take a relatively straightforward example, the UK Offences against the Person Act 1861, s. 20 states:

> Whosoever shall unlawfully and maliciously wound ... any other person ... shall be guilty of a misdemeanour.

On 21 January 1982, a defendant and his friend fired an air-gun in the direction of a group of passers-by. One of these sustained as a result an injury in the form of a bruise below the left eyebrow and 'fluid filling the front part of his left eye [which] for a time afterwards abnormally contained red blood cells'. These facts were not substantially disputed in the case (C.-v-Eisenhower (1981) 3 WLR 537); counsel's statements were broadly compatible. The Prosecution however maintained that the facts as stated constituted an instance of 'unlawfully and maliciously wound[ing] any other person' while the Defence maintained the facts were not an instance of this general statement. Thus the case pivoted on the issue of the linguistic relationship between two (sets of) propositions offered as 'informative'.

The case just mentioned is also an instance of our first point made earlier on, namely that criminal statutes are not read linearly in the way that most written discourses are. There are a large number of sections in the Offences against the Person Act,

1861, but only one section is referred to in the judgements reported in *C.-v-Eisenhower*. Consider the difference between this and a normal informing discourse. In the ordinary situation, the parts are responded to as a whole, but in the case of the criminal statute, each part is capable of being responded to independently of the others.

The emphasis on establishing the relationship between general statements and particular ones inhibits the development of normal discourse patterning. It also gives rise to another of the distinctive characteristics of legal language: the central place given to definition. All statutes carry with them a collection of relevant definitions; volumes of case-law likewise always have an index of words defined in the cases they report. Returning to our example of the passer-by struck by a pellet from an air-gun, it is only possible to determine whether 'firing an air-gun at a passer-by so that he is bruised and his eye bloodshot' is an instance of 'unlawfully and maliciously wound[ing] any other person' if one first determines whether 'bruising and making bloodshot' is an instance of 'wounding'. In other words, the relationship of the statements as a whole pivots on the relationship between the words within the statements, in this case on whether *wound* is defined so as to include or exclude 'bruise and make bloodshot'.

The relationship between statements need not be between the particular statement in the courtroom and the general statement in the criminal statute alone; it may also be (and normally is) between that particular statement and similar particular statements in previous cases. The same triangular relationship between counsel's statements and statements in a previous judgement can be discerned as before, except that this time there need be no general–particular relationship to complicate matters:

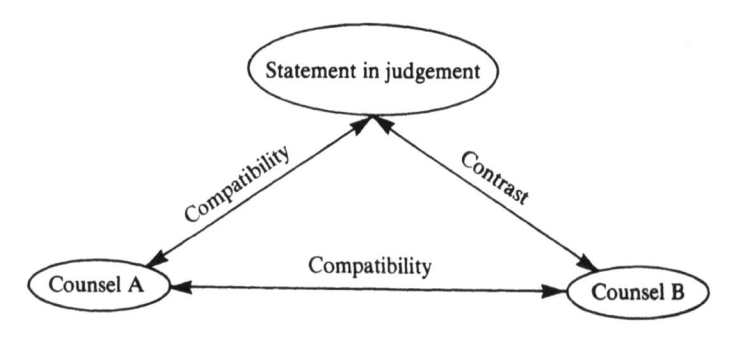

Once again, determining the relationship between statements depends on definition.

Many of the most natural ways of defining however are not available, at least for the draughtsman of legislative documents. There can be no appeal to possible contexts for the word nor lists of overlapping paraphrases. More seriously, the essential fuzziness of words has to be ignored. Few words outside the vocabulary of the professions and the sciences have only one meaning, as a glance at any dictionary will confirm, and the different meanings, moreover, are frequently not discrete but come together in some contexts. None of this usually matters because the reader normally seeks to co-operate in finding a meaning for a word that is compatible with its context, and we rarely need greater exactness for successful communication. In the courtroom, however, the possibility of conflicting readings means that the normal reader strategy is not adequate, and definitions in criminal statutes and similar documents have to be formulated so as to pre-empt unco-operative readings as far as is practicable, which of course also explains the often observed lists of alternative terms found in legislative language. One important effect of the emphasis on precise definition and the relative absence of reliance on co-operative reading is that words in a criminal statute may be assumed to have a constant meaning throughout. The importance of this will become apparent later when we consider ways of uncovering the organisation of such statutes.

The effects of possible unco-operative readings is wider than matters of definition. We mentioned earlier that for a reader to be able to correctly infer the semantic relations holding between the parts of a discourse, he or she has to be co-operative with the writer; unco-operative readings would discover semantic relations that are not intended by the writer. But even co-operatively discovered semantic relations are undesirable in legal language, since it is essential that there be no hidden meanings in a statute. So as soon as one realises that there is the possibility of unwanted inferences resulting from unco-operative readings, it becomes transparently obvious that the criminal statute must be organised so as to inhibit the inference of *any* semantic relations, unwanted or otherwise. In short, it is required of such a statute that it should not have the properties of a normal discourse, i.e. that its sections should be unsequenced. Thus, while sections are internally organised in a manner entirely explicable by current discourse theories, the relationship *between* sections cannot be so explained. And it is right that this should be so: existing discourse models and descriptive systems would be unsatisfactory if they could not distinguish the organisation of a normal discourse from the aberrant lack of organisation of the criminal statute.

This then leads us to the second stage of this paper and to the question with which we began: if the criminal statute is not organised in the same way as other types of discourse, how is it organised? Bhatia (1983) drew attention to one salient fact, namely that sections cross-refer. He shows that a network of cross-references can be drawn between the sections of a statute and between those sections and other statutes. Kurzon (1984) suggests that all legal texts, including statutes, can be shown to be structured in terms of the relation of themes to a hypertheme derivable in the case of a statute from the title. Unfortunately the statute on which he applies his method of analysis is extremely brief. In so far, however, as he demonstrates his case, he shows that the statute does share some properties with other kinds of discourse, though the fact that no theme becomes a subsequent theme in his analysis is further confirmation of the essential separateness of sections in a statute. As will become apparent later, both he and Bhatia are touching on features of the criminal statute that it is possible to make fuller use of in our analysis.

Despite Kurzon's valiant attempt to the contrary, I do not think there is much to be gained from trying to make existing discourse concepts fit on to statutes. It is preferable to consider whether there is not an entirely different way of accounting for such discourses. In an earlier paper (Hoey, 1985), I suggested that an analogy with natural science might be helpful. I should like to expand on that analogy a little here.

If a biologist wishes to provide a detailed description of a complex organism such as a human being, he or she is forced to describe in considerable detail the relationship of all the parts — bones, muscles, organs, nerves, arteries, and so on. It is difficult to describe the heart or the bowel without describing what they are connected to and how they function. The human organism is a single vast interconnecting system, and the biologist's description reflects that. I suggest that a typical discourse is like such an organism, and the linguist's description is tailored accordingly.

The Discourse Properties of the Criminal Statute

Now consider the bee. It too is a complex system which can be described in terms of its interconnecting parts. But a biologist could not be content with a description of its internal system, because it would miss out too much. For the bee is first and foremost part of a social system — the hive — and although there must be a description of its internal system, there must also be a description of the system of which it is a part. That system, however, is not a single organism, but a colony, and must be described in quite different ways. The criminal statute, I suggest, is likewise a colony, and the sections are its bees.

In this the criminal statute is not unique. Other examples of what I am terming the colony are dictionaries, constitutions, examination papers, and the Book of Proverbs. Discourses having some but not all the features of a colony include newspapers and conference proceedings.

The properties of a discourse colony appear to be as follows:

(a) There has to be a hive — a combination of framing sentences and titles that set the bounds for the discourse. In the case of the criminal statute these are the two titles and abbreviation and the statement of enactment that prefaces every statute.

(b) There has to be no inferrable semantic relation holding between the parts that would make one sequence and only one sequence intelligible; in other words, one does not read a colony as continuous prose. It was this property of criminal statutes that led us to identify colonies in the first place. Of course the individual sections of such statutes can be read as continuous prose. It is their juxtaposition that is unusual, not their internal features.

(c) Just as a substantial number of bees perform the same function in a hive, so a substantial number of the parts of a discourse colony must perform the same function in the discourse, e.g. creating offences in the case of a criminal statute, or defining words in the case of a dictionary. In so far as the parts of a colony perform the same function, they are in fact weakly related in a Matching Compatibility relation, but this is not sufficient to give the discourse the continuity associated with normal prose.

(d) There has to be a formal system of reference, usually

either alphabetically or numerically based. In the case of the statute, of course, the section numbering provides such a system.

(e) Individual bees can be isolated: it must be possible to make use of any part of a discourse colony without needing to refer to all the rest.

(f) The bees enter the hive in no order. If the parts are jumbled, the *meaning* of the whole must be the same, though clearly the utility may be radically affected. Thus if sections are re-ordered in a criminal statute, they have exactly the same legal force, despite the loss in accessibility that would result from moving the most important section from near the beginning of the statute.

(g) Just as a bee may rarely change hives, so it is possible in a discourse colony for one or more of the parts to be utilised in a subsequent colony. This is theoretically possible for criminal statutes, but I have not sought to confirm whether it has occurred in practice.

(h) The population of a hive changes through time: old bees die while new ones develop. Likewise a discourse colony is capable of change and development. It is not difficult to delete, replace, or add parts. This is, of course, normal practice in legislation, though the amending statutes tend to co-exist as discourses alongside the statutes they amend.

Such, then, are the basic properties of a colony, of which the statute is a particularly clear example. It will be seen that the statute is not a unique kind of discourse after all but fits quite naturally into a class of discourses. It might be inferred from what we have said, however, that there is no useful way in which we can talk about the relationship between the parts of such a discourse. This is not so. We need, though, first to bring together three insights. Firstly, we recall Bhatia's observation about the cross-referring of sections: he shows in diagrammatic form a simple net of links between sections. Secondly, we recall Kurzon's tracking of themes and note that lexical repetition played an important part in his analysis. Thirdly, we recall that many of the sections are in a weak Matching Compatibility relation because they share the same function.

It is one of the properties of non-narrative discourse that non-adjacent sentences may be semantically related and that this relation may be set up by lexical repetition (Winter, 1974, 1979; Hoey, 1983, forthcoming). Given that criminal statute sections are, by virtue of their forming a colony, non-adjacent, it seems worth exploring in more detail how repetition may help connect the parts of the criminal statute. And with this we move into the third and final stage of this paper.

The analysis that follows has been carried out by hand on an extremely short and therefore untypical statute, the Badgers Act 1973 (UK), an act designed to provide protection for badgers. It clearly needs to be replicated on a much longer statute using a computer before the findings I report can be given more than cautious credence. Nevertheless I believe that, though the suggestions I make here are tentative, they may suggest a way forward in the description of criminal statutes.

The aim of the analysis was to record all the repetitions that connect the sections and sub-sections of a criminal statute with a view to showing how these enable us to say interesting things about the organisation of such a statute. It will be noted that in the analysis the unit worked with is the sub-section, not, as it should strictly have been according to my colony analogy, the section. This is because sub-sections correspond for the most part to sentences.

The method of analysis carried out was relatively straightforward. All grammatical items were excluded, i.e. all closed set items. All lexical items (open class items) were assigned a number on first occurrence. Homonyms were ignored on the grounds that they are rare in legal language and cannot in any case be distinguished conveniently by a computer; my aim in conducting the analysis was to facilitate computer replication. Given the careful nature of legislative language, this seemed a justifiable simplification. Names, indicated by capitalisation, were double-coded both as single lexical items and as multiple items e.g. *Secretary of State* was coded both as one item and as two.

On second and subsequent occurrences of lexical items, a record was made of where they had previously occurred. Repetition within sub-sections was, however, ignored. If an item occurred more than once in another sub-section, it was treated as having occurred only once. Where two lexical items shared a lexical morpheme (e.g. *committed* and *commission*) they were

The Discourse Properties of the Criminal Statute

treated as a single item; but this was not common in the statute I analysed. Explicit references to the Act and to (sub-)sections within the Act were separately recorded but not included in the analysis of repetition. Sections 11 and 12 of the Act were not analysed, as the former consists of definitions and the latter provides the title and date of coming into force.

The result of such an analysis is a complete record of the ways in which the sections and sub-sections of a particular criminal statute refer to each other. First, we have the cross-referencing Bhatia referred to (see Figure 11.1). This is where the sections allude to each other and to the Act as a whole. Even from this a clear sense of the non-linearity of the statute is achieved, though without the references to the Act as a whole the picture would be markedly simpler.

The pattern of repetition is more complex so it is better to begin by representing it in a different manner. Table 11.1 shows all the repetitions that occur in the statute, the sections being listed on both horizontal and verticle axes. Thus, to take a simple

Table 11.1

	1(1)	1(2)	1(3)	2	3	4	5	6(1)	6(2)	7(1)	7(2)	7(3)	8(1)	8(2)	8(3)	9(1)	9(2)	9(3)	10(1)	10(2)
1(1)	✕																			
1(2)	5	✕																		
1(3)	5	5	✕																	
2	7	5	5	✕																
3	4	6	5	4	✕															
4	4	5	4	4	5	✕														
5	4	3	3	3	3	4	✕													
6(1)	1	1	1	1	1	1	0	✕												
6(2)	0	0	0	0	0	0	0	1	✕											
7(1)	8	5	5	7	4	5	3	4	0	✕										
7(2)	8	5	5	9	4	5	4	5	0	14	✕									
7(3)	3	3	3	4	3	4	4	1	0	4	20	✕								
8(1)	8	5	5	8	4	5	3	1	0	9	11	5	✕							
8(2)	4	5	3	6	6	4	2	2	0	5	7	4	6	✕						
8(3)	4	4	4	5	5	4	3	4	0	5	5	3	6	5	✕					
9(1)	4	4	3	5	4	10	1	6(2)	0	6	10	6	5	5	2	✕				
9(2)	0	0	0	0	0	3	0	0	0	1	1	1	0	1	0	4	✕			
9(3)	3	3	3	3	3	6	3	0	1	4	4	4	3	2	4	6	3	✕		
10(1)	5	5	4	8	4	4	9	1	0	5	7	4	6	7	4	6	0	3	✕	
10(2)	4	4	4	4	4	4	4	1	0	4	4	3	4	2	4	2	0	4	4	✕
10(3)	3	4	3	4	3	3	3	2	1	3	4	3	3	2	3	3	0	2	6	5

The Discourse Properties of the Criminal Statute

Figure 11.1: Cross-referencing in Badgers Act 1973 (UK)

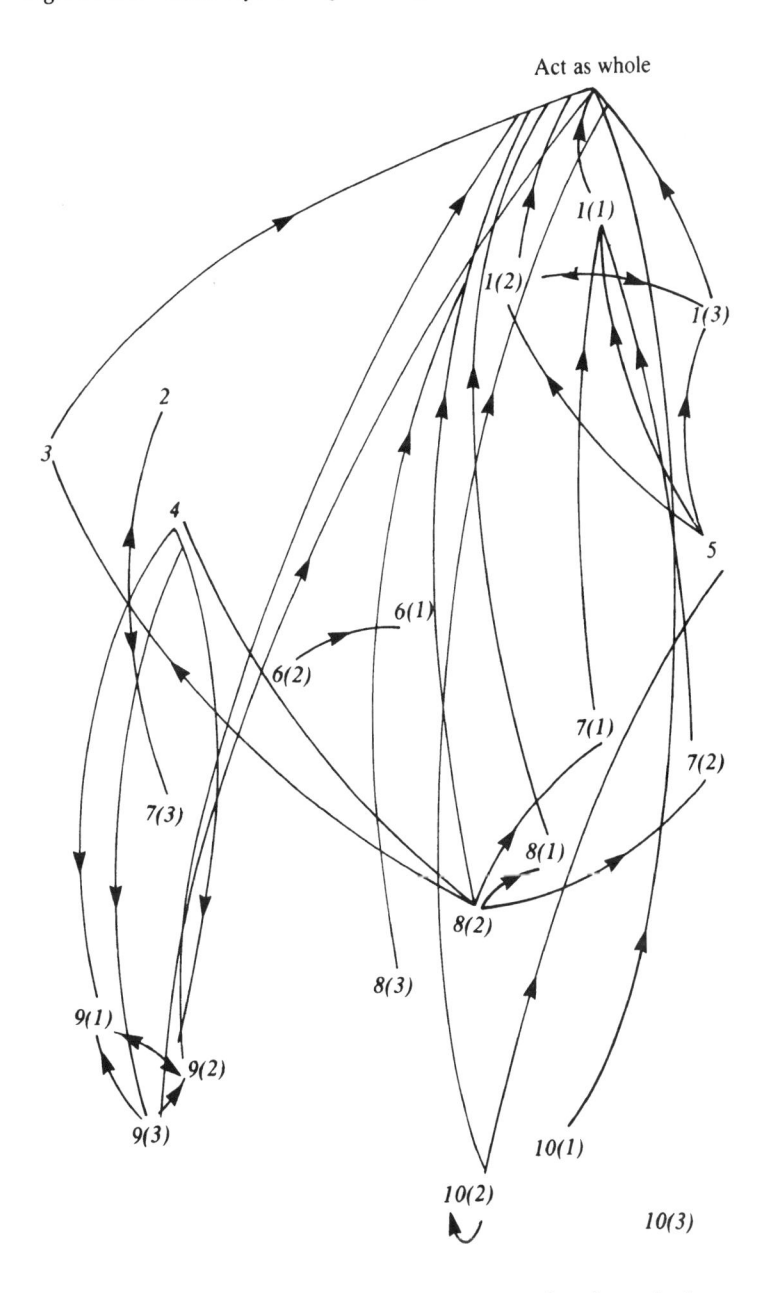

Important: There is *no* significance to the positioning of section and subsection numbers in this and subsequent diagrams. The only relationships the diagram represents are those indicated by line connection.

example, we can see that sub-section 6(2) shares one lexical item with sub-section 6(1), shown in the horizontal column, and one each with sub-sections 9(3)and 10(3), shown in the vertical column.

What this table shows is not only the extraordinary density of repetition, which is presumably no surprise, but also the considerable variation in density of repetition. Thus a glance at this table suggests that 6(2) just mentioned and, to a lesser extent, sub-section 9(2) are marginal to the discourse. Since the former describes the conditions under which an order may be made by Parliament and the latter lists the authorities that may grant licences, neither of which relate directly to what can or cannot be done with badgers, this may be said to be supported by intuition, though no claim is being made that a marginal section is less important than more central sections.

The second observation one can make by glancing at this table is that there is considerable variation in terms of the number of items shared with other sections. Thus, for example, section 7(2) shares 20 items with 7(3), 11 items with 8(1), 7 items with 8(2), and only 1 with 9(2). It would be a reasonable hypothesis that sections sharing a greater number of lexical items are more closely related than sections sharing fewer. As a first step in focusing attention on those more closely related, we may decide to consider only those sections that share above a certain number of lexical items. The threshold is determined pragmatically, at that point at which a distinction is being made between section relations. Thus when five lexical items are taken as the lower limit, we arrive at a picture which is too cluttered for convenient study. If, however, we take six as our lower limit, the picture clarifies dramatically (see Figure 11.2), though even here we are given more than we can comment on in a single paper.

We commented before on the apparent marginality of sections 6(2) and 9(2) as measured by the number of lexical items shared with other sections. Figure 11.2 gives us another possible measure, namely in terms of the number of bonds a section makes with other sections, where a bond is taken to be formed by six or more shared items. It will be noted, for example, that 1(3), 6(2), 9(2), and 10(2) have formed no bonds with any other section by means of repetition. A case can be made that all these sections are marginal in the sense that they are not so much making the law as making it workable. 6(2) and

The Discourse Properties of the Criminal Statute

Figure 11.2: Interrelationships of sections and sub-sections in the Badgers Act 1973 (UK)

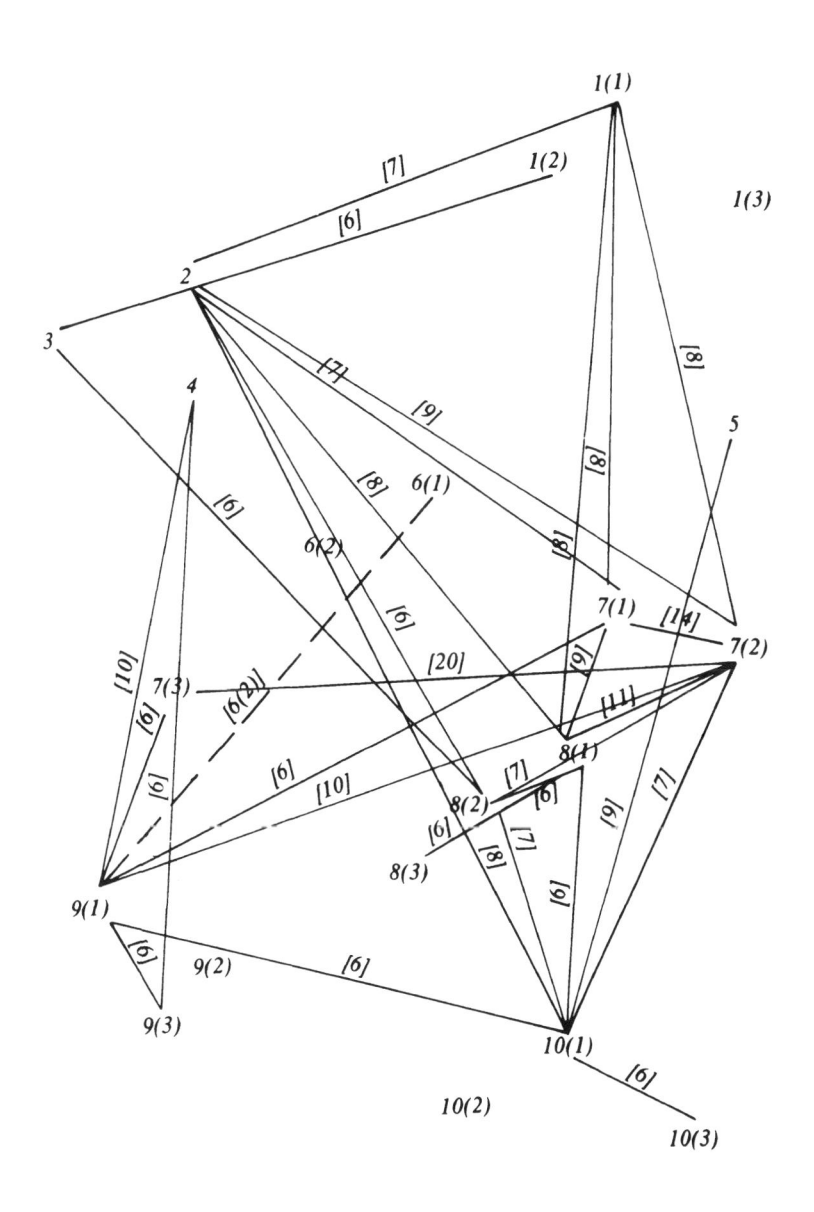

Straight lines represent six or more shared lexical items.

The Discourse Properties of the Criminal Statute

9(2) we have discussed; 1(3) blocks a loophole, while 9(2) spells out the penalties a court may impose. Again, it should perhaps be stressed that I am *not* claiming that these sections are less important as law; I am simply attempting to interpret their marginality in the discourse.

Looking at the diagram again, we note that thirteen of the sections and sub-sections form two or fewer bonds. The remaining eight form four or more. These may reasonably be regarded as the most central to the discourse; they are sections 1(1), 2, 7(1), 7(2), 8(1), 8(2), 9(1) and 10(1). Put together they read like a useful summary of the statute, the only serious omission being section 3, which is needed to make sense of section 8(2). Again, this represents a linguistic not a legal summary; I am fully aware of the importance of the omitted sections. Nevertheless the summary does serve to give the reader an idea of what the Act is about as a preliminary to more detailed investigation, and could be generated straightforwardly with the help of a computer.

We now need to consider how we might interpret the bonds between sections of the statute that we find thrown up by the analysis. We begin by considering relationships formed by section 1(1) with sections 2, 7(1), 7(2) and 8(1) respectively.

There are eight lexical items shared by sections 1(1) and 2, and placed together they very nearly read as if they were continuous prose:

1. If, save as permitted by or under this Act, any person wilfully kills, injures or takes, or attempts to kill, injure or take, any badger, he shall be guilty of an offence.

2. If any person shall
   (a) cruelly ill-treat any badger,
   (b) use in the course of killing or taking, or attempting to kill or take any badger, any badger tongs,
   (c) subject to section 7(3) of this Act, dig for any badger, or
   (d) use for the purpose of killing or taking any badger any firearm other than a smooth bore weapon of not less than 20 bore or a rifle using ammunition having a muzzle energy of not less than 160 footpounds and a bullet weighing not less than 38 grains,
   he shall be guilty of an offence.

The latter section amplifies the protection offered to badgers, turning from the *act* of killing or taking to the *method* of killing and taking; it could be connected to section 1(1) with the conjunct *furthermore*. What the analysis has done then is highlight the closeness of relationship of non-adjacent parts of the discourse.

Another, perhaps more striking, example of a relationship between non-adjacent sections highlighted by the analysis is that of section 1(1) to section 7(1), with which it shares eight lexical items:

1. If, save as permitted by or under this Act, any person wilfully kills, injures or takes, or attempts to kill, injure or take, any badger, he shall be guilty of an offence.

7. (1) Except within an area of special protection, an authorised person shall not be guilty of an offence under section 1(1) of this Act by reason of —
(a) the killing or taking or attempted killing or taking of any badger, or
(b) the injuring of any badger in the course of taking it, or attempting to take or kill it.

Here the latter section spells out an exemption to 1(1), to which it explicitly refers. Again, the tracking of repetition has allowed us to identify the pairing; again, the result is not unlike continuous prose. The relationship of 1(1) to 7(2), with which it shares eight items, will be found to be exactly of the same kind, the exemption applying in this instance *within* an area of special protection.

Another section with which 1(1) shares eight lexical items is section 8(1):

1. If, save as permitted by or under this Act, any person wilfully kills, injures or takes, or attempts to kill, injure or take, any badger, he shall be guilty of an offence.

8. (1) A person shall not be guilty of an offence under this Act by reason only of
(a) the taking or attempted taking of any badger which had been disabled otherwise than by his act and was taken or to be taken solely for the purpose of tending it;
(b) the killing or attempted killing of any badger which appeared to be seriously injured or in such a condition

The Discourse Properties of the Criminal Statute

that to kill it would be an act of mercy;
(c) the unavoidable killing or injuring of any badger as an incidental result of a lawful action.

Once again, the two sections are seen to go together naturally, the latter section describing situations in which killing, injuring, etc. are not offences; it would be possible to connect the sections with *however*.

What is being claimed is that repetition marks those sections which share content and that all such sections are intelligible placed together; in some sense they belong together. I have not chosen my examples carefully to illustrate my point; they are simply the first to be derived from the Figure. To show that it is not because of the central nature of 1(1) that previous bonds produced coherent discourse, we conclude this aspect of our discussion with two instances of bonds between sections from elsewhere in the Act.

It will be seen from Figure 11.2 that sections 5 and 10(1) share nine lexical items. Put together they read as follows:

> 5. If any person shall be found committing an offence under section 1 of this Act on any land, it shall be lawful for the owner or occupier of the land, or any servant of the owner or occupier, or any constable, to require that person forthwith to quit such land and also to give his name and address; and if that person on being so required wilfully remains upon the land or refuses to give his full name or address, he shall be guilty of an offence.
>
> 10. (1) Where a constable has reasonable grounds for suspecting that any person is committing an offence under this act or has committed an offence under this Act and that evidence of the commission of the offence is to be found on that person or any vehicle or article he may have with him, the constable may —
> (a) without warrant stop and search that person and search any vehicle or article he may have with him;
> (b) without warrant arrest that person if he fails to give his full name and address to the constable's satisfaction and
> (c) seize and detain for the purposes of proceedings under this Act any badger whether alive or dead, or any

The Discourse Properties of the Criminal Statute

weapon or article capable of being used to kill or take badgers, which may be in that person's possession.

It will be seen that both sections are concerned with the rights of constables (and others) in their dealings with suspected offenders. Although they are clearly strongly related, they are in no particular order; it would be just as appropriate to read 10(1) first, detailing the constable's rights concerning suspected offenders, and then go on to section 5, in which the rights extend to others as well and where the offence is more definite. This accords with the chains we have made regarding the non-sequential nature of colonies.

As our final unproblematic example, we turn to sections 4 and 9(3) which share six items. Put together they read as follows:

4. If, save as may be authorised by licence granted under section 9 of this Act, any person marks, or attaches any ring, tag or other marking device to, any badger (other than one which is lawfully in his possession by virtue of section 8(2)(a) of this Act or of such a licence) he shall be guilty of an offence.

9. (3) A licence granted under this section may be revoked at any time by the authority by whom it was granted, and without prejudice to any other liability to a penalty which he may have incurred under this or any other Act, any person who contravenes or fails to comply with any condition imposed on the grant of a licence under this section shall be guilty of an offence.

Section 4 describes behaviour that constitutes an offence unless one has a licence, while section 9(3) warns that even such a licence has conditions attached to it and may be revoked. Again, what we have here is nearly acceptable continuous prose in which something mentioned in a subordinate clause becomes the main topic of the next sentence.

Of the thirty-one connections made in this manner by analysis in terms of repetition, twenty-two are in my view unproblematically connected; eight of these are also explicitly cross-referenced. There remain nine pairs connected by the repetition of six or more items that are less obviously related.

The Discourse Properties of the Criminal Statute

Interestingly all but one of these involves either section 2 or 10(1). It may be helpful to consider one of these pairs. Sections 2 and 7(1) share seven lexical items, but when placed together do not approximate to continuous prose nor appear to have much content in common. This fails, however, to take into account the property of a colony, that the bees enter the hive in no order. We are not dealing here with normal linearly read prose and therefore there is no reason why section 2 should be seen as necessarily preceding section 7(1). If we reverse the order of the sections, their relationship becomes slightly more obvious, though it is at first sight still less strong than those we have previously discussed:

7. (1) Except within an area of special protection, an authorised person shall not be guilty of an offence under section 1(1) of this Act by reason of —
(a) the killing or taking or attempted killing or taking of any badger, or
(b) the injuring of any badger in the course of taking it, or attempting to take or kill it.

2. [But] if any person shall —
(a) cruelly ill-treat any badger,
(b) use in the course of killing or taking, or attempting to kill or take any badger, any badger tongs,
(c) subject to section 7(3) of this Act, dig for any badger, or
(d) use for the purpose of killing or taking any badger any firearm other than a smooth bore weapon of not less than 20 bore or a rifle using ammunition having a muzzle energy of not less than 160 footpounds and a bullet weighing not less than 38 grains,
he shall be guilty of an offence.

What we have if we reverse the order is a contrast relation between the two sections which could be marked by the insertion of *but* at the beginning of section 2; the force of section 2 is that any person, whether or not an authorised person, is guilty of an offence if they kill or take badgers in particular ways. Indeed one of the main functions of this section must be to cover the behaviour of authorised persons, since unauthorised persons are in the main already covered by section

1(1). In other words, we are being told that an authorised person commits no offence in killing, injuring or taking a badger outside a protected area unless he has done it in one of the ways described in section 2. Despite immediate appearances to the contrary, the analysis has correctly identified this pair as belonging together; a similar argument can be brought to bear on some of the other problematic pairings.

We have travelled a long way since we started and it may be useful at this juncture to recap the journey we have taken in case anyone wants to take the same route — or work out where I got lost! We began by noting that criminal statutes are unusual in that they are frequently read unco-operatively. This leads on the one hand to a greater attention to definition than is normal in everyday situations and on the other to the absence of the inferred semantic relations that characterise ordinary discourses. Such statutes are, it was claimed, organised instead as colonies, and the properties of colonies were outlined. A method of analysis was therefore suggested that took account of this organisation; this enabled us to make tentative claims about the interrelationship of the sections of a criminal statute.

It has been a long journey, but it has brought us back close to our starting-point. For the method of analysis we outlined depends crucially on the fact that legal language uses lexis consistently, and this is itself a product of the importance of definition. Thus we find that lexical properties and discourse properties are intertwined. In this the criminal statute is a particularly clear example of an interrelationship that exists in all discourses and which has been inadequately described. For this reason, the area of law should continue to provide data of interest to linguists.

Routledge is grateful to Greenwood Press, Inc. for permission to publish 'The Discourse Properties of the Criminal Statute' in *An Historic Tongue*. The original work was presented orally in 1985 by Professor Hoey at the 2nd Annual Conference on Law and Technology at the University of Houston, Houston, Texas, U.S.A., and is being published in revised form in COMPUTER POWER AND LEGAL LANGUAGE, *The Use of Computational Linguistics, Artificial Intelligence, and Expert Systems in the Law*, Charles Walter, Ed. (Quorum Books, a division of Greenwood Press, Inc., Westport, CT, 1988). Copyright © 1988 by Charles Walter. Reprinted with permission of the publisher.

References

Ballard, D.L., Conrad, R.J. and Longacre, R.E. (1971), 'The deep and surface grammar of interclausal relations', *Foundations of Language* 7, 70–118

Beekman, J. (1970), 'Propositions and their relations within a discourse', *Notes on Translation* 37, 6–23

—— and Callow, J. (1974), *Translating the Word of God*, Zondervan Pub., Michigan

Bhatia, V.K. (1983), *An Applied Discourse Analysis of English Legislative Writing*, Language Studies Unit Research Report, University of Aston Language Studies Unit, Birmingham

Graustein, G. and Thiele, W. (1979), 'An approach to the analysis of English texts', *Linguistische Studien* A55, 3–15

—— (1981), 'Principles of text analysis', *Linguistische Arbeitsberichte* 31, 3–29

Hoey, M.P., (1983), *On the Surface of Discourse*, George Allen & Unwin, London

—— (1985), 'The statute as discourse and the lawyer as linguist', *The Eleventh LACUS Forum 1984* (ed. R. Hall) 255–62

—— (forthcoming) *Patterns of Lexis in Text*, OUP, Oxford

—— and Winter, E.O. (1986), 'Clause relations and the writer's communicative task', in *Functional Approaches to Writing: Research Perspectives*, Ablex Pub./Frances Pinter (Pub.) 120–41

Kurzon, D. (1984), 'Themes, hyperthemes and the discourse structure of British legal texts', *Text*, vol. 4, 1/3, 31–56

Longacre, R.E. (1983), *The Grammar of Discourse*, New York, Plenum Press

Sinclair, J. McH. and Coulthard, R.M. (1975), *Towards an Analysis of Discourse*, OUP, Oxford

Van Dijk, T.E. (1972), *Some Aspects of Text Grammars*, Mouton, The Hague

—— (1977), *Text and Context: Explorations in the Semantics and Pragmatics of Discourse*, Longman, London

Winter, E.O. (1968), 'Some aspects of cohesion', in *Sentence and Clause in Scientific English*. Report of the Research Project 'The Linguistic Properties of Scientific English' supported by Grant Y5955 from the Office of Scientific and Technical Information, Communication Research Centre, Dept of General Linguistics, University College London

—— (1971) 'Connection in science material: a proposition about the semantics of clause relations' *C.I.L.T. Papers and Reports*, 41–52

—— (1974), 'Replacement as a function of repetition: a study of some of its principal features, in the clause relations of contemporary English'. Ph.D thesis, University of London. University Microfilms 77–70,036 Ann Arbor, USA, (with minor emendations) (1977)

—— (1979) 'Replacement as a fundamental function of the sentence in context', *Forum Linguisticum*, 4.2, 95–133

12

Varietas Delectat: Forms and Functions of English Around the World[1]

Manfred Görlach
University of Cologne

Barbara Strang's *History of English* was one of the first language histories to take account of the importance of the international spread of the world language. However, when she wrote the book in 1968/69, very little research had been done on varieties of English outside Britain and the United States (see her note on p. 76), so that the book contains far less on the topic than it would have done if it had come out ten years later — or if a second edition of her work had been published. The following account is intended to sum up progress in the field of world English mainly during the 1970s and 1980s, not to add a chapter to her book.

1. History of research

The world-wide spread of English has taken 500 years in all to complete, but the major developments have taken place in the course of the last 200 years. It is surprising that the problems connected with the topic have found less scholarly interest than might well have been expected.[2] Although there have been a great number of studies on the question of English as an international *auxiliary* language, and national varieties, such as those of the United States and Australia have been discussed, important data and hypotheses are still lacking in the field: it even remains doubtful how far traditional linguistic methods can be applied to the subject. It may be symptomatic for the state of knowledge (and the interest) that most histories of the English language, even of recent date (excepting Leith, 1983) deal with the topic only in passing, although the relevant phenomena are, linguistically and historically, well documented, or at least much better than the favourite playgrounds of historical linguistics. As regards the history of research, the preference given to older periods by traditional philologies and the homogeneity of language systems postulated, or at least tacitly assumed, by various structuralist schools and their transformational heirs, which stressed the systematic aspects and the competence of the ideal native speaker, explain why problems of ordered variation did not get into focus. Scholarly interest in 'New Englishes' and their functions would have been difficult to justify: most colonial forms of native English were considered provincial, backward, incorrect and not quite respectable (similar criticisms were formerly levelled at AmE). Second-language varieties fared even worse: most were discarded as gibberish; their apparent lack of system did not make them serious candidates for Ph.D. theses or other forms of scholarly attention.

It was the rediscovery of the social and communicative functions of language, and of variation as a phenomenon governed by social and functional rules, together with the growing national self-confidence of peoples using English, that made the time ripe for new research. Such tendencies were reinforced by Labov's work in quantificational sociolinguistics, by American interest in minority dialects, particularly Black English, and by an increase in the linguistic attention paid to such areas of study as language acquisition, bilingualism, and pidgin and creole languages. Finally, traditional dialectology turned to the social causes and effects of variation, and began to take account of urban dialects and class distinctions in speech.

After these conditions for new research had been created in the 1960s, the wealth of scholarly publications from 1973 on illustrates how results were collected, sifted, compared and made available for academic teaching.[3] When looking at publication dates, one must be aware of the fact that handbooks take years to get into print. The proportion of publications from Germany (partly *in* German) seems particularly remarkable. With all these books available, it now seems worthwhile to summarise, and comment on, the results and critical insights of a new discipline.

2. The spread of English

The spread of English was a much slower and more laborious process than its present distribution would lead one to expect. Around 1500 the New World was divided up by Papal edict between Spain and Portugal, and a little later on, the Dutch and the French became serious competitors for naval supremacy on the seven seas and at the trading posts established on the coasts. England had internal problems to settle in the 16th century: there could be no thought of exporting English settlers and the English way of life (including the English language) until the late 16th century. Only then did the anglicisation of Wales and Ireland begin (Leith, 1983; Bailey, 1984); in 1603 the Union of the Crowns joined England, Scotland and Ireland into one kingdom, and bound the new provinces to London speech norms. Also, this was the period in which the first attempts at English settlements in Newfoundland and Georgia fall (both in 1582). Daniel's much-quoted prophetic words of 1599 illustrate the accompanying change in linguistic attitudes towards the vernacular,[4] in the wake of England's first bid for world power after the defeat of the Armada:

(1) And who in time knowes wither we may bent
       The treasure of our tongue, to what strange shores
       This gaine of our best glorie shal be sent.
       T'inrich vnknowing Nations with our stores?
       What worlds in th'yet vnformed Occident
       May come refin'd with th'accents that are ours?
                          (Samuel Daniel (1599) *Musophilus*)

In North America, parts of the Caribbean were wrested from the Spanish, and other colonies were taken from the Dutch and Swedes in 'New England' in the 17th century, while the French were routed in Canada in the 18th. Whereas the spread of English was fairly successful on the American continent, it was very slow elsewhere. The period 1788–1835 marked a breakthrough with first settlements in Australia and New Zealand, the conquest of Cape Province, and also the beginning of the anglicisation of the school system in India. These expansions laid the foundations for the stabilisation of the Victorian Empire in which peoples with a great multitude of cultures and languages were administered from a tiny mother country with the help of one language — English. This world-wide expansion is particularly noteworthy when one considers the blow the British had suffered through the breakaway of their major colony in North America. The final phase came with the erosion of the Empire (though parts of it live on in the Commonwealth) and — in spite of a certain loss of ESL functions — the unpredicted growth of English internationally, as a consequence of the supremacy of English-speaking nations such as Great Britain, the U.S.A., Canada, South Africa, Australia and New Zealand in trade and industry, science and technology, and politics.

The fascinating history of this expansion is a mixture of colonial force and deliberate submission, economic convenience on the part of the Europeans, and faith in progress or pragmatic utility on that of non-Europeans. The history of English in India has often been adduced as evidence for such mixed motives. In 1823 Raja Rammohadan Roy proposed

(2) employing European gentlemen of talent and education to instruct the natives of India in mathematics, natural philosophy, chemistry, anatomy and other useful sciences, which the natives of Europe have carried to a degree of perfection that has raised them above the inhabitants of other parts of the world,

thus stressing the importance of the English language for the modernisation of the country. The value of anglicisation for the colonial administrators was clearly stated in Macaulay's *Minutes* of 1835:

(3) That Minute proclaimed the need to form a subculture in India: 'a class who may be interpreters between us and the millions we govern, a class of persons, Indians in blood and colour, but English in taste, in opinion, in morals and in intellect'
(R.R. Roy and T.B. Macaulay, quoted from Kachru, 1982a:355)

It is especially illuminating to compare the successes of English with the overseas expansion of Spanish (Milan, 1983) and of French (Gordon, 1978; Valdman, 1979), and, to a lesser

Varietas Delectat

degree, with that of Portuguese and Dutch.[5] The following features seem to be typical of the historical spread of English:

1. English began to spread when the language had achieved homogeneity in its written form (and, by and large, also in the phonemic structure of its spoken form) and been accepted as the standard. Kurath (1972:68) claimed convincingly that this was the state of early AmE, and if it is true of AmE, then certainly also of the English of later settlements elsewhere.

2. English was *successful* to a surprising degree. Unlike Spanish, French and, especially, German settlements abroad, there has never been a sizeable English-speaking group of settlers (since the Anglo–Irish of the Middle Ages) that gave up their mother-tongue.[6] The only ones in danger of doing so today are comparatively small groups of speakers of (creole) English in Central America (on the Atlantic coast of Nicaragua, Costa Rica and Panama, cf. Holm, 1983). Where English has ceased to function as a second language (as is the case in Tanzania, Malaysia or the Philippines, cf. Llamzon, 1986), its uses as an international *foreign* language are unchallenged and are, in fact, expanding.

3. Colonial communities unquestioningly accepted metropolitan norms (in language and other areas involving value judgements) until the First World War (in the USA at least until 1776), an attitude that was bound up with inferiority complexes regarding cultural independence and a strong desire for prescriptive rules, e.g. in the form of grammars.

4. Outside settler communities the integrative functions of English were much weaker. Imitation of the British way of life was found in an extreme form in the 19th-century Krio community in Freetown and in some circles in colonial India (where reading Shakespeare, Milton and Wordsworth was considered an indispensable part of all English-medium education), but pragmatic values, for both sides, always complemented, and often dominated, such cultural functions world-wide.

   These politically neutral utilitarian considerations made

possible the continued use of English in post-colonial societies and its impressive expansion as an international language after 1945.[7]

The success of English in its function as an international auxiliary language has often been regarded as the measure of its adequacy for the job, and scholars have tried to account for it with reference to the type of language English is. In particular, its reduced inflectional system (which was largely identical with 'grammar' for Latin-influenced grammarians) has been mentioned as favouring such international functions. These reflections have led on to further plans for deliberate simplification and attempts to make English even easier to teach and to learn.[8]

Brosnahan (1973) tried to systematise the factors responsible for successes and failures in language spread; he names the following variables:

1. imposition as a consequence of military conquest;
2. length of colonial rule;
3. linguistic heterogeneity of the conquered population;
4. material rewards.

Fishman *et al.* think that the significance of these factors is difficult to judge; they add the following, based on the historical facts of the spread of English (1977:80–1):

5. urbanisation;
6. economic development;
7. educational development;
8. religious composition (of the population);
9. political affiliation (of the government in question).

All these factors are interdependent and therefore do not permit operational quantification. Fishman *et al.*, in their accounts of the status of English, further add (1977:83):

10. official status;
11. language of government administration;
12. lingua franca within country;
13. technical language;
14. first foreign language studied by most students;

15. use in universities;
16. percentage of daily newspapers in English;
17. use on radio;
18. percentage of books published in English;
19. medium, or subject, of instruction in primary or secondary schools;
20. percentage of population in primary and secondary school English classes.

Of these, 10, 11 and 14 have proved to be especially relevant; they closely correlate with the factors 'former British colony' and 'multilingualism of inhabitants': in fact, the more or less unilingual countries of the Third World are found mainly among non-British ex-colonies, whereas former British 'possessions' such as Ghana, Nigeria, Cameroon, Kenya, India, Singapore or Papua New Guinea are characterised by extreme multilingualism. The usefulness of English as a supraregional standard with high international prestige is obvious. Further additions to the list, such as English as the dominant language in industry and trade have been proposed, but they overlap with those already mentioned.

3. Settlement history and new varieties

The Scandinavian settlement of 10th-century England is still an indispensable factor in understanding some of the regional peculiarities of present-day BrE dialects; the fact that settlers in 17th-century Ulster came from Scotland and the West Midlands accounts for many regional distinctions in the modern dialects of the area. To what extent does the origin of settlers help to account for non-European varieties of English?

The settlement phase of English continued until about 1860; it spread, almost without exception, EngE speech forms — the last expansion of Scots dates back to the 17th century, in the course of the Ulster Plantations and the scotticisation of the Orkney and Shetland Islands; the Bahamas, Sierra Leone and especially Liberia were recipients of American settlers.[9]

Four overseas areas may serve to illustrate the interdependence of settlement history and modern varieties:

1. Kurath (1972:40-2) has convincingly shown that the tri-

Varietas Delectat

partition of the dialects of AmE reflects the geographically separate settlement areas (and speech communities) of the 17th century and later westward migration starting from these bases (cf. Map 12.1). The developments of the 18th and 19th centuries, however, make clear how strong the levelling tendencies were, which made AmE more homogeneous than BrE has ever been. The history of AmE is especially important as an explanatory model for New Englishes in other regions, because AmE is the earliest and best-documented settler variety.

2. The Caribbean region provides less relevant material than might have been expected. Apart from the levelling, also found in AmE, this is mainly because the number of whites (i.e. of native speakers of English) was dwarfed by that of blacks early on, and their pidgin and creole speech forms 'melted down' dialectal features of the white settlers beyond recognition. But it is remarkable that the isolation of individual islands did not lead to the preservation of settlers' dialects: this might have been expected on Montserrat, a tiny island of 12,000 inhabitants where a high percentage of the original settlers came from Ireland.[10]

3. The most convincing illustration of how settlement history has affected regional varieties of English abroad are the varieties of SAfE (Lanham 1982).[11] The Dutch had been present as a colonial power in the Cape Province from 1652; the English, who had long been interested in forts in this region, which would enable them to make the route to India safer, took the Cape Province in 1806. Shortly after, some 4–5,000 Englishmen from the south of England, mostly lower class, settled in the eastern half of the new colony, where Lord Charles Somerset made the English language official in 1822 and forced it, at least for public use, on the Dutch population — with the help of great numbers of teachers and parsons imported for the purpose. The Great Trek of the Boers from 1838 onwards then transported Dutch and Cape English into the new republics of the interior.

A second settlement was started in Natal (1848–62), which consisted mainly of officers and other members of the middle class, who here created a bourgeois Victorian

Varietas Delectat

Map 12.1: *The speech areas of the eastern United States*

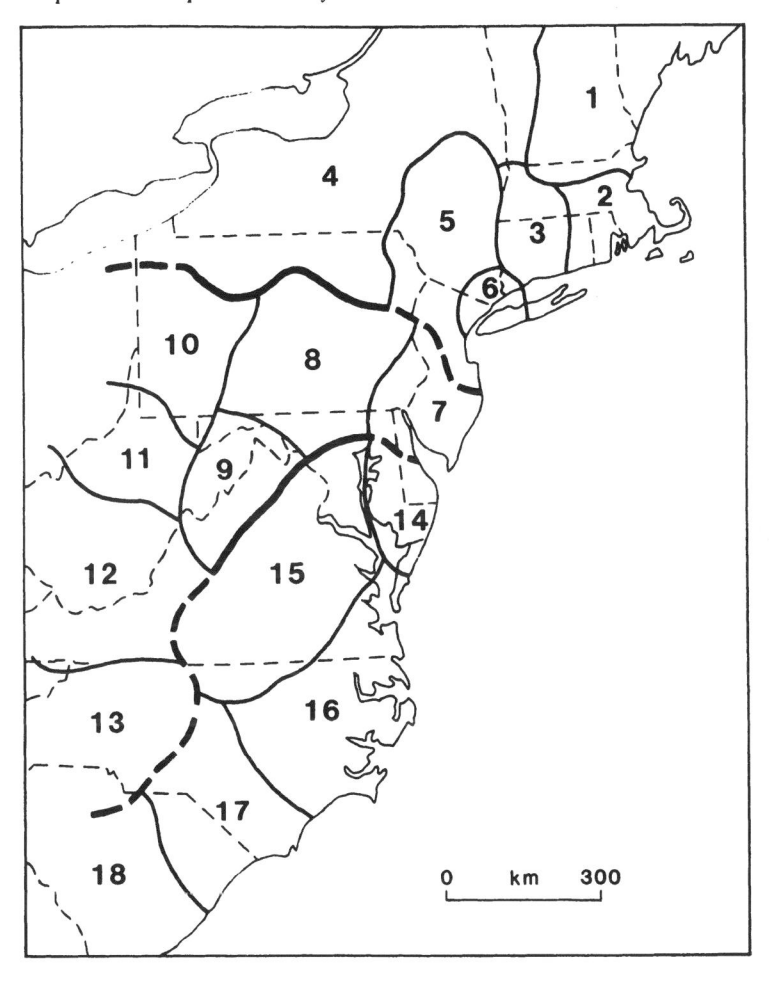

THE NORTH

1. Northeastern New England
2. Southeastern New England
3. Southwestern New England
4. Upstate New York and W. Vermont
5. The Hudson Valley
6. Metropolitan New York

THE MIDLAND

7. The Delaware Valley (Philadelphia Area)
8. The Susquehanna Valley
9. The Upper Potomac and Shenandoah Valleys
10. The Upper Ohio valley (Pittsburgh Area)
11. Northern West Virginia
12. Southern West Virginia
13. Western North and South Carolina

THE SOUTH

14. Delamarvia (Eastern Shore of Maryland and Virginia, and southern Delaware)
15. The Virginia Piedmont
16. Northeastern North Carolina (Albemarle Sound and Neuse Valley)
17. The Cape Fear and Peedee Valleys
18. South Carolina

After Kurath (1972)

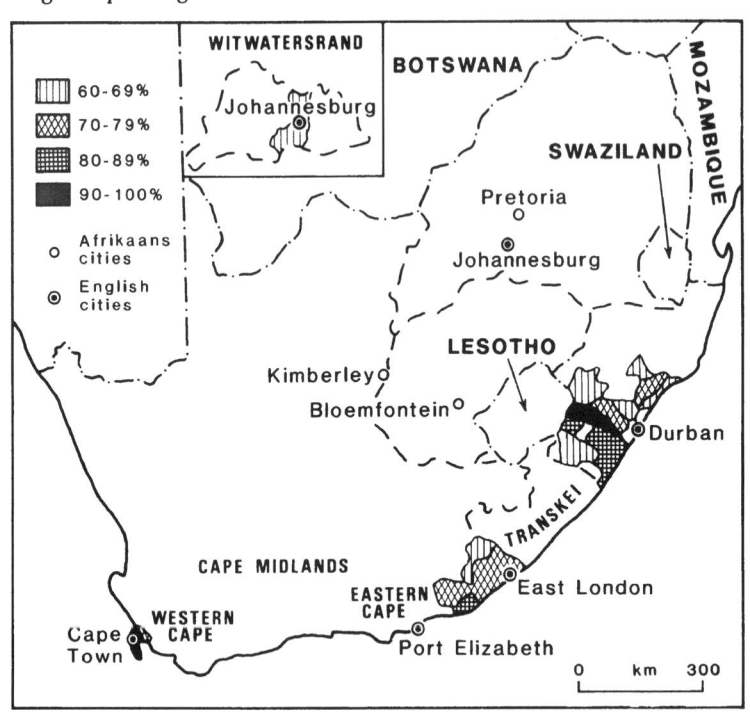

Map 12.2: *English-speaking South Africa: major concentrations of English-speaking whites*

After Lanham and MacDonald (1979)

Little England and cultivated standard BrE as a prestige form. This Natal English provided a model for Johannesburg, when it came to develop into an industrial and commercial English centre deep in the Boer hinterland from 1880. See Map 12.2.

Even today, it is claimed, the broad Cape dialect is stigmatised partly because of its closeness to Afrikaans English, whereas Natal English sounds slightly archaic, but is fully acceptable.

4. A comparison of South African and Australian settlement history is enlightening (cf. Lanham and McDonald 1979:90–2). The early settlers of both colonies came from the same regions and classes (even though South Africa was, of course, never a penal colony). In Australia, unlike South Africa, dialectal levelling must have occurred very

early, possibly spreading from Sydney across the vast continent; but the details of this movement, and the reasons why AusE and NZE are so similar are still not clear. Again in contrast to South Africa, where the English-speaking whites are a minority within a minority, a local (spoken) norm of AusE became acceptable when political and cultural independence began to develop from the early 20th century.

4. Values and new norms

Even native colonial English, where it differed from London usage, was commonly regarded as 'erroneous, corrupted, not respectable'. The list of such negative judgements is particularly long and impressive for AmE, and one might perhaps select as particularly interesting the caustic evaluation of AmE by the Scotsman Witherspoon (in Mathews, 1931:17), who criticised American deviances in much the same way as Scotticisms had been castigated and purged by educated Scots during the 18th-century Edinburgh Enlightenment. Similar judgements are found in Pettman (1913) on the subject of the English spoken in South Africa:

(4) It gives an Englishman, who loves the sentence that is lucid and logical, a shock to hear his native tongue maltreated by those who are just as English in blood as himself.

Even Edward Morris, who saw his *Austral English* as a complement to the OED, thought it necessary to defend the words listed in his dictionary against the criticism of 'precisians':

(5) It may be thought by some precisians that all Australasian English is a corruption of the language. So too is Anglo-Indian, and *pace* Mr. Brander Matthews, there are such things as Americanisms, which were not part of the Elizabethan heritage, [...] When we hear railing at slang phrases, at Americanisms, some of which are admirably expressive, at various flowers of colonial speech, and at words woven into the texture of our speech by those who live far away from London and from Oxford, and who on the outskirts of

> the British Empire are brought into contact with new natural objects that need new names, we may think for our comfort on the undoubted fact that the noble and dignified language of the poets, authors and preachers, grouped around Lewis XIV., sprang from debased Latin. [...] It is too late a day to close the doors against new words. This *Austral English Dictionary* merely catalogues and records those which at certain doors have already come in. (Morris, 1898:xvi)

The linguistic independence of AmE was established in the 19th century, that of AusE/NZE in the 20th. However, acceptance of local norms in AusE was restricted to pronunciation and lexis, and a few features in spelling and grammar: AusE/NZE (and SAfE) norms of usage still lean heavily on prescriptive models *à la* Fowler.

In the multilingual countries Canada and South Africa the situation is more complex. Canada (outside the francophone areas) bears the stamp of both British immigrants and American Royalists. The feeling of endangered independence, with a huge neighbour looming large from the South, has always strengthened the British element and certainly contributed to the proclamation of CanE as a distinct entity (e.g. through the efforts of Avis).[12]

Many of the 1.5 million English-speaking South Africans, barred from political power since 1948, and with the somewhat uncertain future of the country in view, must find difficulty in defining their role (and that of English) in a future South Africa (or Azania?). Perhaps it is this uncertainty (not confined to linguistic matters) that has led to unswerving loyalty to British norms. What the English of the future will be like when it has, perhaps, merged with Afrikaans-coloured English and Black English it is difficult to imagine.

New norms also develop through the 'export' of new varieties: Native AmE partly forms the basis of Hawaiian and Liberian English; ESL in the Philippines is modelled on 20th-century AmE. Since 1945, AmE has increasingly influenced EFL varieties outside the former British Empire, e.g. in Japan, Thailand or in Arab countries. Finally, it interferes with BrE in Australia and the Caribbean, and its impact on certain domains and registers, for example in the media (newspapers, radio, television and films) and in pop music is world-wide.

The linguistic independence of New Englishes in ESL countries is even more difficult to achieve than that of ENL varieties. Even today a large number of Indian students regard BrE as their model (and possibly they also believe they speak BrE).[13] The government of Singapore denies the existence of SgE as a local norm (but cf. Platt, 1982 and Fraser Gupta, 1986), while Sey (1973:10) is realistic in his summary of the attitudes of his educated countrymen towards local forms of English:

(6) The linguist may be able to isolate features of Ghanaian English and describe them. But once these are made known to him, the educated Ghanaian would strive to avoid them altogether. The surest way to kill Ghanaian English, if it really exists, is to discover it and make it known.

The social history of pidgins and creoles makes it clear that attitudes towards these forms of speech are commonly even more negative: many speakers of such varieties (at least when research began) could not understand why scholars were interested in such 'broken speech'. A comparison of the number of theses written in West Africa and India on Shakespeare or Milton with the figures for serious studies of local forms of English (or pidgins) still reflects the very hesitant acceptance of these — as means of communication or as objects of scholarly research.

5. English as a second and as a foreign language

Moag (1982) has made the most detailed proposal so far for a classification of national uses of English. He distinguishes 26 factors determining individual and societal uses without attempting to weight the factors. They can conveniently be grouped together under two headings:

1. *Acceptance:* The official status of English (as of any language) can range from recognition as a national language (possibly with the aim of integrating minorities using different languages) to regional use only. It may be promoted by obligatory functions in education and the

Varietas Delectat

media, on traffic signs and stamps — or tolerated in the private domain, with open or tacit discouragement of official, public or all written uses. In statistics of existing language use, official statements and realistic informed guesses often diverge widely, but quantifications are precarious where attitudes and evaluations tend to bias the figures.

2. *Frequency of use*: Who uses English with whom, and in what situations, on what topics, in spoken or written form? Frequency is largely determined by the extent of the role of English in education, administration and the media.

Moag suggests classifying English-using speech communities on the basis of his 26 factors as follows (here complemented by the ESD type of community):

(a) ENL = English as a native language, used for all standard and informal functions. This is the case with more than 86% of the population in Great Britain, Ireland, the USA, Australia and new Zealand; in Canada and South Africa only certain sections of the population are ENL users.

(b) ESD = English as a second dialect. The community in which a native English-related creole coexists with standard English in written uses appears, in view of its special problems, to demand a category to itself (Jamaica, Guyana, Belize — the last multilingual — and other Caribbean countries).[14] It is doubtful whether extreme cases such as Sierra Leone (with Krio vs. English) or Papua New Guinea/Solomon Islands/Vanuatu (with Tok Pisin/Solomon Pijin/Bislama vs. English) should be placed in this category or whether it should be limited to cases where a continuum exists bridging the two poles of the country's linguistic spectrum.

(c) EBL = English as a basal language. Possible cases of this constellation always have an English-related *creole* dominated by a non-English standard. The historical successes of English (cf. 2. above), which have but rarely involved groups of English speakers under foreign rule,

Varietas Delectat

have restricted this situation to certain Caribbean communities (Holm, 1983).

(d) ESL = English as a second language, usually inherited from the (former) colonial administration, but retaining important functions as a supraregional language for *intra*national uses in education, administration and the media (Nigeria, Ghana, Kenya, India, etc.).

(e) EFL = English as a foreign language, fulfilling only international functions, and serving as a book language in secondary and, especially, tertiary education, all other standard functions being performed by an indigenous national language (Western Europe, USSR, Japan, etc.).

This kind of neat classification into five types obviously cannot do full justice to the multiplicity of existing situations; for example, the complex pattern discernible in present-day West African countries may be summarised as follows (cf. Maps 12.3 and 12.4 and Görlach, 1984b):

Cameroon:	ESD in Western Cameroon for the pidgin-speaking community; ESL in other parts of Western Cameroon; EFL (realistically) in other parts of Cameroon which are increasingly affected by French; transition to EBL status in W. Cameroon is possible.
Nigeria:	ESL throughout, but ESD in Southern Nigeria in pidgin-using areas.
Dahomey, Togo, Ivory Coast:	EFL (second language: French), but some pidgin English (EBL) along the coast.
Ghana:	ESL (with little pidgin worth speaking of according to Ghanaians).
Liberia:	ENL for a small minority along the coast, American-based, especially in Monrovia; ESD for speakers of pidgin/creole; ESL throughout the country.
Sierra Leone, Gambia:	ESD — if Krio can be classified as a 'dialect' of English; ESL throughout.

Map 12.3: European expansion in West Africa after 1890

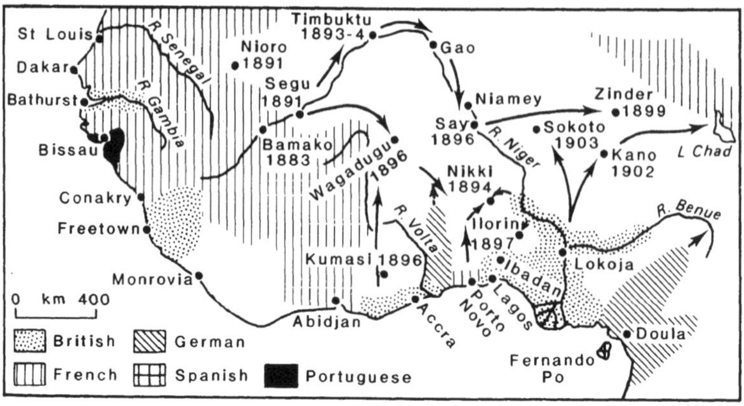

After Isichei (1977), p. 172

It must also be stressed that any classification can be valid only for one particular stage in a country's linguistic history: all ESL countries started as EFL ones, and political independence after 1945 has prompted many countries to select one native tongue and make it into a national language. In this context it was intended to reduce English to EFL status in India, too, an effort that was more successful in Malaysia and the Philippines, classical ESL countries until around 1970. To develop a national language so that it can function as a modern standard for all public functions, ranging from law to the training of technicians, means that great idealistic and financial sacrifices have to be made. Such language planning has therefore been successful in only a few cases (Malaysia, the Philippines, Somalia, Tanzania and, in quite different circumstances, Israel); the chances of success were greatest straight after independence, when use could be made of anticolonial sentiments. A leader entitled 'National Language' in the Tanzanian daily *The Nationalist* of 5 January 1967 begins as follows:

(7) A nation without a national language is a nation without a soul. A nation with a national language which is not very much cared for is a crazy nation. Such a state of affairs cannot be tolerated in Tanzania.

Map 12.4: West Africa's colonial language legacy

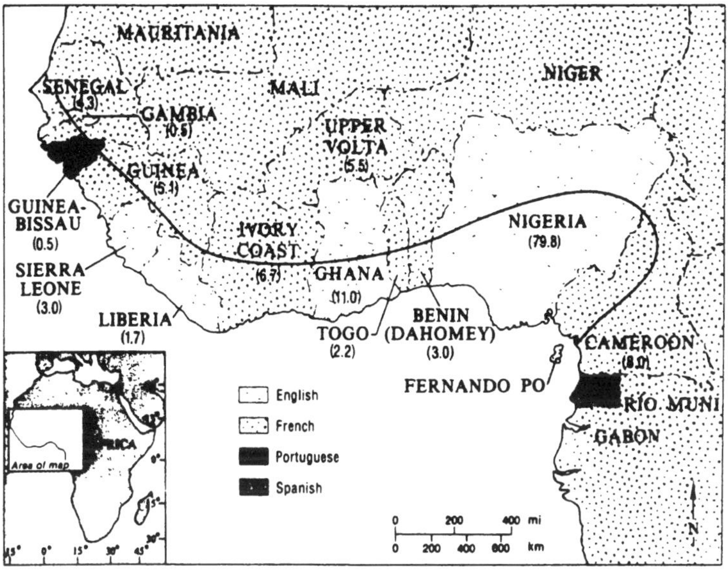

The dark solid line indicates the approximate extent of the use of pidgin English along the coast as a lingua franca.

Todd (1982b), p. 282

Even when successful, the shift to a new national language brings with it considerable problems. In Tanzania (cf. Schmied, 1985), Malaysia and the Philippines the new national language has to be taught in the schools as a second language (or a second dialect at least) to a large proportion of the pupils, which reduces the time that can now be reserved for the learning of English. This means that the quality of English is changing: it is used more rarely, and while the norms aimed at may well be closer to international standards, the degree of individual competence achieved is often considerably lower. This development has caused ministries of education in Malaysia and Singapore to attempt to counteract the 'corruption of English' by employing greater numbers of native-speaker teachers. 'Stopping the rot' is the significant phrasing of the title of an article on this phenomenon in *Asia Week* of 15 October 1982.

Two factors favour the preservation of ESL status after

independence (or at least slow down the return to EFL status):

1. Multilingualism without one dominant language: English may then be seen as a neutral compromise and therefore as politically opportune (Nigeria, India).
2. The small size and low income of the population concerned. The full development of a national language even in monolingual countries is unlikely in cases ranging from such countries as Lesotho (1,600,000 inhabitants) to Nauru (8,000 inhabitants).

Multilingualism, small size and poverty coincide in such countries as Mauritius (official language: English; spoken: French Creole and Indian languages) or Fiji (official language: English; spoken: Fijian, Indian languages). Small size and a difficult choice between indigenous languages may even make development from ESL to ENL possible: the multilingual states of Singapore and Fiji have seen within their borders a remarkable expansion of the neutral world language with its ability to bridge the divisions caused by ethnic diversity, and English might well be accepted as the first language of the majority of their populations.

The schools play the most important role in the development of the ESL:EFL distinction. It is typical of ESL countries that children receive their primary education in English (so that many children never learn to read and write their mother tongue). In Africa this appears to be largely the case in Gambia, Sierra Leone, Ghana, Nigeria, Uganda, Kenya, Botswana, Swaziland and Zimbabwe. But even where children are first taught in their mother tongue, knowledge of both native and foreign languages often remains deficient. This is the case with the Bantu-speaking Black majority of South Africa: since there is little motivation to read and write the mother tongue, the children will not attain full competence in either their Bantu language (say Xhosa) or Afrikaans or English. On the other hand, ESL countries provide many opportunities of acquiring minimal communicative competence in everyday domains, learnt in unmonitored situations in the market-place or at work.

EFL countries exhibit the reverse pattern: English is learnt more or less exclusively through the schools, its uses within the country are very limited and it functions virtually only as a means of international communication and as a book language.

Percentages or absolute numbers of speakers of English are, then, not the proper way to distinguish between ESL and EFL countries[15] — the proportion of speakers of English is likely to be higher in Western Europe than it is in India for example. It is, rather, the actual use of the language in native contexts that separates ESL countries from EFL ones.

6. How many varieties of English?

With the preceding discussions in mind, one might now ask whether it is possible to determine how many distinctive Englishes there are. Whether a speech form can be regarded as a dialect of English is an open question in the case of European varieties such as Scots (formerly a quasi-independent language) or Anglo-Romani (a relexified English used by English Travellers). Similar problems with classification also arise for English-related pidgins and creoles world-wide. The criteria of linguistic distance from English, expansion of the range of uses, and (incipient) standardisation make a decision easy for the languages of Surinam (Sranan, Saramaccan, Djuka) and of the Southwestern Pacific (Tok Pisin, Solomon Pijin, Bislama, Australian Kriol) as well as for Krio in Sierra Leone: even though there are unmistakably English components in all these, their modern forms must be classified as independent languages. A decision is much more difficult in cases with continua bridging the poles of basilect and close-to-standard acrolect, as found in Jamaica or Southern Nigeria. It seems legitimate to treat these modern varieties, frequently in advanced stages of decreolisation, i.e. of closing the gap between them and Standard English, as dialects of English — however differently their 18th- or 19th-century predecessors would have been classified.[16]

How many separate varieties ought to be distinguished within what is undoubtedly 'English' cannot be conclusively decided (nor can the question of how many dialects of English there are in England). However, the question is not purely an academic game, because it forces the scholar to list the defining characteristics of the postulated variety and thereby to show whether a label such as 'Indian English' can be accepted as a linguistic term or whether some non-committal designation such as 'English in India' is preferable.

Mühlhäusler (1985) has analysed the pidgins of the Southwest Pacific to show what criteria can serve to differentiate related or similar varieties and to demonstrate how contradictory criteria stand in the way of satisfactory solutions to the problem. Factors obviously involved are:

1. the degree of standardisation in the spoken and written forms;
2. prestige, and users' awareness of speaking a particular language;
3. range of uses;
4. linguistic distance from the historical 'ancestor' (e.g. from BrE) and from neighbouring varieties.

Features from various linguistic levels are, of course, involved in classifying an individual speech form. A very raw and simplifying classification[17] on the basis of phonetic/phonemic features alone is provided by Trudgill and Hannah (1982:5):

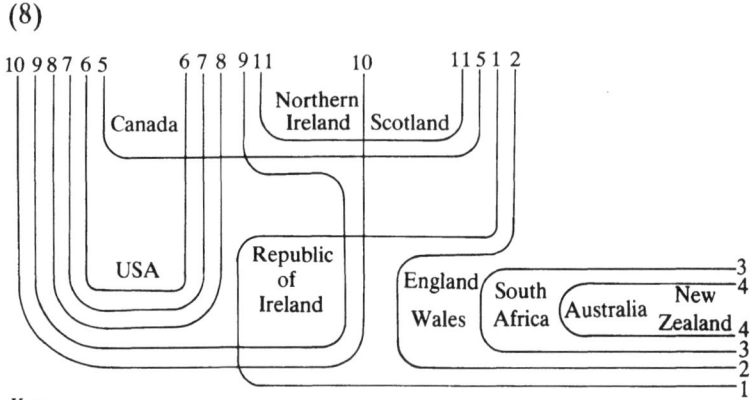

(8)

Key
1. /ɑː/ rather than /æ/ in *path* etc.
2. absence of non-prevocalic /r/
3. close vowels for /æ/ and /ɛ/, monophthongisation of /ai/ and /au/
4. front [aː] for /ɑː/ in *part* etc.
5. absence of contrast of /ɒ/ and /ɔː/ as in *cot* and *caught*
6. /æ/ rather than /ɑː/ in *can't* etc.
7. absence of contrast of /ɒ/ and /ɑː/ as in *bother* and *father*
8. consistent voicing of intervocalic /t/
9. unrounded [ɑ] in *pot*
10. syllabic /r/ in *bird*
11. absence of contrast of /ʊ/ and /uː/ as in *pull* and *pool*

Varietas Delectat

The four cases below may be adduced to exemplify the problems of classification:

A. Is there such an entity as 'Canadian English'?
   As mentioned above, scholars agree that the degree of homogeneity and distinctiveness of the English now existing in Canada is not sufficient to allow 'CanE' to be delimited on purely linguistic grounds. Dialectologists before 1965 never questioned that Canadian forms of English should be treated within the framework of North American English, and the independence of CanE postulated by many linguists after Avis seems to be contradicted by the sociolinguistic facts: the more US-oriented speech of the younger generation and of the normative region of central Ontario in general indicates that there is an ongoing process levelling the few remaining distinctions in speech north and south of the border (cf. Bailey, 1982; Chambers, 1986).

B. Is there a West African (or Pan-African) English?[18]
   West African communities with ESL (or EFL) and possibly an indigenous PE (cf. chapter 5 and map 5) use individual mixtures and regional conventions composed from the following factors:

   1. the degree of users' competence/fluency ranging from minimal/broken to fluent/perfect;
   2. the combination of PE and English, or creole and English;
   3. AmE or BrE as historical norms;
   4. ethnic differences in E/in the use of E, reflecting different mother tongues;
   5. national differences (e.g., a 'NigE' possibly forming part of a larger entity, describable as 'WAfE').

   The present state of research does not appear to permit clear classification of existing speech forms as well-defined 'varieties' (cf. Görlach, 1984a) nor indeed any prognostications about a future WAfE norm. However, Jibril (1982, 1986) has shown that a levelling process is in progress in Nigeria, which might well lead to a NigE standard.

C. Is there a South Asian English?
   The hypothesis that the region should be seen as a linguistic

whole, also in the description of its ESL forms, seems reasonable — but SAsE has not been properly described so far, nor have its subvarieties been properly delimited: what is the relation between the IndE ⧧ Lankan English contrast on the one hand and forms characterised by a common L_1 such as the 'Tamil' English found in both India and Sri Lanka on the other? (The assumption that national distinctions exist is plausible in this case, since the colonial history of the two states has been so different, and English has played different roles in each since independence, too.)

D. What is the (systemic) difference between AusE and NZE? All scholars (and all native speakers) agree that AusE is exceptionally homogeneous (and that variation mainly depends on sociolect and style). Many features of the English of New Zealand are similar to or identical with AusE ones, a fact that can only be partly explained by settlement history. Most Australians claim that they can identify NZE (and vice versa) — but a coherent description of NZE, and its differences from AusE (and possible 20th-century convergence) remains an urgent desideratum (cf. now Bauer, 1986).

7. Challenges to linguistic theory

It will have become apparent that dealing with varieties of world English poses problems of theory and method that are largely unsolved, but which must not stop us from attempting descriptions. Some of the basic assumptions of older or more recent grammarians which are based on European languages and uses in more or less monolingual societies are obviously not applicable to, for instance, English in Africa:

1. Not all speakers have an obvious native language — because they grew up using more than one language, or because a second language (such as NigPE) became dominant in early childhood. Moreover, such speakers are less able to judge the acceptability of utterances — or even to classify them as realisations of one particular language. This does not seem to be possible for them even in the case of

widely divergent linguistic systems, let alone where the systems have become mixed (as is the case in Kupwar, India, according to Gumperz and Wilson's classic description of 1971), or where elements of two languages occur in apparently irregular code-mixing. The distinction becomes even more precarious if two similar languages are involved, as with pidgins and their related European languages.

2. The concept of 'speech community', difficult to define even in western societies considered monolingual, becomes useless in multilingual situations. Even a widening of the concept of 'competence' to include communicative competence and a refining of the methods of description (by the identification of grammatical variables and the use of statistical methods in the description) leads to fundamental problems. Thus Daswani (1978) complains that there is no systematic description of IndE in which it is contrasted with BrE: a list of details (deviances, additions, losses, gaps) does not constitute a description, especially since the geographical and social distribution of individual phenomena is normally not investigated. Apart from the problem of deciding which speakers of English in India can be regarded as speakers of IndE (so that a description could be based on data collected from them), there is also the question of how to accommodate apparently irregular features within a systematic analysis. For instance, deviance in the use of the articles can be accounted for neither by subclassifying nouns according to their semantic syntactic features, nor as interference from Indian languages in any way that would make their distribution predictable.

As for the correlation of linguistic data with social reality, there are now large numbers of sociolinguistic investigations of western communities so that methods and results can be evaluated (cf. the very critical summary in Hudson, 1980:138–90). However, of Third World communities only Singapore appears to have been treated adequately so far (Platt, 1982). A promising start on the quantification of southern and northern pronunciations in NigE has been made by Jibril (1982), but the number of studies is not sufficient to permit any judgement of the applicability of his methods to other cases or of what modifications of his models might be necessary. It may be significant that Lanham (1982) claims that he is providing a Labovian analysis, while in his social history of SAfE he, in fact, uses only a few Labovian concepts, and that R.B. Le Page — after thirty years of work on the sociolinguistic description of language use in multilingual societies in the Caribbean (mainly St Lucia and Belize) — came to the conclusion that a satisfactory method is still not in sight (Le Page, 1980, but now cf. his recent major contribution in Le Page and Tabouret-Keller, 1985).

What is needed are new theoretically well-founded descriptions of language contact and multilingualism as individual and societal phenomena, of the rules governing code-switching, of models for learners' interim grammars of the target language, and finally evidence of the extent to which quantitative analyses can be expected to be fruitful.

8. The genesis of ESL varieties

Kachru (1983:4) quotes a statement by Dustoor which in content *and* form[19] impressively illustrates the consequences of the transplanting of English to Indian surroundings:

(9) Our mental climate will always foster plants that do not flourish in England or America; and such plants, just because they are somewhat exotic, add to the charm of a garden. All lovers of English will, therefore, encourage them to grow in the world-wide garden of English. It is only the weeds, which spring up whenever ignorance, carelessness or pretentiousness infects the air, that need to be pulled up by the roots.

Settlers' ENLs and overseas ESLs have to use (and where necessary modify) the lexicon of what was initially a purely European language to refer to the objects and ideas of new situations and cultures: phenomena such as lexical expansion by way of new meanings, new word-formations and loanwords are consequently common to both ENL and ESL varieties. However, the similarities end here: whereas settlers' languages continue to develop the full range of stylistic choices that the immigrants brought with them, ESLs depend on the texts chosen for use in language teaching either haphazardly or from a limited range of preferred registers, or on what is considered important in unmonitored language acquisition.

This limited input has problematic consequences for the use of English in various domains: the range of styles acquired is limited — traditionally literary English from the texts of English classical writers (Shakespeare, Milton, the Authorised Version of the Bible, Victorian novels and poems), registers from public domains such as administration and legislature or jurisdiction, and increasingly in recent years the English of newspapers and radio, films and pop music — often without learners being aware of register differences. This explains the frequent uncertainty in stylistic matters and (from an ENL point of view) register misuse. A particularly obvious instance of this is the traditional use of a grandiloquent style in everyday contexts, the penchant for the florid and the preference for a Latinate vocabulary, observable in India and West Africa, a tendency reinforced by the prestige traditionally attaching to elaborate diction in native Indian and West African languages. Passages from a football report (Cameroon 1979) and from a popular novel belonging to the Onitsha Market literature (Nigeria 1972) may serve to illustrate such phenomena:

(10) How for goodness sake the team we saw last Sunday lost 0:3 to the Guineans is hard to fathom.

Once more, Cameroon fell by the way side in the African Nations football tournament.

Our only consolation is that we seem to organize better for club competitions than for national tournaments. May be that is a virtue. Then so be it....

Milla gave his team all that they could hope for: he is a subtle thinker and a tactician in his own right.

His game as a striker relies on stealth rather than strength, and man, he can take diabolical chances even when the chances initially appear hopeless to an onlooker. Milla is quick, flexible and versatile. His three goals were scored under such tricky and cheap situations that it looked easy even to a neophyte.

The penalty aside, Milla was worthy of his hire ... Indeed,

it was a pirate victory last Sunday. But Cameroon is used to such circumstances.

In 1972, when Cameroon organized the 8th African Nations Cup, Congo nipped victory just when the public was celebrating ...
(from Todd, 1982a:37–9)

(11) She was in her maiden form and remained untampered with, since her generate days. Even to meddle with her zestful glamour of beauty, nobody had ever succeeded. The grim enthusiasm of her ardent lust was bubbling on her romantic face, and her youthful glances of shyness. She had got all the zests of the West and mettled her senses, to bolster up alacrity, to crack love, romance and joke, up to their highest mediocre of acme. It was a day for love maniacs to come and a day for Rosemary to travel too.
(Miller O. Albert, Rosemary and the Taxi-Driver,
from Obiechina, 1972:135)

Possibly even more significant in this context is the following passage of scholarly expository prose, the content of which is also relevant to the points here made:

(12) Creative writing is altogether a different matter, however. As is widely accepted, creative writing has a unique self-identificational and self-expressive value for the community which begets it, providing for its people a means of exploring themselves and discovering who they most distinctively are, and of giving a special satisfying kind of expression to their most vital thoughts and feelings and experiences. If this is true, then it will not be too difficult to see that the switch is bound to have fatal consequences. The system that these writers turn so carelessly away from is that which is interwoven with the very pith and marrow of their unique symbiotic lives. For them to shake off the distinctive forms and rhythms of the everyday speech which expresses the system is, thus, to debilitate themselves, to cut their writing off disastrously from the very source of its life and vitality, impoverishing it and rendering it artificial, sterile, anaemic. To make

matters worse, the formal academic standard with which they replace it keeps them too consciously preoccupied with scholarly norms of grammar and correctness to allow them to truly relax and come into their own in such writing.

(Kandiah, 1981:75-6)

Kachru (1982c:325ff.) mentions the following types of texts (using Indian specimens), which are said to show signs of linguistic adaptation (nativisation, indigenisation) as a consequence of contextualisation in Indian communicative patterns: reviews, matrimonial advertisements, obituaries, invitations, letters and acknowledgements (e.g. in prefaces). This list was compiled empirically and not analytically, and it would be interesting to see to what extent the type of text determines the degree of adaptation and whether Kachru's Indian list is parallelled by texts from other ESL cultures: a comparative analysis of various types of text from different parts of the world is an urgent desideratum. Here are a few matrimonial advertisements from India (1980) and an obituary from Nigeria (1981) to illustrate various forms of nativisation:

(13) WANTED CHARMING, CONVENT EDUCATED MATCH FOR HANDSOME AGARWAL BOY, 25 YEARS, 172CMS., CHEMICAL ENGINEER, OFFICER IN STATE BANK. ONLY FAMILY OF STATUS NEED CORRESPOND BOX 125321-CH, HINDUSTAN TIMES, NEW DELHI-110001.

BEAUTIFUL, slim, short medico/B.D.S./studying girl for a handsome doctor (Capt) in army (Punjabi Khatri, 24½ yrs., 161 cm). No dowry, caste no bar. Box 122566-CH, Hindustan Times, New Delhi-110001.

SUITABLE match for well-settled Agarwal, Engineer, M.B.A. 27, emoluments Rs 3000/-. Respectable, cultured family. Full particulars first instance. Box 502020-CA, Hindustan Times, New Delhi-110001.

MATCH for Punjabi Arora boy, M.Com., 28, 172, Bank 1700/-. Box 39433-CA, Hindustan Times, New Delhi-110001.

GUPTA, Mittal Gotra boy, 25, 168, Inspector, D.E.S.U. degree in Electrical. Studying Master of Engineering. Girl's merits main consideration. Box 39412-CA, Hindustan Times, New Delhi-110001.

MATCH for Engineer, Good, handsome boy, 23. 173 cms., own business near Delhi. Income high four figures. Send full details. Box 39450-CA, Hindustan Times, New Delhi-110001.

WANTED beautiful, homely match for well-settled, Khatri, Engineer, age 40 — 169 cms. Three daughters 9, 13 and 15. Salary four figures. Independent, high standard living. No dowry. Caste no bar. Widow, divorced acceptable. Box 122608-CH, Hindustan Times, New Delhi-110001.

PRETTY bride for 28, Arora, businessman, respectable family. Income four figures, Father brothers in business. Box 122609-CH, Hindustan Times, New Delhi-10001.

WANTED a 'Beauty Queen' girl, Graduate, homely, sweet and expert in domestic work, for handsome Garg boy of Ludhiana, 23 years, 161 cms. Higher Secondary, own engineering industry. Income six figures yearly. Dowry not acceptable. Please apply only for a Beauty Queen. Status no bar. Box 122610-CH, Hindustan Times, New Delhi-110001.

(14) **IN MEMORIAM**

In cherished and affectionate memory of our devoted, kind and industrious mother, aunt and grandmother.

MADAM LYSTER BENE WOKOMA

who was translated into transition on the 1st day of January, 1973.

Mother, eight years have rolled by without your loving presence. Although the blow was hard and the grief too great to bear, our consolation lies in the belief that your soul is now forever with the Almighty who understands everything. Your place in the family will forever remain vacant; we pray to the Almighty to give you perfect rest until we meet to part no more.

MR F.M. EFEREBO
MRS IBIERE I. PRINCEWILL
(for the family)

Categories gained from an analysis of texts that have not been systematically collected are unlikely to represent the full range of adaptations. Richards (1982) has claimed that the transfer of native principles of textual structure and of paralinguistic features of communication is the most characteristic type of deviance in ESL texts. Indeed such features, which are less susceptible to monitoring and conscious correction, remain remarkably stable even generations after a language shift has occurred within a speech community (cf. 'Africanisms' in CarE).

Adaptations to suit ESL communicative needs are, then, necessary and to be expected. Kachru's statement on the subject ought, therefore, to be self-evident and not in need of any apology: 'Indianisms in Indian English are, then, linguistic manifestations of pragmatic needs for appropriate language use in a new linguistic and cultural context' (1983:2).

However, linguistic insights and postulates derived from them do not match social reality. The linguist is certainly not some kind of language referee who can make grammatical deviance from a foreign norm acceptable, i.e. turn the 'mistakes' of a prescriptive tradition into permissible alternatives on the grounds that they are the consequences of necessary adaptation.

9. Literature written in a second language

The use of English for literary purposes is an important, but often exaggerated, function of the world language; however, works written by local authors on local themes for local audiences in local forms of English illustrate how far nativisation has proceeded in many ESL countries. Obviously the kind of features mentioned can occur in quite unexpected distributions: many works are still written with an eye on the London publisher, who may regard the use of local Englishes (or even pidgins) as incorrect English and at best permit a diluted form of local English to give the work a certain local flavour. A fundamental distinction must also be made between ENL literature in, say, Australia and ESL writings, where the knowledge of English at the command of writers and intended local audiences may permit only a narrow range of stylistic options, and the transfer of English to new subject matter and different narrative traditions may call for commensurate stylistic adaptation. Such experiments have been most plentiful in West Africa and India, and it is no coincidence that these are regions which have important literatures in local languages, and in which spoken forms of English have diverged far from London standards. (The Caribbean region is particularly important for its use of creole languages for literary purposes, and there are various texts in Krio or NigPE, too). The independence of literary forms of ESL has been stressed by Chinua Achebe in a much-quoted passage (1975:61):

(15) The African writer should aim to use English in a way that brings out his message best without altering the language to the extent that its value as a medium of international exchange will be lost. He should aim at fashioning out an English which is at once universal and able to carry his peculiar experience. I have in mind here the writer who has something new, something different to say. The nondescript writer has little to tell us, anyway, so he might as well tell it in conventional language and get it over with.

In practice such writing, placed as it is between two cultures and languages, creates great problems. An author has a number of different forms of adaptation to choose from:

1. He can employ a native literary form, which may include the use of textual and narrative structures diverging from those of BrE.
2. He can use throughout a local variety of English, which is deviant in spelling, syntax and vocabulary.
3. He can use coexisting local varieties for dialogue only, the speech forms serving to characterise personae as individuals and as members of particular social and regional speech communities.
4. He can freely transfer structures from native languages to his English; this process may include deliberate 'mistakes' or comprise the creation of an entirely new literary diction.

All this shows that literary texts (not only from ESL literatures!) must be treated with the utmost caution if used as corpora for linguistic analysis; but if interpreted with circumspection, they can provide valuable data for establishing both linguistic structures and language attitudes (cf. Görlach, 1983). This applies even to parodies such as that by R. Parthasarathy below, which is very successful if the stereotypes are recognised and correctly interpreted by Indians and Europeans alike. (It should be unnecessary to say that such interpretation must also precede literary analysis.)

Varietas Delectat

(16) *What is Your Good Name, Please?*
What is your good name, please?
I am remembering we used to be neighbours
in Hindu Colony ten fifteen years before.
Never mind. What do you know?
5   You are in service, isn't it?
I am Matric fail. Self-employed.
Only last year I celebrated my marriage.
It was inter-caste. Now I am not able
to make the two ends meet.
10 Cost of living is going up and up everyday.
Sugar, for example, is costing much.
I am eschewing sugar therefore since last two months.
Also I am diabetes. It is good, no?
Excuse me, please, where are you putting up?
15 Never mind, you will be coming to my place
one day surely, I am hoping.
Not to disappoint.
You are Madrasi, no? How I make out?
All Madrasis talking English language wonderfully.
20 I am knowing intimately one Srijut Dandayudhapani
from Brahmanwada.
He is foreign-returned from U.K.
Pronunciation is A1, I am telling you.
Some people are lucky.
25 He is officer in State Bank, Drawing Rs. 2.000.
We are always discussing about politics.
Congress government I am saying
is still best for delivering goods.
What you opine?
30 Beg pardon, I am going.
I am forgetting to go to Gandhi Market
for purchasing the Aspro
Since today morning I am suffering
from headache pain.
35 I am taking your leave, yes, for the time.
                    (R. Parthasarathy, in Gokak, 1975)

Even expository prose (such as (12) above — and the structure of Kandiah's complete article as originally submitted) is often fully comprehensible only within a non-English tradition. It is obvious that such differences in the structure and function of texts involve basic problems of intelligibility which have not, however, attracted much scholarly attention until recently.

If such independence is possible (and desirable) in ESL writing, could similar adaptation be permitted in EFL countries? Since these have a foreign norm, usually that of the ENL country closest in geographical or historical terms, the kind of development that takes place in ESL communities appears to be impossible at first sight. However, certain local usage preferences *within the norm* indicate that EFL speakers exploit the range of existing choices differently from native speakers, and even this alone can be interpreted as a form of nativisation. The following factors may be regarded as symptomatic:

1. Loanwords in the contact languages involved are indicators of lexical and semantic preferences; it is likely that these will also be preferred when speakers switch to English.
2. Two types of syntactic structures are likely to be preferred: those which have equivalents in the native language, and those which are frequent in English.
3. Textual and stylistic features and expectations are likely to be transferred to English.
4. Reference to non-English objects is necessarily expressed by extension of meanings and by new coinages (as in ENL/ESL communities).

These considerations hardly permit one to speak of 'German English' or a 'West European variety of English' in the way one may speak of IndE, but descriptional models will have to be found to deal with such deviant language use that does not involve conflicts with native-speaker grammatical norms.

10. Consequences for English language teaching

What kind of English should, then, be taught and which methods employed? Wong (1982:264) rightly stresses the chasm that exists between the age-old efforts to teach native-speaker English in ESL countries and linguistic reality. A solution to this dilemma is difficult in view of:

1. budgetary constraints causing

2. classes with too many pupils, insufficient teaching materials, and badly trained and badly paid teachers, which results in
3. uses of English diverging further and further from the proclaimed norm, while
4. the demand for a knowledge of English is unabated — because of its high prestige, job requirements within the country, and its usefulness abroad after emigration.

Only two solutions appear to be feasible:

1. Either English is taught only to those who can prove that they need it; however, to decide who does is impossible, and any selection would produce new social inequality and injustice.
2. Or an effort is made to teach the form of English that is accessible to learners in their own particular circumstances.

The reflections presented here mesh with the ongoing discussion on English as an international auxiliary language. After all, English is in a much better position than other natural languages (being more widespread and having a simpler grammar) and than artificial languages (learners being able to expand their knowledge to achieve full integrative competence, permitting them to participate in one of the richest cultures in the world).

It might be possible to get linguists to agree on what kind of simplification of English should be aimed at in order to make the language easier to learn. For instance, a core vocabulary — surrounded by concentric spheres of an expanded general vocabulary or sectors of special terminologies (ESP) — could be defined by scientific methods; such things *have* been done by the staffs of dictionary and school-book publishers. It may well be of decisive importance to avoid the word 'auxiliary' or 'vehicular', and to allay any suspicion on the part of learners that such language planning is a neocolonial plot to fob them off with a second-rate variety of English. Such fears, which are easy to understand in view of the colonial past and of continuing political and economic dependence, must be taken very seriously if any language planning in this direction is to be successful. Therefore a solution respecting the interests of ESL/EFL users would appear feasible on the lines suggested by Wong

(1982:261-86). It is significant that she quotes Kachru, with whom she fully agrees:

(17) It is obvious that in the Third World countries the choice of functions, uses and models of English has to be determined on a pragmatic basis, keeping in view the local conditions and needs. It will, therefore, be appropriate that the native speakers of English abandon the attitude of linguistic chauvinism and replace it with an attitude of linguistic tolerance. The strength of the English language is in presenting the Americanness in its American variety, and the Englishness in its British variety. Let us, therefore, appreciate and encourage the Third World varieties of English too. The individuality of the Third World varieties, such as the Indianness in its Indian variety, is contributing to the linguistic mosaic which the speakers of the English language have created in the English speaking world. The attitude toward these varieties ought to be one of appreciation and understanding.
(p.263)

However, the practical difficulties of the proposal should not be neglected:

1. Attitudes towards New Englishes would have to change, in particular in the countries affected. More than before, it would be necessary to accept that degree of individual competence in English appropriate to the communicative needs of the individual users.
2. Local usage would have to be codified in order to permit teachers to distinguish between mistakes and acceptable local features of English.
3. Necessary conditions would be that
   (a) international intelligibility is retained as far as possible, though without creating conflicting norms of international vs. national (regional) Englishes;
   (b) the denotative and communicative ranges of English are impaired as little as possible.

This kind of language planning, which takes better account of existing regional diversity would not lead to a fully homogeneous world language — but since fluency in and frequency of use of local Englishes would increase, intelligibility, even internationally, would not be likely to suffer.

11. Conclusion

English as a World Language is still not a properly demarcated scholarly discipline employing well-defined terms within a theory developed for the purpose. Indeed, it is doubtful whether such methodological foundations are necessary for an interdisciplinary subject, especially in view of the long list of desiderata which must be met before a theory proper can evolve. As a subdiscipline of English Studies, a consideration of English as a world language provides an ideal opportunity to expand the social, historical and geographical aspects of English Studies — and it will hardly be necessary to point out that partial reorientation along these lines might well serve to enhance the appeal of a traditional and somewhat ageing discipline.

Notes

1. The present article is an updated and rewritten English version of a state-of-the-art account that first appeared in German as a commissioned paper in *Studium Linguistik* 15 (1984), 10–35 (Görlach 1984b). The limited readership for this original German version makes it worthwhile to broach my ideas in English, thus making them accessible to a more 'world-wide' readership. I wish to thank the editors of *SL* for allowing me to do so, and am grateful to Helen Weiss for helpful comments on the English version.

The following remarks reflect my own thinking over the past ten years, but they may also owe more than I am aware of to my editing of Bailey and Görlach (1982) and of *English World-Wide* (1980–7) and *Varieties of English Around the World* (1979–87). Developments of the discipline are here summarised up to 1985, the year when the original manuscript was submitted; no attempt is made to update the arguments and references now that the text goes to the printer (late 1987). More recent reflections on related topics are found in Görlach (1988), an account which can be read as a complement to the present article.

The following abbreviations for regional varieties of English have been used (as suggested in *EWW* 1:1, 1980, 8–10): AfE = African E., AmE = American E., AusE = Australian E., BrE = British E., CanE = Canadian E., CarE = Caribbean E., EngE = English E., IndE =

Indian E., IrE = Irish E., NigE = Nigerian E., NZE = New Zealand E., PE = Pidgin E., SAfE = South African E., SAsE = South Asian E., SgE = Singapore E., WAfE = West African E — and St E = Standard E.

2. John Holm (1984), in his review of Bailey and Görlach (1982), pointed out that the entity 'English as World Language' makes better sense from a standpoint *outside* Britain or America; if the problem is looked at from London or Washington, there is always the danger of prescribing a certain norm, or letting oneself be influenced by political considerations.

3. An exhaustive documentation, itself an indicator of the new wave of scholarly interest, can be found in the bibliography of Viereck *et al.* (1984), whose 'world English' section is based on Görlach (1979). The fact that 1965 was chosen as the cut-off date in these compilations reflects the change in linguistic interest. A selective bibliography of books on the topic is found in Bailey and Görlach 1982: 467–79, but it may be useful to list here the most important handbooks and journals etc. (1973–86) illustrating the trend:

1973 R.W. Bailey and J. Robinson, *Varieties of Present-Day English.*
1974 D. Bähr, *Standard English und seine geographischen Varianten.*
1977 K. Wächtler, *Geographie und Stratifikation der englischen Sprache.*
J.A. Fishman, *The Spread of English. The Sociology of English as an Additional Language.*
1979 J.C. Richards, ed., *New Varieties of English.*
Varieties of English Around the World.
1980 W.R. O'Donnell and L. Todd, *Variety in Contemporary English.*
English World-Wide.
1981 L. Smith, ed., *English for Cross-cultural Communication.*
1982 R.W. Bailey and M. Görlach, eds, *English as a World Language.*
J.C. Wells, *Accents of English.*
P. Trudgill and J. Hannah, *International English.*
B.B. Kachru, ed., *The Other Tongue. English Across Cultures.*
J. Pride, ed., *New Englishes.*
1983 B.B. Kachru, *The Indianization of English.*
1984 J.T. Platt, *et al., The New Englishes.*
L. Todd, *Modern Englishes: Pidgins and Creoles.*
1985 English Today
World Englishes (revived)
1986 B.B. Kachru, *The Alchemy of English. The Spread, Functions and Models of Non-Native Englishes.*
P. Trudgill, *Dialects in Contact.*
R. McCrum *et al., The Story of English.*

4. The decisive period in the growth of confidence in the English vernacular is usually dated around 1575, cf. Jones, 1953:168–213;

Leith, 1983; Görlach, 1985a. The passage from Daniels is quoted in Görlach 1988, and chosen as a motto for Bailey and Görlach: note the unique fusion of educational and mercantile aspects in the metaphors employed.

5. A detailed comparative history of the imposition and acceptance of English and French would be particularly rewarding. Apart from political considerations, the different role of French is generally seen as a matter of attitude: the stress placed on its *mission civilatrice*, on correctness *à la* Paris, and on the integrative function of French as a second language (which makes its speakers participants in French *culture*) have certainly been more dominant than in the history of English abroad. (These aspects of the French tradition are, however, exaggerated in Gordon 1978.)

6. This remark even applies to individual immigrants: the only exception to the rule in modern history appears to be the case of Israel, where American Jews, under some pressure from the community, gave up their English or at least did not pass it on to their children.

7. This aspect is central in Mazrui (1975); note that the highly positive evaluation of English in this context has given way to a more sober view today.

8. Such attempts may apply to orthography only or they can include other levels of speech. Probably best known in this context are BASIC English, Michael West's attempts to set up a core vocabulary, or recent discussions of Nuclear English. Opinions vary on whether 'simplicity' of language is open to scholarly definition. Also compare section 10.

9. This simplifying statement passes over some Scottish-based features of Southern NZE, Irish and Scottish features in Ottawa Valley English, and similar instances — all of which retain but few and usually recessive features, showing that even a high level of homogeneity in immigrants' speech and the relative isolation of settlements did not suffice to preserve very distinctive dialects in non-European surroundings; in this they differ from German dialects such as Palatinate-based Pennsylvania Dutch etc.

10. Richard Blome states in his *Britannia* (1673:341): It is most inhabited by the Irish, who have here a Church for Divine worship. Wells (1982:586) corrects this widespread error: It is popularly claimed that Montserratians speak with an Irish accent ... there is no justification for this claim.

11. Research in progress by Roger Lass, Cape Town, suggests that some of Lanham's tenets may well have to be modified, but the major findings will not be affected.

12. The later Walter S. Avis stressed the distinctive character of CanE in a great number of articles (Avis, 1978) and in a series of dictionaries published by Gage, Toronto. For a sober summary of the question see Bailey (1982).

13. Cf. Kachru (1982a:373); this does not exclude the possibility that English in internal use (by Indians for Indians) should be recognisably Indian — speech forms too close to the British model are considered inappropriately formal or presumptuous in many contexts.

14. This is the classic situation for diglossia. In Europe, the historical situations in Scotland (most conspicuously in the 18th century), in Northern Germany (cf. Görlach, 1985b) and in Luxemburg and German-speaking Switzerland can be compared, even though the historical foundations diverge widely.

15. I here refrain from giving estimates of my own; the varying numbers of speakers given (especially for ESL/EFL countries) appear to be the result of (a) inadequate investigation and (b) failure to define what a statement like 'Mr X speaks English' should be understood to mean. Serious statistics ought to contain detailed analyses of when and where speakers of English make use of their competences; these investigations can then serve to account for stages of progressive language shift, as illustrated by the analysis made by Platt (1982:391) — whereas the study published by Tay (1982), though it is exemplarily diligent in other respects, lacks the statistics which are so vital for multilingual Singapore. If prognostications are at all possible, it appears that the number of ESL speakers will become smaller as a consequence of emerging national languages, but that the number of EFL speakers is likely to grow as a consequence of the expansion of secondary education (and possibly of recruiting among speakers breaking away from French). The important, but vast and complex field of ESP 'English for special purposes' is here neglected. (Cf. the review article by H. Weiss, 1982.)

16. Todd (1982a) presents an excellent survey of the Englishes coexisting in Cameroon (book and accompanying cassette).

17. Features of quite a few dialects tally with those of other dialects rather than with the superordinate variety. Thus the homophony of *cot*: *caught*, found in Canada, N. Ireland and Scotland does not apply to all dialects of these regions nor, on the other hand, is it restricted to speakers from these areas. Simplified contrastive analyses such as the graph reproduced here also conflict with the insight of sociolinguists (like Trudgill), viz. that it is often the frequency of features that is characteristic for individual varieties rather than their total presence or absence.

18. Cf. the detailed summary in Görlach (1984a). Angogo and Hancock (1980), Hancock and Angogo (1982) and Bokamba (1982) tend to suggest that an 'AfE' exists or is likely to evolve, but the close linguistic contacts and political–economic unification of anglophone African countries which would be the necessary conditions of greater linguistic homogenisation are obviously lacking.

19. The following specimens, examples 8–11, manifest nativisation of English in the form of unusual metaphors, non-British collocations and meanings. However, deviant syntax is quite rare (since this would be regarded as unacceptable and 'need to be pulled up by the roots', example 8). The transition to texts 12–13 is blurred: here the foreign content leads to deviant expressions, mainly in word-formation or meaning. By contrast, English-related pidgins and creoles from the Caribbean, West Africa or the Southwest Pacific exhibit structural divergence in phonology, lexis and syntax. But the problems of pidgin and creole languages (for which cf. Todd, 1984) are outside the scope

of the present article; I therefore do not give illustrative texts and analyses.

References

Achebe, Ch. (1975), 'The African Writer and the English Language' in Achebe, Ch., *Morning Yet on Creation Day*, Heinemann, London, pp. 55-62

Angogo, R. and Hancock, I.F. (1980) 'English in Africa: Emerging Standards or Diverging Regionalisms?' *English World-Wide 1*, 67-96

Avis, W.S. (1978) *Essays and Articles*, Royal Military College, Kingston, Ont.

Bailey, R.W. (1982) 'The English Language in Canada' in Bailey and Görlach (1982), pp. 177-209

—— (1984) 'The Conquests of English' in Greenbaum, S. (ed.) *The English Language Today*, Pergamon, Oxford, pp. 9-19

—— and Görlach, M. (eds) (1982) *English as a World Language*, University of Michigan Press, Ann Arbor

—— and Robinson, J.L. (eds) (1973) *Varieties of Present-Day English*, Macmillan, New York

Bauer, L. (1986) 'Notes on New Zealand English Phonetics and Phonology' *English World-Wide 7*, 225-58

Bokamba, E.G. (1982) 'The Africanization of English' in Kachru (1982b), pp. 77-98

Brosnahan, L.F. (1973) 'Some Historical Cases of Language Imposition' in Bailey and Robinson (1973), pp. 40-55

Cooper, Robert L. (ed.) (1982) *Language Spread, Studies in Diffusion and Social Change*, University Press, Bloomington, Ind.

Daswani, C.J. (1978) 'Some Theoretical Implications for Investigating Indian English' in Mohan (1978), pp. 115-28

Fishman, J.A. et al. (1977) *The Spread of English. The Sociology of English as an Additional Language*, Newbury House, Rowley, Mass.

Gokak, V.K. (ed.) (1975) *Twenty-One Anglo-Indian Poems*, Madras

Gordon, D.C. (1978) *The French Language and National Identity*, Mouton, The Hague

Görlach, M. (1979) 'A Selective Bibliography of English as a World Language', *Arbeiten aus Anglistik und Amerikanistik 4*, 231-68

—— (1983) 'The Function of Texts in the Description of Varieties of English' in Riemenschneider, D. (ed.) *The History and Historiography of Commonwealth Literature*, Narr, Tübingen, pp. 233-43

—— (1984a) 'English in Africa — African English?' *Revista de Estudios Ingleses 6*, 33-56

—— (1984b) 'Weltsprache Englisch — eine neue Disziplin?' *Studium Linguistik 15*, 10-35

—— (1984c) 'A Selective Bibliography of English as a World Language' (1965-1983)' in Viereck, W. *et al.* (1984), pp. 225-319

—— (1985a) 'Renaissance English' in Greenbaum, S. (ed.) *The English Language Today*, Pergamon, Oxford, pp. 30-40

—— (1985b) 'Scots and Low German: the Social History of Two Minority Languages' in Görlach, M. (ed.) *Focus on Scotland*, John Benjamins, Amsterdam and Philadelphia, pp. 19-36

—— (1988) 'English as a World Language — the State of the Art', *English World-Wide 9*, 1-32

Gumperz, J.J. and Wilson, R. (1971) 'Convergence and Creolization. A Case from the Indo-Aryan/Dravidian Border' in Hymes, D. (ed.) *Pidginization and Creolization of Languages*, Cambridge University Press, Cambridge, pp. 151-67

Hancock, I.F. and Angogo, R. (1982) 'English in East Africa' in Bailey and Görlach (1982), pp. 306-23

Holm, J. (ed.) (1983) *Central American English*, Groos, Heidelberg

—— (1984) 'Review of Bailey and Görlach (1982)', *Word 34*, 42-5

Hudson, R.A. (1980) *Sociolinguistics*, Cambridge University Press, Cambridge

Jibril, M. (1982) 'Phonological Variation in Nigerian English' Ph.D., Lancaster.

—— (1986) 'Sociolinguistic Variation in Nigerian English', *English World-Wide 7*, 47-74

Jones, R.F. (1953) *The Triumph of English*, Stanford University Press, Stanford

Kachru, B.B. (1982a) 'South Asian English' in Bailey and Görlach (1982), pp. 353-83

—— (ed.) (1982b) *The Other Tongue. English Across Cultures.* University of Illinois Press, Urbana

—— (1982c) 'Meaning in Deviation: Toward Understanding Non-native English Texts' in Kachru (1982b), pp. 325-50

—— (1983) *The Indianization of English*, Oxford University Press, Delhi

Kandiah, Th. (1981) 'Lankan English Schizoglossia', *English World-Wide 2*, 63-81

Kurath, H. (1972) *Studies in Area Linguistics*, Indiana University Press, Bloomington

Lanham, L.W. (1982) 'English in South Africa', in Bailey and Görlach (1982), pp. 324-52

—— and MacDonald, C.A. (1979) *The Standard of South African English and its Social History*, Groos, Heidelberg

Leith, D. (1983) *A Social History of English*, Routledge, London

Le Page, R.B. (1980) 'Theoretical Aspects of Sociolinguistic Studies in Pidgin and Creole Languages' in Valdman, A. and Highfield, A. (eds) *Theoretical Orientations in Creole Studies*, Academic Press, New York, pp. 331-68

—— and Tabouret-Keller, A., (1985) *Acts of Identity*, Cambridge University Press, Cambridge

Llamzon, T.A. (1986) 'Life Cycle of New Englishes: Restriction Phase of Filipino English', *English World-Wide 7*, 101-25

Mathews, M.M. (1931) *The Beginnings of American English*, University of Chicago Press, Chicago

Mazrui, A. (1975) *The Political Sociology of the English Language: An African Perspective*, Mouton, The Hague

Milan, W.G. (1983) 'Contemporary Models of Standardized New World Spanish' in Cobarrubias, J. and Fishman, J.A. (eds) *Progress in Language Planning*, Mouton, The Hague, pp. 121-44
Miller, T.R. (1969) *Graphic History of the Americas*, New York
Moag, R.F. (1982) 'On English as a Foreign, Second, Native and Basal Language', in Pride (1982), pp. 11-50
Mohan, R. (ed.) (1978) *Indian Writing in English*, Orient Longman, New Delhi
Morris, E. (1898) *Austral English*, Macmillan, London
Mühlhäusler, P. (1985) 'The Number of Pidgin Englishes in the Pacific' in *Papers in Pidgin and Creole Linguistics 4*, Pacific Linguistics A-72, Pacific Linguistics, Canberra
Obiechina, E.N. (ed.) (1972) *Onitsha Market Literature*, Heinemann, London
Pettman, Ch. (1913) *Africanderisms*, Longmans, Green & Co., London
Platt, J. (1982) 'English in Singapore, Malaysia and Hong Kong' in Bailey and Görlach (1982), pp. 384-414
—— et al., (1984) *The New Englishes*, Routledge, London
Pride, J. (ed.) (1982) *New Englishes*, Newbury House, Rowley, Mass.
Richards, J.C. (1982) 'Rhetorical and Communicative Styles in the New Varieties of English' in Pride (1982), pp. 227-48
Schmied, J.J. (1985) *Englisch in Tansania*, Groos, Heidelberg
Sey, K.A. (1973) *Ghanaian English: An Exploratory Survey*, Macmillan, London
Smith, L. (ed.) (1981) *English for Cross-Cultural Communication*, Macmillan, London
Sridhar, K.K. (1985) 'Sociolinguistic Issues in Non-native Varieties of English' unpubl. paper, New York
Tay, M.W.J. (1982) 'The Uses, Users and Features of English in Singapore' in Pride (1982), pp. 51-70
Todd, L. (1982a) *Cameroon* (Varieties of English Around the World T1), Groos, Heidelberg
—— (1982b) 'The English Language in West Africa' in Bailey and Görlach (1982), pp. 281-305
—— (1984) *Modern Englishes. Pidgins and Creoles*, Blackwell, Oxford
Trudgill, P. (ed.) (1984) *Languages of Britain*, Cambridge University Press, Cambridge
—— and Hannah, J. (1982) *International English. A Guide to Varieties of Standard English*, Edward Arnold, London
Valdman, A. (1979) *Le français hors de France*, Paris
Viereck, W., et al. (eds.) (1984) *A Bibliography of Writings on Varieties of English, 1965-1983*, John Benjamins, Amsterdam and Philadelphia
Wächtler, K. (1977) *Geographie und Stratifikation der englischen Sprache*, Bagel, Düsseldorf and Bern
Weiss, H. (1982) 'ESP Literature' (Review Article) *English World-Wide 3*, 92-6
Wells, J.C. (1982) *Accents of English*, 3 vols, Cambridge University Press, Cambridge.

Whitworth, G.C. (1907) *Indian English. An Examination of the Errors of Idioms Made by Indians in Writing English*, Letchworth, Herts

Wong, I.F.H. (1982) 'Native-speaker English for the Third World Today?' in Pride (1982), pp. 259–86

Year Book Australia (1980), Canberra

13
'Talking Proper': Schooling and the Establishment of English 'Received Pronunciation'

John Honey
Leicester Polytechnic

It is customary for definitions of 'Received Pronunciation' (RP), when referring to its origins, to cite the English public school.[1] Daniel Jones, who did more than anyone else to promote the use of the term RP, originally[2] labelled it PSP (public school pronunciation), and though the label was changed in 1926 the relationship of this variety of accent to this set of schools continued to be widely acknowledged. But — understandably, considering the undeveloped state of serious historical and sociological analysis of these educational institutions until recently — the nature of that relationship was never clearly specified, nor, indeed, what was meant by the term 'public schools'.

The nineteenth century saw the creation of a public school system in a new sense.[3] The reality of the Arnoldian revolution and, no less significantly, the power of the Arnold legend, led to the uneven transformation of the original Clarendon schools; the adaptation, on this new model, of several old-established grammar schools; and the foundation of purpose-built new public schools. One feature of the term 'system', as we can use it after c.1870, is the relationship of schools to one another, to a very limited extent by means of an organisational device, the Headmasters' Conference, but more significantly by means of interaction at games, cadets and other activities which in this period were coming to be regarded as typical for this purpose.[4] Another feature is their relationship to an infrastructure of preparatory schools, modelled no longer after 1870 on the domestic system, but now run as miniature public schools with the whole panoply of games, prefects, etc. etc.[5] This facilitated a consolidation of the public schools by age which accompanied a partial consolidation in terms of social class as some of the old-established schools dreamed up devices for disembarrassing themselves of the local poor.

It was these features of the 'system' which after 1870 made possible that further characteristic of the public school system: its fitness to be the recipient of the bizarre traffic in children which represented the transfer of function between home and school, to an extent where it became the common expectation that the sons of the upper and upper-middle classes should be educated in this way, whereas in the first half of the century this had by no means been the case, even for the aristocracy.[6] Between 1870 and 1900 this expectation became so well established that few could resist it, and various kinds of disability were experienced by those who did. A new caste was created in British society, the caste of 'public school man', whose traces are with us even now. His image was stamped upon the consciousness of the nation not just by the activities of such men at every level of prominence in national life, but by the enormous public attention given to the public school 'way of life' in the contemporary press and in literature, especially by the new genre of public school story, in novels, magazines and annuals, which reached down into every corner of society, and certainly far beyond those classes whose children would have any chance of personal experience of that type of schooling.[7] No section of the education industry — the endowed grammar schools, the new secondary schools afer 1902, girls' schools, the teacher-training colleges, the inspectorate, even the elementary schools — was left untouched by the educational assumptions, the institutions or the practices of the public school system, sometimes as a result of direct colonisation of this new sector by public school products and public school masters. Even the Borstal system was to be founded and developed by public school men on public school lines.

Around 1870 the question 'Where were you at school?' began to become crucial for appointment to jobs, commissions in the army, entry to clubs, and in terms of general social acceptability.[8] Biographical reference books began to record details of schooling, and (for example) Oxford University matriculation registers suddenly, for the first time, began in the 1890s to take note of entrants' previous schooling. One of the curiosities of the situation was the great imprecision about which schools actually constituted the 'public school system',[9] so that reference books, school registers, and the newly invented device of the Old School Tie could only confirm the credentials to public school status of those who had attended the better-known public schools. The other recognition device invented by the public school system, a specific accent, served by its absence to exclude all those who could not have been to public schools, but gave the benefit of the doubt to those who, having gone to some trouble to acquire it elsewhere, advertised their identification at second-hand with that system.

The public school system after 1870 did not, of course, *invent* RP, though the schools were indeed to contribute some distinctive linguistic forms to standard English. The achievement of the public school system — prep schools and public schools, and I would add Oxford and Cambridge as an extension of this process — was rather to *establish* RP as the most socially acceptable spoken form of British English, and thus to furnish what was to become, for at least a century after 1870, the most important superficial index of social class.

The distant origins of this newly established standard form of English pronunciation are well known to linguists: they can be traced to the late Middle English period, especially around the time of the change-over to the use of English in central government records in the 1430s.[10] The variety which this administrative development happened to promote represented a fusion of South Central Midlands influences with existing London speech forms. The evolution of this new standard through the sound changes of the Great Vowel Shift and the loss of post-vocalic *r* (*card, port*), until it had achieved by 1800 a form not essentially different from current RP, was accompanied at all stages by recurrent manifestations of social prejudice against other varieties of accent.[11] These prejudices were given particularly strong expression in the eighteenth century, when the efforts of dictionary makers and orthoepists, and the burgeoning London industry of teachers of elocution, were reinforced by judgements like that of Mrs Elizabeth Montagu — born in 1720, brought up in York and in Kent but thoroughly assimilated into genteel society in London. In a letter in April 1773 to a relative, she wrote

> I am glad you intend to send my eldest neice [sic] to a boarding school. What girls learn at their schools is trifling, but they unlearn what could be of great disservice — a

provincial accent, which is extremely ungenteel ... I dare say you will find great improvement in her air and her speech by the time she has been there a year, and these are points of great importance. The Kentish dialect is abominable, though not so bad as the Northumberland and some others; but in this polished age, it is so unusual to meet with young ladies who have any patois, that I mightily wish to see my neice cured of it.[12]

We find expressions of prejudice by a Yorkshire squire against the local 'Yorkshire tone' in 1778, and a Gateshead parent sent his young sons away to boarding school in High Wycombe in 1789, but after four terms at the school the father complained that their accent — and especially their North Country intonation — had not been eradicated. The headmaster, the Rev. Thomas Lloyd, assured him that 'a proper cadence' would be acquired 'in time'.[13] The head of another gentry family in the North East, Admiral Collingwood, wrote thus of his daughters' schooling, 'Being in London, I hope, will correct their language'.[14] The father of Matthew Boulton (who with Watt contributed to the technology of the industrial revolution) was advised by his son's dayschool headmaster to let him board with him in his house, rather than that as a day boy in Birmingham he would 'acquire a vicious pronunciation and vulgar dialect'.[15]

From these and many other examples we know, therefore, that in high society in London in the eighteenth century there were prejudices that were also felt against certain specific accents elsewhere. We note that for several of the critics cited above, the remedy lay in a boarding education. What was lacking to such critics — indeed, what was lacking before Arnold's reforms and the establishment of the public school system — was a form of boarding education sufficiently viable to become widely and generally usable by the classes who were likely to be most susceptible to these prejudices.

Nor, indeed, was a boarding school education in the eighteenth century — or the first half of the nineteenth — any guarantee of the standardisation of accent, for even in the small number of acknowledged[16] public schools of that period — like Eton, Harrow, Winchester or Rugby) there was as yet no expectation of a standard accent among boys or masters. One indication of this is the number of national political figures in that period who, like the majority of magnates and gentry outside London, were still influenced, in varying degrees, by pronunciation forms which reflected local dialects.

This was true of Sir Robert Walpole, despite Eton and Cambridge, the 14th Earl of Derby (Eton and Oxford), the 15th Earl of Derby (Rugby under Arnold, and Cambridge) who, according to Disraeli, 'talked a Lancashire patois'; and it was even to a slight extent true of Gladstone himself (Eton and Oxford), of whose speech Disraeli wrote tersely 'Gladstone was provincial, but a very fine voice'.[17] Sir Robert Peel (1788–1850) grew up in Staffordshire, and attended Harrow and Christ Church, Oxford. Disraeli's account suggests he pronounced 'put' as 'putt'; 'to the last [he] said "woonderful" and "woonderfully". He guarded his aspirates with extreme care. I have known him trip.'[18] A good number of later Victorian public school headmasters, as well as leading Oxford and Cambridge dons, who had attended their public schools before 1870, retained marked traces of regional accent.[19]

Some among the social élite seem to have made a special point of doing this. Writing in the latter part of the century, Thomas Adolphus Trollope (born 1810, brother of Anthony) mentions two examples in the 1820s and 1830s, in Devon and in Cumberland, of 'highly educated people whom I had known to affect provincialisms of speech' — i.e. to speak in the accents of their locality, and cites these as 'one more illustration of the change in manners, feeling, and decencies',[20] implying that such would not happen in later nineteenth century England. Even by 1874 the House of Commons had some expectation of a certain degree of standardness of spoken English. The parliamentary correspondent of the *Gentleman's Magazine* in that year described the ageing Sir John Pakington (Eton and Oxford) as having been treated by his fellow MPs 'with a consideration which English gentlemen are, happily, always ready to pay to mediocrity when it is well-off, is highly connected, and can express its ideas without violence to the rules of grammar or the principles of accent'.[21]

One element in the account so far is defective. We are required to envisage a transitional stage (say c.1870–1900) in which boys with non-standard accents entering a given school in the public school system are induced to adapt to the standard. (The evidence suggests that this was done less by explicit teaching than by the ruthless shaming of those who spoke otherwise, and it seems to have been more effective in southern public schools than in that minority of public schools which are in the north.[22]) Such a process would certainly have to allow for the continued presence in the school of masters — even a headmaster — who spoke with marked non-standard features: we have evidence that this was the case, and that the boys adopted various degrees of tolerance to accommodate that fact. Boys from 'non-standard' homes would be returning in the holidays (though at less frequent intervals than is the case nowadays) to be with parents for whose non-standard accent allowances would have to be made. More importantly, they would be seeking relationships with — and, before long, brides from among — girls who might in many cases be speaking non-standard, unless we can trace a similar process at work in the education of girls. It would be interesting to discover how far this factor was a preoccupation with the parents of such girls as attended the girls' boarding schools of the later Victorian period; or how far this was a prerequisite in the qualifications for a governness at that time. So far I have not found enough evidence. Certainly the accent-consciousness of Victorian women had the potential to be crucial, unless they are to be counted an exception to the sociolinguists' generalisation that women strive more than men towards speech forms that are considered 'correct', and expect these in their children.

The degree of prescription of English pronunciation exercised first by the public schools and then by their imitators in the rest of the school system for at least a century after 1870 has been one of the great unexamined aspects of our social history. In 1895 a Rugby master asked a colleague about the newly appointed head: 'Tell me, is James a gentleman? Understand me, I don't mean, does he speak the Queen's English but — had he a grandfather?'[23] It would be the achievement of the public school system to substitute for ancestry as the criterion of 'gentleman' status, first, membership of that public school caste itself, and secondly, the ability to speak the Queen's English with the specific accent and intonation which the public school system was now establishing as standard. It is salutary to reflect that it is barely two decades since the death of a well-known Englishman — diplomat, politician and author: public school and Oxford — who once declared that he found himself unable to take seriously anyone who spoke with what he called a 'common voice'. It takes an effort to recollect that Sir Harold Nicolson was a member of the *Labour* party.

Compelling and pervasive though the influence of RP may have been, two important qualifications must be stated. First, it is necessary to distinguish betweeen a general, mainstream form of RP and a more exclusive, 'posh', 'U' form which perpetuated certain features of a long-established aristocratic class dialect;[24] and, secondly, there were certain specific provincial varieties which had greater power to resist the onslaught of the standardising force of RP. These included educated varieties of Scottish, Irish and to a lesser extent Welsh English, each reflecting the existence of a local intelligentsia of teachers, ministers of religion and other professional groups who set a local standard of 'educatedness'. When the antiquarian and amateur philologist F.T. Elsworthy (1830–1907) wrote in 1875 that 'speaking from my own experience, I have often been amused at the very marked provincialisms in the pronunciation of educated men and women in the Northern and Midland counties',[25] he drew attention to the existence even then of a hierarchy of acceptability which the social history of the next hundred years would consolidate, which put RP at the top, followed closely by certain 'educated' provincial forms (especially Edinburgh Scots), with northern and midland forms well down the scale, and the vernacular accents associated with large industrial areas around London, Birmingham, Liverpool and Glasgow in bottom place.

After 1922 the role of the public schools in regard to the maintenance and diffusion of a standard accent passed to Sir John Reith's BBC, both in the selection of radio voices and also in the establishment of the Advisory Committee on Spoken English (1926), chaired initially by the aged Poet Laureate, the Etonian Robert Bridges. When he died he was succeeded by George Bernard Shaw, a lone maverick Irishman on a committee which in the twelve years of its active life (until 1938) contained, besides a few anglicised Scots or Welshmen, and the naturalised American Logan Pearsall Smith, an overwhelming preponderance of public school/Oxbridge figures, including the headmaster of Rugby itself. Shaw, with a lifelong interest in phonetics which he embodied in *Pygmalion*, had a simple criterion for the ultimate acceptability of a given pronunciation: as he wrote to Reith in 1937, 'If the announcer can give the impression that he is a gentleman, he can pronounce as he pleases'[26] — a specification which we remember was reinforced by the (unseen) radio announcer's having to be properly dinner-jacketed when reading the news. A flood of protests at the use of any speakers with non-standard accents confirmed the BBC in its policy of using RP speakers, especially public school and Oxbridge men, and the influence of such presenters and newsreaders has been even greater than that of the Committee which pontificated on the pronunciation of individual words, some of whose recommendations give a remarkably dated impression.[27]

It was not until around 1960 that the BBC pointedly reversed its policy of limiting the representation of non-standard accents to the statutory weather forecaster, gardeners' programme contributor, and a few others, and by the end of the 1960s the BBC had joined the contemporary generation of boys in public schools in trying to escape from RP. Nevertheless, there is good evidence that from the 1920s to the 1960s many people from non-standard accent backgrounds were influenced in the direction of standard by the model represented by BBC radio.[28] Thus, we can expect to find many entrants to élites over the past century who had had no public school education, but we will find relatively few among them who had not adjusted their regional accents, especially in the case of the less prestigious ones, in the direction of RP.

Popular discussion of this subject often invokes the example of Sir William Robertson (1860–1933), the first soldier to rise from the rank of private to become Field Marshal, and Chief of the Imperial General Staff in the crucial war years of 1915 to 1918 — a man of lowly birth in Lincolnshire, of whom it tends to be said that 'for most of his life he dropped his aitches' or that he 'talked with a cockney accent'. In fact, Robertson's skill as a linguist had enabled him to qualify in official examinations in six languages in India: he was clearly able to cope with the demands of 'code-switching' and to choose appropriate occasions on which to drop his aitches or retain them. His general accent was, in fact, classless apart from what is reported as 'a roughish intonation'. (Incidentally we also note that at a stage when he was an impoverished officer on half-pay, Robertson made it the first charge on his tiny income to send his son to Charterhouse.[29])

In October 1919 the boys at the public school Lancing were examined for their cadet corps Certificate A by a visiting officer. Instead of the expected 'Guards major' type, they were disgusted — and even the master-in-charge was put out — to find that the visitor was what the 16-year-old Evelyn Waugh described as 'the most blatantly risen-from-the ranks I've ever seen' — and Waugh and the other senior boys set out systematically to sabotage the Cert.A exam, organising the dropping of rifles etc. The blatancy of the examining officers' class origins was, of course, advertised by his accent: Waugh explained that 'he was not even a Temporary Gentleman but a Permanent Oik' — the word *oik* aptly emphasising the phonemic alternation in many southern vernaculars of /ɔɪ/ for /aɪ/.[30]

None of the boys stopped to ask themselves what conspicuous gallantry or leadership in battle had caused the man's promotion from the ranks; instead he was disqualified from any right to command because he spoke with the wrong accent. Britain's massive military casualties in World War I put an enormous strain on the selection of officers and on the criterion of accent, so it is not surprising to find that in the last year of that war an enterprising lecturer in English at the Midland Institute, Birmingham, Mr Frank Jones, should be publishing a manual which set out to describe phonetically, and to correct, the peculiarities of pronunciation in Birmingham and neighbourhood. 'From "Brummagem" English (and all other dialects, for instance the Cockney) all educated men and women are free', quoted the *Times Educational Supplement* reviewer approvingly. 'If parents only knew the truth', the reviewer went on, 'they would know that their clever boy had no greater obstacle in his material progress than those peculiarities of pronunciation which differentiate him from his fellows in the new sphere to which he is to be called. For instance' — and here the reviewer again quoted from Mr Jones — 'to no one is the absence of local dialect more important than to the young officer in the army'.[31] The popular assumption that things had changed little in this respect in World War II is given credence by such evidence as the claim by the public-school-educated actor Dirk Bogarde (born in 1921) that in that war the sole reason for his promotion from the ranks to an officer's commission was his accent.[32] We see all these tendencies at work in the decision in 1916 by an old established Midlands day-school, Queen Mary's School, Walsall — shortly to achieve recognition as a 'public' school by admission to the Headmasters' Conference — to introduce its 'New Scheme for Improving the Pronunciation of English in the School'. This 'unique system', introduced by a headmaster who was a product of public school and Cambridge in the 1880s, involved 'a vowel sound for each week, with its appropriate prose or verse exercise which the boys chanted together first period every morning'.[33]

Even so, this complex of attitudes linking RP with 'educatedness' and general social acceptability did not go unchallenged even in the privileged sector of education. A remarkable leading article in the recently established *Times Educational Supplement* in 1917 criticised, in the period before the term RP had become general, what it called the 'class dialect', namely, 'Public School and University English' — especially in the mouths of Anglican clergymen who were graduates of Oxford and Cambridge — as tending to lack both precision and expression:

> Just as the Cockney dialect expresses a desire to be knowing, the Midland dialect an air of sturdy independence, and the North Country dialect a placid shrewdness, so the University dialect expresses an ambition of easy refinement.

What we ought rather to be teaching in our schools and universities, the *TES* writer went on, is 'a normal and classical English which no one will be able to laugh at because there will be no class-consciousness in it, but only the desire for excellence'.[34]

But what of popular education? When was it, and how was it, that this new ingredient of 'educatedness' began to reach down into elementary schools, and impose itself upon the mass of the people?

In his now famous article in *Past and Present* (1970), the Marxist historian Richard Johnson presents the classic statement of the connexion in Britain between the origins of state provision of popular education and the ruling classes' concern with 'social control'.[35] In the course of his argument Johnson commits himself to the interesting statement that in the 1840s HMIs — the school inspectors appointed to monitor the effectiveness of central government grants towards elementary education — 'waged war' upon 'provincial dialect and indistinct articulation', 'coarse provincial accents', and 'faults and vulgarities of expression'. For this he cites, as example, one reference in the Minutes of the Committee of Council for 1845.[36]

This example is, I suggest, profoundly misleading, and the more so because of the weight of the case that has been built upon it. My own reading of HMI reports to the Committee of

Council in that period yields a quite different conclusion. I find detailed comments from HMIs, both in general reports and in references to specific schools, on such things as reading, dictation, and grammar, without any trace of a reference to pronunciation or accent. A report that children who on leaving school for work 'become much worse in their language and manners' clearly means 'bad' language in the moral sense. Indeed, morality, character, discipline, punctuality, hygiene, 'general intelligence and moral tone', truthfulness, 'habits of industry' are the preoccupations of HMIs, *not* accent or dialect.[37] A report on a school in the Liverpool area must have involved pupils whose Lancashire accents were undergoing that invasion by Irish accents which was to produce Scouse: the HMI comments only that 'they read fluently and with correct expression'.[38]

Johnson's one quoted reference in fact derives from HMI Mr F.C. Cook in his Report for 1845 on the Eastern district, in the section on 'The Improved Style of Reading'. A careful study of the context of his observations makes it clear that HMI Cook's comments on accent are made in respect of pupils' general intelligibility to others, and their own understanding of what they are saying. Thus, for example, in his report on the Examination of Monitors, he seriously queries how far the methods of teaching the Catechism are effectively 'teaching the children to pronounce the words articulately and correctly — to perceive the divisions and connexions of the sentences — to understand their meaning ...'. And he goes on:

> I could easily make out a long list of the gross mistakes, omissions, and mispronunciations of the principal words, and perversions of the sense, which are almost universally made by the young children, and which are in many cases unobserved, or uncorrected, by the monitors. It is painful to dwell upon this subject, but it is necessary to state that, even in the Lord's Prayer, nothing is more common that to hear the children say: 'Our father *charter heaven*', and when they are requested to divide the words, or, if sufficiently advanced, to write them, they generally persist in the error.[39]

His HMI colleague Mr Moseley is keen to observe the deportment of training college students when giving lessons (as models for 'the manners and character of the child') but he makes no comment on accent, which must indeed have been non-standard.[40] In his visitation of St Mark's Training College, Chelsea, in the 1843–44 Minutes, Mr Moseley is keen to notice the 'correct expression of their thoughts in writing', their 'command of language', their 'power of literary exposition'. His comment on 'examples of that more opulent diction and more elevated tone of thought and expression which characterise a highly educated mind' may be the nearest we get to a direct observation on accent.[41] In general the cry from HMI Mr Watkins (Northern Division): 'We must have educated men to educate the uneducated' shows in its context[42] hardly a trace of any presuppositions about the compatibility of certain accents with educatedness. Hardly a trace — how could it have been otherwise? The HMIs themselves, like their fellow-clergymen and their government officials, and like the academics and country gentlemen they might expect to move amongst, would in that period be quite likely to speak with marked traces of a non-standard variety of English accent. I find nothing to support the claim that in the 1840s HMIs 'waged war' against non-standard accents among elementary school pupils. Indeed, how could they have waged such a war?

Matthew Arnold was a penetrating observer of popular education in mid-Victorian England, and as HMI his Reports over the three decades 1852–1882 reveal above all his passion for the teaching of literature — and especially poetry — as a means of spreading 'sweetness and light'. When he writes of lack of culture or 'low degree of mental culture and intelligence' or 'want of taste' among the pupils, it is clear that this has nothing to do with their accent, for his remedy is that they should learn to paraphrase.[43] For Matthew Arnold familiarity with literary masterpieces, learned by heart for recitation, cultivates the power of perception, promotes general intelligence, and tests the memory. Attention to rhythm and diction are urged in the interests not of correct pronunciation but of the promotion of wider vocabulary, ideas and intelligence. The cockney urchins in his central London elementary schools were commended by Arnold for the 'quite remarkable purity and delicacy of tone and accent' of their reading, 'in spite of some faults of pronunciation'.[44] But, in general, I venture the guess that there are more references in his educational writings to hygiene (and there are few enough of those) than to accent.[45]

This is not to say, of course, that there is no evidence of any prejudice at all among inspectors or other commentators against the speech forms common in schools for the masses in this period — such as the observer who commented in 1840 on the 'very uncouth pronunciation' heard among pupils whose reading he inspected in dame schools in Coventry.[46] What we do not find in this period, however, is any clear assumption that it is the task of the school to transmit a form of accent which itself was as yet imperfectly established as standard among the educated class. A.J. Ellis could write in 1869 of how 'anxious and willing' the 'social inferior [was] to adopt the pronunciation of the superiorly educated', but at that date it was still possible for him to deny there was any general means whereby those 'inferiors' could learn it;[47] this availability was yet to come.

We must look to HMIs of the *later* nineteenth century for traces of accent-consciousness which could impinge upon the school system they inspected. But not among the older HMIs even then. A.J. Swinburne was at Merchant Taylors' in central London in 1859, then at Oxford, and was an HMI for 35 years from 1876, in Suffolk and Lancashire. Many of the conversations he reproduces in his memoirs are in dialect, but he gives no evidence of any attitude of explicit prescriptiveness employed as HMI.[48] Exactly the same can be said of E.M. Sneyd-Kynnersley — Rugby in the 1850s and Balliol, an HMI from 1871 — whose memoirs (1908) contain plenty of comment on dialect in Cheshire, etc., but no suggestion that he set himself to discourage it in schools;[49] similarly with T.G. Rooper, Harrow 1862 and Balliol, HMI from 1878 to 1903.[50]

Yet the closing decades of the century suggest a changing picture, and the HMI General Reports in the 1880s and 1890s do begin to show how a new consciousness of standard English among public school and Oxbridge HMIs was beginning to influence the rest of the school system. The prominence given to reading, recitation and dictation (the latter involving the HMI under the now crucial examinations of the Revised Code from the 1860s to the 1890s) opened the way to some HMIs to comment on 'mispronunciation', 'intonation and inflection', 'expression' such as we find occasionally in HMI Reports in the 1880s: HMI Mr Blakiston recommended the 'kindly and judicious use of ridicule' on the 'inarticulate utterances' of South Yorkshire schoolboys in 1886.[51]

By 1898 such HMI comments are much more common: not

so much condemnation of, but condescension towards, 'picturesque provincialisms' (HMI Mr Whitwell, North East division⁵²); HMI Mr Carter on reading in Bradford schools: 'much time is devoted to securing proper enunciation'.⁵³ And in the general HMI Report on the North Eastern Counties the prescription 'It is a more valuable accomplishment to know when to write *his* and when *is* than to be able to spell words of seven syllables'.⁵⁴ Noteworthy too is the frequency with which the Teacher Training HMIs ram home in their reports at the very end of the century their recommendations for the provision in training colleges of lessons in voice production and elocution. Sir H. Oakeley's General Report on the Colleges contains comments on this at college after college.⁵⁵ The HMI who visited the Training College Department for Cheltenham Ladies' College was 'much pleased with the accuracy, taste and distinctness with which the exercises [in reading and recitation] were rendered'.⁵⁶ Oakeley himself rejoiced that more 'persons of good university antecedents were being appointed to training college staffs, especially to principalships: of 44 principals in 1886, only 14 now [1898] remained in office'; he also rejoiced that principals now did more actual teaching — with all the direct influence on students' 'state of culture' which that could be held to imply.⁵⁷

HMI Mr Munro was quite explicit in 1898 about the direct effect of all this on the schools: 'a constantly increasing number of students who have received a good college training, and speak and read with a purified tone, accent, and expression, is to be found in the schools, and such teachers leave their mark upon the reading and recitation'.⁵⁸ And by that same year (1898), the Education Department's Circular 407 on reading existed to recommend to teachers the ideal method of pronouncing the vowels. Four years before, HMI Mr Scott Coward, when addressing the committee which controlled the teacher training department of what is now Newcastle University, emphasised the needs of these students for help 'to overcome the peculiarities of local pronunciation', and he was soon strongly recommending the provision of lectures on elocution.⁵⁹

The autobiography of F.H. Spencer, HMI after 1912, illustrates this process and its implications. Spencer was born into a working-class family in Swindon in 1872, the son of a fitter and turner. From an elementary school he became a pupil-teacher and then went to Borough Road College at Isleworth in 1892. Despite his lifelong pride in his working-class origins, he later wrote candidly about what — significantly — he called the 'evil side' of his own elementary schooling, which he specified as follows: 'In speech I acquired the accent and intonation of the common people.' His contemporaries at Borough Road were students from all parts of England and Wales; moreover, he gives examples of the reactions of (say) North Country students to doing teaching practice alongside elementary school teachers with West Country accents.[60] He arrived at Borough Road soon after the appointment of a new Principal, P.A. Barnett, who had himself gone on from a London day-school to take a first in Greats at Oxford, and his appointment to the Principalship in 1889 was for Borough Road a new departure compared with the Anglican colleges, like St Mark's, with their established tradition of Oxbridge principals. Barnett was quick to introduce Oxbridge graduates as college tutors, alongside the traditional staff made up of former students of the college. Spencer comments on Barnett that he was 'a born teacher', and goes out of his way to say what I think is very revealing: 'It was not unfortunate for us that he affected an "Oxford" manner and speech ...'. Significantly, Barnett left Borough Road to become an HMI, and later indeed to become Chief Inspector of Training Colleges, exercising a notable influence 'both by his teaching and his example' on the world of teacher education.[61] His successor at Borough Road in 1893, H.L. Withers, came from a Balliol 'first' in Greats and the personal recommendation of Jowett — and, we notice also, from a teaching post at a leading public school (Clifton).[62]

As the established middle classes began to feel competition from among the newly educated masses, so they hit back where they could. 'The elementary school teacher', proclaimed a writer in the *Fortnightly Review* in 1899, 'is a small middle-class person ... unintellectual, parochial in sympathies, vulgar in the accent and style of his talking ... What we want is educated ladies and gentlemen as teachers'.[63] It is difficult not to suspect that the conception of 'educatedness' embodied here had a lot in common with that underlying the strictures in the notorious Holmes Circular of 1911, in which inspectors drawn from among elementary school teachers were deemed 'uncultured and imperfectly educated' in comparison with those HMIs who 'have been educated first at a Public School and then at Oxford or Cambridge' — though nowhere in that Circular is accent ever referred to explicitly.[64]

The Conference on the Teaching of English in London elementary schools (1909) reported that

> The cockney mode of speech, with its unpleasant twang, is a modern corruption without legitimate credentials, and is unworthy of being the speech of any person in the capital city of the empire.[65]

However, in an interesting article in 1977, B. Hollingworth showed us, at an elementary school in Rochdale in 1890, not only an interesting preservationist inspector (HMI Mr Wylie) at work, and generating controversy in the local press, by his attempts to foster the use of local dialect in school; but also the response of some parents, which is no less illuminating: 'Keep the old Lancashire dialect out of the schools, Mr Wylie, for I want my children to talk smart when they're grown up'.[66]

Philologists had noted in the 1870s the eroding effect on dialects of 'railways, telegraphs, machinery and steam', and now after 1870 of 'board schools in every village'.[67] Every mass system of state education in Western Europe had some effect in standardising pronunciation, as part of a wider standardisation of national languages, but in England such a system, though it came relatively late, produced within thirty years a marked influence on local speech forms. As a historian of Cockney has written, 'the gibes of critics in the eighteenth and early nineteenth centuries had little effect: when they were taken up by thousands of school teachers they became steam-rollers'.[68]

Notes

1. For references to the connexion between public schools and RP by Daniel Jones, H.C. Wyld, David Abercrombie, Randolph Quirk etc., see John Honey, 'Acrolect and Hyperlect: the Redefinition of English RP', in *English Studies*, June 1985, vol. 66, no. 3, p. 244
2. Daniel Jones, *English Pronouncing Dictionary*, editions from 1917 to 1924
3. John Honey (1977) *Tom Brown's Universe*, especially Chapter 3
4. Honey (1977), Chapter 4; J. Honey 'The Nature and Limits of the Victorian Public Schools Community', in Brian Simon and Ian Bradley (eds) (1975), *The Victorian Public School*, pp. 19–33
5. D.P. Leinster-Mackay (1984) *The Rise of the English Prep School*
6. Honey (1977), Chapter 3 and T.W. Bamford (1961), 'Public Schools and Social Class', *Br. Jnl Sociol.* XII, pp. 224

7. For one especially telling example, see Robert Roberts (1971) *The Classic Slum*, Chapter 8

8. Honey (1977) Chapter 4

9. Ibid; and Honey (1985) p. 243

10. See especially three papers, by A. McIntosh, M.L. Samuels and E.J. Dobson respectively, reprinted in Roger Lass (1969) *Approaches to English Historical Linguistics*

11. For early examples of this, see Cecily Clark (1981) 'Another Late Fourteenth Century Case of Dialect Awareness', *English Studies* pp. 504–5

12. Dr [John] Doran (1873) *A Lady of the Last Century*, pp. 181–2

13. F.M.L. Thompson (1963) *English Landed Society in the 19th Century*, pp. 85–6; Edward Hughes (1952) *North Country Life in the 18th Century*, vol. I, pp. 364–5

14. Hughes (1952) p. 366

15. A.E. Musson and E. Robinson (1969) *Science and Technology in the Industrial Revolution*, p. 201

16. Honey (1977) p. 239

17. Benjamin Disraeli, *Reminiscences* (written in early 1860s), Helen and Marvin Swartz (eds) (1975) p. 93; H.C. Wyld, appendix to *The Best English* (Society for Pure English) Tract No. 39, 1934; Honey (1977) pp. 231, 389

18. Disraeli (1975) p. 93

19. Honey (1977) pp. 231–2

20. T.A. Trollope (1887) *What I Remember*, vol. I, 37, and vol. II, 34–5. See also L.E.O. Charlton (ed.) (1939) *The Recollections of a Northumbrian Lady*, p. 123

21. H.W. Lucy (1874) *Men and Manners in Parliament, by the Member for the Chiltern Hundreds*, p. 7

22. Honey (1977) p. 286; Honey in Simon and Bradley (eds) (1975) p. 32

23. Frank Fletcher (1937) *After Many Days*, p. 80

24. Honey (1985) p. 249

25. F.T. Elworthy (1875) *The Dialect of West Somerset*

26. Quoted in programme on early years of BBC broadcasting, compiled by Paul Ferris, broadcast on Radio 3, December 1977 and again April 1978

27. Ibid.: A. Lloyd James (1935) *The Broadcast Word*, BBC *Broadcast English*, 1928, 3rd edn, 1935

28. From among a great battery of possible evidence, note e.g. Henry Green (1940/1979) *Pack My Bag*, p. 238

29. Article on W.R. Robertson by F. Maurice in *DNB 1931–40*; Victor Bonham Carter (1963) *Soldier True*; A.J.P. Taylor (1965) *English History 1914–45*, p. 47, n.4; P.T. Bauer (1978) *Class on the Brain*, p. 6

30. Michael Davie (ed.) (1976) *The Diaries of Evelyn Waugh*, 31, pp. 149–50

31. *Times Educational Supplement* (*TES*) 3 October 1918 p. 419: review of *Brummagem English*, by Frank Jones, Powis, Walsall, 48 pp.

32. Dirk Bogarde, interviewed on BBC 1 television programme *Omnibus*, 27 March 1983

33. D.J.P. Fink (1954) *Queen Mary's Grammar School*, Walsall, pp. 336, 347, 359
34. *TES*, 11 October 1917, p. 393. I owe this reference to Mr C.A. Stray of University College Swansea
35. Richard Johnson, 'Educational Policy and Social Control in Early Victorian England', in *Past and Present* no. 49, November 1970
36. Committee of Council on Education (1846) *Minutes* for 1845, vol. 1, p. 140
37. Report in 1845 *Minutes* (1846) especially HMIs Watkins, Bellairs, Fletcher, etc., pp. 334–407
38. Ibid.: p. 392
39. 1844 Report (1845) p. 143
40. HMI Mr Moseley, 1843-4 Report (1845) p. 304
41. Ibid.: p. 303
42. HMI Mr Watkins, 1845 Report (1846) p. 334
43. Matthew Arnold, *Reports on Elementary Schools 1852-82*, (ed. Sir F. Sandford) (1889) pp. 18–19 (1852), p. 94 (1861)
44. Ibid.: pp. 210–11 (1878); pp. 42–3 (1855)
45. In any case, 'accent' for Matthew Arnold usually refers to the allocation of stress in polysyllabic words, which, he complained, foreigners often got wrong in reading his poems. G.W.E. Russell (ed.) (1895) *Letters of Matthew Arnold*, 1848–88, vol. I, p. 128
46. D. Leinster-Mackay, 'The Dame Schools of Coventry in 1840: a Research Note', *History of Education Society Bulletin*, no. 35, Spring 1985, p. 15.
47. A.J. Ellis (1869) *On Early English Pronunciation*, p. 629
48. A.J. Swinburne (1911) *Memories of a School Inspector*
49. E.M. Sneyd-Kynnersley (1908) *Passages in a Wandering Life*
50. T.G. Rooper (n.d.) *School and Home Life*, e.g. pp. 94–5, 367–97
51. *Reports of Commissioners, Education (England and Wales), for 1886* (1887) XXVIII, p. 317
52. General Report for N.E. Division, p. 163
53. Ibid.
54. Ibid.: p. 165.
55. *Reports of Commissioners, Education (England and Wales)*, Sir H. Oakeley's Report on Training Colleges for 1898, vol. XXI (1899)
56. Ibid.: p. 47
57. Ibid.: p. 1
58. Ibid.: p. 221
59. J.C. Tyson and J.P. Tuck (1971) *The Origins and Development of the Training of Teachers in the University of Newcastle upon Tyne*, pp. 46–7; and Minute Book of Committee of Durham College of Science Normal Department, entry for March 1894
60. F.H. Spencer (1938) *An Inspector's Testament*, pp. 66, 125, 145
61. Ibid.: pp. 129, 131, 152; G.F. Bartle (1976) *A History of Borough Road College*, p. 45
62. Bartle (1976) p. 54
63. Quoted in Asher Tropp, *The School Teachers* (1957) p. 148n

64. Peter Gordon, 'The Holmes–Morant Circular of 1911: a Note', *Jnl of Educ. Admin. and History*, vol. 10, no. 1, Jan. 1978

65. Report of a Conference on the Teaching of English in London Elementary Schools (based on sessions 1906–8), 1909 (ILEA Education Library) p. 4

66. Brian Hollingworth, 'Dialect in School — an Historical Note', *Durham and Newcastle Res. Rev.* vol. VIII, 39, Autumn 1977, pp. 15–20

67. Elworthy (1875) p. 3

68. William Matthews (1938/72) *Cockney Past and Present* Preface, p. xv

14
The Methods of Urban Linguistic Surveys

Graham Nixon
University of Sheffield

1. Introduction

The idea of an urban linguistic survey was dear to the heart of Barbara Strang for a variety of reasons, and she was instrumental in setting up the Tyneside Linguistic Survey (TLS). Tentative directions for such a survey were discussed many years ago (Strang, 1968), and developed and refined by other workers (Pellowe *et al.*, 1972; Jones-Sargent, 1983; etc), but perhaps the most influential work from the point of view of theory and methodology was Pellowe (1967). The sociolinguistic climate at this time was largely influenced by Labov, and his seminal study carried out in New York (Labov, 1966). Because of the overshadowing influence of what has come to be known as the 'Labovian paradigm' for such research, and also perhaps the technical nature of the non-linguistic aspects of TLS methodology, the TLS has never really been sufficiently accessible to a wide enough audience to gain the recognition which I believe it deserves.

The aims of the remainder of this paper will therefore be threefold: (i) to point out some of the characteristics of the Labovian paradigm with which dissatisfaction was felt, and thereby justify the rather radically different approach taken by the TLS; (ii) to explain, in what is hoped will be a clear fashion, what that approach involves and how it works; (iii) to reflect on further improvements and alterations suggested in the light of work now being carried out under the aegis of the Survey of Sheffield Usage (SSU), whose methods are themselves in part derived from and influenced by those of TLS.

2. The Labovian paradigm

Labov's important work is too well known to require extensive rehearsal here. It would be unfortunate, however, if concentration upon a relatively small number of points of critical comment were to detract from the value and importance of that work to the development of sociolinguistics in general during the past twenty years or more.

The linguistic variables chosen by Labov for investigation were both few in number (five) and phonological in nature (1966:50–6). Does a small number of phonological variables adequately characterise the way a person speaks? The answer to this question must depend upon a measurement of the predictive value of such variable-usage for other features of the speech variety in question, which in turn demands an analysis of all such other features, in a large number of varieties, as well as of the few of particular interest. Now Labov was interested in discovering '... in the apparently irregular fluctuations in the speech of New Yorkers, a coherent linguistic structure. ... a regular pattern of social variation and a regular pattern of stylistic variation.' (1966:207). It is not altogether surprising that such regular patterns were there to be found, since the variables were chosen on the basis of *a priori* and intuitive knowledge of linguistic variation in New York. They were ones which New Yorkers felt to have some (high) degree of social significance. They are not claimed, of course, to be the only variables to demonstrate such patterning, but TLS wished to discover which other variables did so, and to what degree. This meant, of course, that very large numbers of variables needed to be considered (approximately 450 in one form of the analysis) independently of whether the research workers intuitively believed that they would eventually prove to be significant. (In fact there was frequently, and expectably, disagreement between workers of different linguistic background on such matters.) The motto became: 'If it moves, catch it.' More formally stated this would imply that if between any two members of the speech community in question, there is observable linguistic variation in comparable environments, then there is a variable with at least the *potential* to exhibit regular patterning. The vast majority of variables so identified would be 'interviewed for the purpose of elimination' so to speak, but at least they are eliminated systematically. And many, of course, prove to be of unexpected significance. An essential difference between TLS and Labov seems to be that Labov at that early stage was primarily concerned to describe the systematic co-variation of linguistic variables and social (and stylistic) attributes, while TLS was concerned to identify whole varieties (by means of their constituent variables) and relate them in some systematic way to social features: 'Under the rubric of *ecology* we aimed, having identified the speech varieties themselves, to determine the relative commonness or rarity of each, and to define their distribution across social attributes (Pellowe *et al.*, 1972:1). The concentration upon whole speech varieties, rather than individual variables, predicts not only the inclusion of large numbers of variables, but also that those variables should range across levels of analysis other than the simply segmental phonological, in particular the supra-segmental phonological, lexical and syntactic. In turn, the non-phonological levels especially produce variables which are essentially quantitative in nature rather than qualitative. The analytical task is therefore considerably greater than that required for a Labovian study involving similar quantities of raw data.

These, I believe, are the most important differences between the two approaches. There are others, of course, some to do with the structure of interviews and the construction of samples of the population, which reflect differences of purpose rather than of philosophy. Some others certainly do reflect differences of philosophy, particularly attitudes to classification, but these will be elaborated in the following section.

3. TLS method

As has been seen, the concept of variety is central to TLS method, and the first step in analysis is to characterise the speech varieties collected by means of interviews. This is done by coding each speaker('s variety) in terms of each of the variables used in the analysis to yield a Variety Profile. It will be appreciated that with 450 variables, each with a number of possibles scores, or 'states', the number of different profiles available will be sufficiently high to ensure that each is effectively unique to the speaker being analysed. A classification of varieties is then made possible such that varieties with a high similarity are grouped together. This similarity is measured by comparing the Variety Profiles of each possible pair of speakers, and deriving a percentage of the total number of variables on which the performance of the two speakers was the same. Thus a similarity coefficient is yielded for each pair of speakers, and this is then used as the basis for placing speakers(' varieties) into groups or 'clusters'. A successful clustering routine is well described in Jones-Sargent (1983), for those with a computational turn of mind. It is dependent upon the principles of numerical taxonomy (e.g. Sokal and Sneath, 1963), which is a non-hierarchical or 'polythetic' approach to classification.

Thus far, we have a set of groups of linguistic varieties ('clusters' within a 'Variety Space'). These clusters are to some extent manipulable, depending upon the similarity levels at which they are formed. That is, you can have a large number of small clusters or fewer bigger ones, but they still represent groups with a high level of internal homogeneity and a lower external level. These may then be scanned from the point of view of the variable-usage represented within them. For example, the use of a particular state of a variable may be a necessary or sufficient condition for membership of a particular cluster, or it may simply be a high frequency feature amongst members of a cluster but not restricted to them. These (and other) varying levels of association of states of variables (or groups of states of variables) with membership of clusters are reflected in the 'diagnostic' value of a state, that is, the state's ability to predict membership of a cluster on the part of a variety having it.

We have, then, at this stage a sophisticated classification of linguistic varieties, which owes nothing to social attributes. What happens next is that social attributes of the speakers who provided the linguistic data are treated in precisely the same way. Social profiles are constructed, clustered in a social space, and states of social variables evaluated for their diagnostic value in predicting membership of particular social clusters. It is only now that linguistic features come together with social ones. The two spaces (Variety and Social) are scanned for clusters having a degree of commonness in the 'owners' (informants) of the linguistic and social varieties represented therein. Thus the extent to which a cluster in one space shares members with a cluster in the other, coupled with the diagnostic values of a linguistic variable state and a social one, represent the extent of genuine sociolinguistic correlation between them. The value of this admittedly rather complex way of arriving at such correlations lies principally in the fact that they are, as far as possible, precluded from being constructs of the investigators' assumptions and perceptions. The claims of all linguistic variables to correlate with all social ones are tested in an empirical fashion.

4. Phonetic similarity — a new metric

If we consider for the moment only segmental phonological variables, it will be seen that the overall units of comparison resemble a phoneme inventory of RP (with nods in the direction of localised varieties). The function of these is solely to ensure that like is compared with like. However, it is open to question whether phoneme-like units are best suited to this form of comparison of sound systems,[1] and there are two major reasons why I feel that this part of the methodology has room for improvement.

The first is that in respect of the *individual features* being compared it ignores the *degree* of difference observable. That is to say, it allows a variable where very great phonetic disparity is observed between the two varieties under consideration, to contribute to the overall measure of similarity precisely the same value as one where the realisations concerned differ in only the finest observable phonetic detail. A counter argument to this criticism might claim that, given a sufficiently large number of variables, such cases would be rare enough not to affect the results significantly. This is not convincing, however, if one envisages two varieties being compared where one has, say, an articulatory set characterised by slight, but observable, advancing compared with the other. In such a case it would be possible to score the varieties as completely different, giving no recognition to the slight and systematic nature of that difference.

The second point concerns the practice of taking the most frequently occurring realisation of each variable for the purpose of constructing profiles. Here no allowance is made for the effects of phonetic environment, in that although speakers A and B might each have an identical (in terms of the delicacy permitted by the analytic framework) pair of phonetically conditioned realisations of /ɛ/ in the words 'bell' and 'tennis' ([ɛ̃] and [ɛ̞] respectively), speaker A, who chose to use the word 'tennis' frequently in his interview (for the data are characteristically taken from a free-wheeling interview) would be scored differently in respect of variable /ɛ/ than would speaker B who used many realisations of 'bell'.

Let us consider, then, a method of measuring similarity which does not fall prey to these objections, assuming in the first instance that we have isolated a number of comparable segments from several linguistic varieties. For the purpose of the present work consideration is restricted to segments containing stressed vowel variables, these segments being considered comparable by virtue of their occurrence in the same words in each of the varieties, and the articulatory feature-values which will be ascribed to each variable referring to the point of peak (perceived) prominence of the syllable in which it occurs. One further restriction is to syllable peak realisations which are not distinctively non-monophthongal. (Further criteria will need to be adduced in order to handle realisations which are distinctively diphthongal.) A conventional (impressionistic) phonetic transcription of such a point would express, implicitly at least, judgements concerning placement on several scales. The vertical and horizontal dimensions of the vowel quadrilateral, which co-ordinately locate place of articulation by means of conventional symbols and diacritics, probably lend themselves best to direct conversion to numerical scales. It is a relatively simple matter to superimpose an arbitrary grid pattern on the vowel quadrilateral, and thereby create a reference system in terms of two scales, viz. height and backness. Difficulties arise when we come to consider questions concerning the nature of these scales. How many points does each require? (That is, what are the limits of analytic discriminability in respect of each feature?) Are the points, however many, equally spaced along the scale? (Does discriminability vary according to the portion of the scale involved?) Is discriminability on one scale dependent upon position on another? (Is it, for example, easier to distinguish between backness and frontness in respect of a high vowel rather than a low one?)

The arbitrary imposition of this particular grid pattern upon the vowel quadrilateral may be defended on two grounds. The first is a matter of operational necessity; we must have a way of coding or scoring our phonetic analysis in numerical form if we are to compute similarity in numerical terms, and a grid pattern of some sort appears to correspond most nearly to the reality of judgements of vowel position. Secondly, although little is known about the levels of discrimination employed by speaker/hearers (which is not the same thing as their maximum theoretical discriminatory capacities), we do have some information about the abilities of phoneticians, in respect both of levels of discrimination and consistency (Ladefoged, 1960; Laver, 1965; Hurford, 1969). It is therefore necessary to choose a grid pattern which allows full rein to these abilities, and the initial choice of ten-point scales is more than adequate for this having regard to the results of the investigations cited above.

It is at this point that the use of the acoustic correlates of articulatory scales might be considered, though there are two reasons why this line is not pursued here. First, Ladefoged's (1967:55) pessimistic remark that 'phonetic similarity in this sense seems only to be definable in terms of judgement by the trained observer' would appear to reflect some of the technical and theoretical obstacles to such a scheme, but more importantly, it must be remembered that the clustering procedure this measure of similarity is designed to facilitate is part of a model of *sociolinguistic* behaviour. There is thus an argument against the use (at this stage) of analytic techniques which are different *in kind* from those available to real speakers/hearers. We shall therefore establish a set of scales whose primary reference is to articulatory features. The first two of these scales are quite independent of each other in a way that the features listed by Ladefoged (1969:5) are not. Those features included (i) high; (ii) mid; (iii) low; (iv) front; (v) central; (vi) black; etc., and since they were all interpreted binarily were clearly interdependent, e.g. + high implies − low, etc. The undesirability of this interdependence is recognised in his movement towards 'independent multivalued feature specifications' (1969:10), which are essentially the types of scales proposed here. Two further scales which are in some sense obvious candidates may be represented by lip-rounding and length. We should not be deterred by the notorious difficulty of making consistent judgements of features such as length on a multivalued scale. Since we know that its acoustic correlate, duration, varies consistently from speaker to speaker and from vowel to vowel (House, 1961) it may reasonably be assumed that a hearer *might* make use of it in his sociolinguistic perceptual behaviour. That it must be represented by a scale having relatively few discrete values, however, has been shown by a preliminary study (Bownass,

1977).[2] A not inconsiderable difficulty for a phonetician making such judgements consists in dismissing from consideration prior knowledge of results obtained instrumentally, e.g. those of Peterson and Lehiste (1960).

These four articulatory scales comprehend one set of features which might be referred to as distinctive for English vowels, but if what we are eventually to investigate is sociolinguistic significance, then the similarities must be expressed not solely in these terms. 'Voice quality' features may also be expressed in the form of such scales. Nasality, retroflexion, breath, creak, etc. are possibilities here though they will, like length, have relatively few discrete values and the score on the scale will frequently be zero. It must be emphasised at this point that the analytical framework here proposed is intended as a starting point for the investigation of the behaviour of speaker/hearers. It provides an *empirical* measure of similarity based upon the (exhaustive) observations of linguists, and it does not assume that the set of criteria used by speaker/hearers in their perceptions of similarity will necessarily coincide with those established for the measure. What is assumed, however, is that the criteria used by speaker/hearers will be a proper subset of those which are potentially observable by the linguist, and will be accessible experimentally by an eliminative procedure. This experimentation would also need to determine the 'weighting' given by speaker/hearers to individual criteria since in the measure the scales are not inherently weighted. Methodologically this would compare with, say, the isolation of phonologically distinctive features from the set of observable phonetic ones. Any observable articulatory feature may thus constitute a feature scale provided only that there is a potential for inter-varietal variation. Figure 14.1 illustrates some typical scores for three informants' varieties on one variable in respect of five criteria:

Figure 14.1

Inf.	Ts.	Feature Scales				
		Ht	B'ck.	L.R.	Dur.	Nas.
A	ï	8	2	1	2	1
B	ï	9	1	0	2	2
C	ï	8	1	1	1	0

The Methods of Urban Linguistic Surveys

Here, environmentally comparable realisations of variable /I/ for three informants, A, B, and C, are scored with respect to the five feature scales of height, backness, lip-rounding, duration and nasality. Each scale is regarded for convenience as having ten discrete values labelled 0–9, which means that the greatest possible distance between two realisations on any one of the scales is nine units. A first approximation, therefore, to the measurement of similarity between two realisations might be to express the sum of absolute differences on each of the five scales as a proportion of the maximum potential difference (here 45). Thus, Sim AB $= (x-y)/x$ where x is the maximum potential difference, and y the sum of actual differences over all scales (in figure 14.1 = 4 between informants A and B). The overall similarity between A and B would then be the mean of similarities on all variables. So for figure 14.1:

$$\text{Sim AB} = \frac{45-(1+1+1+0+1)}{45} = 0.911.$$

$$\text{Sim BC} = \frac{45-(1+0+1+1+2)}{45} = 0.88.$$

$$\text{Sim AC} = \frac{45-(0+1+1+0+1)}{45} = 0.933.$$

There are, however, a number of disadvantages associated with this method. First, the similarity betwen A and B does not depend in any way upon the value or even existence of C, and an absolute value of similarity is therefore meaningless from the point of view of the system of speakers as a whole (A,B,C,...n). The similarities (or differences) between any two speakers should ideally be expressed in a form which takes account of the existence and form of other varieties. (This is merely a formalisation of the fact that for a Londoner the localised speech of Leeds will be judged to be further from or nearer to his own, depending, *inter alia*, upon whether or not the speech of, say, Glasgow, is part of his linguistic experience.) Secondly, since the number of points on the feature-scales is arbitrarily imposed, there is no guarantee that a contribution to the coefficient of one unit of difference from one scale will be of the same order as one unit of difference from another scale. A large (in the sense of statistically significant) variation might be represented by one unit in the case of a scale where, say, the distribution of all realisations is unevenly divided between two adjacent points, compared with the lesser significance of one unit from a scale which displays greater inherent variability.

Both these objections are resolved by adopting the following procedure: the individual scale differences between a pair of speakers on one variable are taken from the raw scores such as those in figure 14.1; each difference may now be converted from an absolute value to a contributing one by adjusting it according to the variability of scores exhibited over the relevant scale by the whole sample of speakers in respect of the particular variable. The most appropriate function for this is the mean square deviation ($E[(x-\mu)^2]$), or variance. The absolute difference is divided by this factor in order to arrive at the contributing difference. Contributing differences are then summed as in the previous example to yield an index of difference for a pair of speakers in respect of one variable. The mean of such indices for all variables represents the overall index of difference between that pair of speakers. When a list of overall differences has been computed for each permutation of pairs this is ordered, inverted and rescaled over a percentage range. This yields percentage similarities which are suitable for use in a conventional clustering routine, and which are maximal in their discriminating capacity.

Thus, for the data in figure 14.1 the mean square deviation for the height scale is 0.22, as it is for backness, lip-rounding and duration. For nasality it is 0.66. Therefore,[3] in respect of variable /I/,

$$\text{Diff AB} = \sum_{1\ldots n} \left(\frac{|x_a\ x_b|}{E[(x-\mu)^2]} \right)$$

$$= (\tfrac{1}{0.22}) + (\tfrac{1}{0.22}) + (\tfrac{1}{0.22}) + (\tfrac{0}{0.22}) + (\tfrac{1}{0.66}) = 15$$

Similarly, Diff BC = 16.5, Diff AC = 10.5
By ordering and rescaling

Sim AC (Diff 10.5) = 100%
Sim AB (Diff 15) = 25%
Sim BC (Diff 10) = 0%

The 0 and 100 per cent points are understood as signifying 'most similar' and 'least similar', and provide the limiting points *for a particular sample of speakers.* Introduction of further speakers alters the spread over the scale of the original sample, just as we may assume that changes in the linguistic exposure of individuals can lead to changes in their perceptions of previously known varieties.

For example, figure 14.2 adds two speakers to the three already analysed:

Figure 14.2

Inf.	Ts.	Ht	B'ck.	L.R.	Dur.	Nas.
D	ẹ̃	7	2	0	2	0
E	ĩ	8	1	0	2	3

This changes the mean square deviation for the scales to 0.4, 0.24, 0.24, 0.16 and 1.36 respectively and the computation yields the following ordered percentage similarities:

Pair	Difference	% Sim
BE	3.235	100
AD	7.401	69.91
DE	8.871	59.30
AE	9.802	52.57
BD	10.636	46.55
AC	11.151	42.83
AB	11.567	39.83
CE	12.621	32.22
BC	14.387	19.46
CD	17.082	0

It will be noted that while the spacing of similarities between the pairs AB, AC and BC has changed in response to the introduction of new data, their relative order has not. An advantage of taking the mean of individual variable differences as the overall similarity measure is that a small proportion of variables not recorded will not disturb either the process or the results unduly. It might also prove possible, though this has not yet been attempted, to isolate diagnostic variables (those whose realisations are highly predictive of the form of realisations of other variables in the same variety) by comparing a sufficient number of individual variable differences with the corresponding overall mean differences.

Implementation of this type of measure in a cluster analysis involving more variables demands, of course, further development. The principal difficulty is in the handling of distinctively non-monophthongal syllable peaks. (There is a tacit assumption otherwise that the analysis of a point of peak prominence as though it were representative of a steady-state vowel is reasonable.) Here the choice seems to lie between the construction of multivalued feature scales capable of representing degree and direction of glide, which could be useful even in the case of distinctively monophthongal peaks, and the separate analysis and coding of two (or more) points in the relevant syllable peak. Consonants, too, are not dealt with here in view of the quite different problems posed. Since there are significant differences in mode of perception, e.g. categorical versus non-categorical (Liberman, 1963), there is some reason to suppose that there may also be differences in the amounts of sociolinguistic information conveyed by vowels and consonants. This would introduce the question of 'weighting' the contribution of different variables depending upon the purpose of the measure at that time.

One final advantage of the method suggests itself. This is concerned with the identification of features, whether at an articulatory or acoustic level, used by hearers in making sociolinguistic judgements about their interlocutors. If, as Ainsworth (1975:104) suggests, some kind of perceptual normalisation (of intrinsic acoustic features, in particular F_1 and F_2) is part of the process of vowel recognition, then one way of arriving at these features would be to eliminate those features where it does not occur. To this end an empirical measure of phonetic similarity which may be controlled in respect of the features contributing to it would seem to be of some importance for comparison with the subjective reactions and judgements of linguistically naive informants.

It is assumed by most authors that phonetic similarity is not the same thing as phonological similarity, but the nature of the relationship is not generally stated ('The similarity condition refers to phonological similarity ... It does not refer to phonetic similarity, however that might be measured' (Foley, 1977:79)). Although what is proposed here is a phonetic measure, the value of such a basis for statements of phonological similarity in whatever general phonological theory seems self-evident.

Accepting, therefore, some restrictions (e.g. the addition of one or more members to the sample requires reprocessing of the existing data) and some assumptions (e.g. the reasonableness of the construction and choice of the feature scales themselves) we hope to have moved towards the development of an alternative framework both for the classification, and the description of the distribution, of speech varieties. This framework aims to be sufficiently flexible and responsive as to facilitate also experimentation with similarities perceived and reported by non-linguists,[4] primarily by providing a basis for comparison of perceived with analysed similarities, together with the ability to manipulate a model of a single speaker's linguistic experience through the inclusion of differing sets of sample members.

Notes

1. Whether or not analyst-imposed segmentation of the data into phoneme-like units of comparison is a sound basis for a model of language *use* is a separate question, but much psycholinguistic evidence (e.g. Liberman, 1970, on the rate of perception of sound segments and Oettinger, 1972, on the phoneme as a product of perception) points to a prosodic/syllabic approach for such a model.

2. Potapova (1975) reports more optimistically on the ability of phoneticians to discriminate auditorily between segments of small, instrumentally determined duration differences in certain sentence positions.

3. A similar, multidimensional sum-of-differences technique, without allowance for scale variation, is employed by Plomp (1976:95) in the determination of interpoint distances within a multidimensional space representing the sound spectra of certain stimuli.

4. This is facilitated by an auditory model of peripheral perception such as that contained in Bladon and Lindblom (1979).

References

Ainsworth, W.A. (1975) 'Intrinsic and Extrinsic Factors in Vowel Judgements' in Fant, G. and Tatham, M.A.A. (eds) (1975) *Auditory Analysis and Perception of Speech*, London

Bladon, R.A.W. and Lindblom, B, (1979) 'Auditory Modelling of Vowels'. Paper presented to Acoustical Society of America, June 1979

Bownass, S. (1977) 'Consistency in Phonetic Analysis'. Unpub. B.A. dissertation, University of Sheffield

Foley, J. (1977) *Foundations of Theoretical Phonology*, London
House, A.S. (1961) 'On Vowel Duration in English', *JASA 33*, 1174-8
Hurford, J.R. (1969) 'The Judgement of Vowel Quality', *Language and Speech 12*, 4, 220-37
Jones-Sargent, V. (1983) *Tyne Bytes: a Computerised Sociolinguistic Study of Tyneside*, Frankfurt
Labov, W. (1966) *The Social Stratification of English in New York City*, Washington, D.C.
Ladefoged, P. (1960) 'The Value of Phonetic Statements', *Language 36*, 387-96
—— (1967) *Three Areas of Experimental Phonetics*, London
—— (1969) 'The Measurement of Phonetic Similarity', *Int. Conf. on Comp. Ling.*, preprint no. 57, Stockholm
Laver, J.D.M.H. (1965) 'Variability in Vowel Perception' *Language and Speech 8*, 95-121
Liberman, A.M. (1970) 'The Grammars of Speech and Language', *Cognitive Psychology 1*, 301-23
Liberman, A.M., Cooper, F.S., Harris, K.S. and McNeilage, P.F. (1963) 'A Motor Theory of Speech Perception'. Paper D3 in *Proc. of the Speech Communication Seminar, Stockholm, 1962*, vol. 2, Stockholm
Oettinger, A.G. (1972) 'The Semantic Wall', in David, E.E. and Denes, P.B. (eds) (1972) *Human Communication: a Unified View*, New York
Pellowe, J.N.H. (1967) 'Studies towards a Classification of Varieties of Spoken English'. Unpub. M.Litt. thesis, University of Newcastle-upon-Tyne
—— (1967) 'The Tyneside Linguistic Survey' unpublished M.Litt. thesis, University of Newcastle-upon-Tyne
——, Nixon, G., Strang, B.M.H., and McNeany, V. (1972) 'A Dynamic Modelling of Linguistic Variation: the Urbabn (Tyneside) Linguistic Survey', *Lingua 30*, 1-30
Peterson, G.E. and Ilse Lehiste (1960) 'Duration of Syllable Nuclei in English', *JASA 32*, 6, 693-703
Plomp, R. (1976) *Aspects of Tone Sensation*, London
Potapova, R.K. (1975) 'Auditory Estimate of Syllable and Vowel Duration in Sentences', in Fant, G. and Tatham, M.A.A. (eds) *Auditory Analysis and Perception of Speech*, London
Sokal, R.R. and Sneath, P.H. (1963) *Principles of Numerical Taxonomy*, London
Strang, B.M.H. (1968) 'The Tyneside Linguistic Survey', *Zeitschrift für Mundartforschung NF 4*, 788-94

15
A Bibliography of Barbara Strang

Richard N. Bailey
University of Newcastle-upon-Tyne

Barbara left no complete list of her publications. What follows has therefore been assembled from a variety of sources but, given the range of her interests, may well be incomplete.

Articles and books

as B.M.H. Carr

'A History of the Kentish Dialect with Special Reference to Agricultural Terms', M.A. Dissertation, University of London, 1947
'"The Ettrick Shepherd", Two Unnoted Articles', *Notes & Queries*, CXCV, 1950, 388–90
'Neglected Sources for the Vocabulary of Kentish and Some Neighbouring Dialects in the Eighteenth and Nineteenth Centuries', *Trans. Philol. Soc.*, 1950, 34–59
'On "The Prelude", II, 399–420', *Notes & Queries*, CXCVIII, 1953, 65–6

as B.M.H. Strang

'Types and Tokens in Language', *Proc. Univ. Durham Philos. Soc.* I(B), 1958, 17–25
'William Somner's "Dictionarium Anglo-Saxonicum"', *Notes & Queries*, n.s. VI, 1959, 424
'Dryden's Innovations in Critical Vocabulary', *Durham Univ. J.*, n.s. XX, 1959, 114–23
'Who is the Old Man in "The Pardoner's Tale"?', *Notes and Queries*, n.s. VII, 1960, 207–8
'Piers Plowman, B, Prologue 132–8', *Notes and Queries*, n.s. VII, 1960, 436

A Bibliography of Barbara Strang

'Two Wulfstan Expressions', *Notes & Queries*, n.s. VIII, 1961, 166–7

Modern English Structure, Arnold, London, 1962; repr. 1963, 1964, 1965; 2nd edn revised 1968, 1969, 1970, 1974; corr. repr. 1978

'Memorabilia', *Notes & Queries*, n.s. IX, 1962, 322–3

'The Study of Modern English', *Talks to Teachers in English*, II, 1962, 5–12

(with J.C.M.), 'English Studies in Korea', *Notes and Queries*, n.s. X, 1963, 162

'Piers Plowman, B-text, Passus V, 491–2', *Notes and Queries*, n.s. X, 1963, 286

'Theory and Practice in Morpheme Identification', *Proc. 9th International Congress of Linguists, Cambridge, Mass., 1962*, (ed. H.G. Lunt), Mouton, The Hague, 1964, 358–65

'Metaphors and Models', (inaugural lecture), The University, Newcastle-upon-Tyne, 1965

'Some Features of S.V. Concord in Present-day English', *English Studies Today*, (eds I. Cellini *et al.*), 4th series, Rome, Edizioni di Storia e Letteratura, 1966, 73–87

'Lecturing', *J. Newcastle-upon-Tyne Univ. Inst. of Educ.*, XVII, 1966, 145–8

'Swift and the English Language: a Study in Principles and Practice', *To Honor Roman Jacobson*, III (Janua Linguarum: Series Maior XXXIII), Mouton, The Hague, 1968, 1947–59

'The Tyneside Linguistic Survey', *Zeitschrift für Mundartforschung*, NF, 4, (Verhandlungen des Zweiten Internationalen Dialektologenkongresses), Wiesbaden, Franz Steiner Verlag, 1968, 788–94

'Swift's Agent-noun Formations in -ER', *Wortbildung, Syntax und Morphologie: Festschrift zum 60 Geburtstag von Hans Marchand*, (eds H.E. Brekle and L. Lipka), Mouton, The Hague, 1968, 217–29

'Further Thoughts on Speech Studies', *Speech and Drama*, XVII, 1968, 29–34

'Memorabilia', *Notes & Queries*, n.s. XVI, 1969, 362–3

'Aspects of the History of the -ER Formative in English', *Trans. Philol. Soc.*, 1969, 1–30

'Some Problems in Defining the Lexicon of English', *Actes du xe Congrès International des Linguistes 1967*, Bucharest, L'Académie de la république socialiste de Roumanie, 1970, 633–45

A History of English, Methuen, London, hardback edn, 1970, repr. 1975; paperback edn 1974, repr. 1975, 1976, 1979, 1982, 1986

(Commentary on Paper 3 by D. Crystal), *CILT Reports and Papers*, 6, *Interdisciplinary Approaches to Language*, London, Centre for Information on Language Teaching and Research, 1971, 53–6

(with J. Pellowe *et al.*), 'A Dynamic Modelling of Linguistic Variation: the Urban (Tyneside) Linguistic Survey', *Lingua*, XXX, 1972, 1–30

(with J. Pellowe), 'English Language', *The Year's Work in Eng. Studs (1971)*, LII, 1973, 34–64

'A Supplement to OED: A–G', *Notes & Queries*, XXI, 1974, 2–13

(with J. Pellowe), 'English Language', *The Year's Work in Eng. Studs (1972)*, LIII, 1974, 37–66

(with J. Pellowe), 'English Language', *The Year's Work in Eng. Studs*

A Bibliography of Barbara Strang

(1973), LIV, 1975, 37–68
'Obituary — J.C. Maxwell', *Durham Univ. J.*, n.s. XXXVIII, 1976, 3
(with J. Pellowe), 'English Language', *The Year's Work in Eng. Studs (1974)*, LV, 1976, 34–75
'The Influence of International Trade on the English Language', *J. Royal Soc. of Arts*, CXXIV, 1976, 426–42
'A Supplement to OED: H–N', *Notes & Queries*, n.s. XXIV, 1977, 388–99
(with J. Pellowe), 'English Language', *The Year's Work in Eng. Studs (1975)*, LVI, 1977, 35–62
(with M. Brennan), 'English Language', *The Year's Work in Eng. Studs (1976)*, LVII, 1978, 11–42
'The Ecology of the English Monosyllable', *Studies in English Linguistics for Randolph Quirk*, (eds S. Greenbaum *et al.*), Longman, London, 1980, 277–93
'Some Aspects of the History of the BE + ING Construction', *Language Form and Linguistic Variation: Papers Dedicated to Angus McIntosh, Current Issues in Linguistic Theory, XV*, (ed. J. Anderson), John Benjamins, B.V. Amsterdam, 1982, 427–74
'Appendix 1: John Clare's Language', *John Clare: The Rural Muse*, (ed. R.K.R. Thornton), Carcanet, Manchester, 1982, 159–73

Reviews

as B.M.H. Carr

B. Thuresson (1950) *Middle English Occupational Terms*, in *Rev. Eng. Studs*, n.s. III, 1952, 65–7
S. Rubin (1951) *The Phonology of the Middle English Dialect of Sussex*, in *Eng. Studs*, XXXVI, 1955, 67–9
A. Rynell (1952) *Parataxis and Hypotaxis as a Criterion of Syntax and Style, especially in Old English Poetry*, in *Eng. Studs*, XXXIV, 1953, 30–2
A. Cohen (1952) *The Phonemes of English: A Phonemic Study of the Vowels and Consonants of Standard English*, in *Rev. Eng. Studs*, n.s. V, 1954, 104–6
V. Brown (ed.) (1952) *þorgils saga ok Hafliða*, in *Durham Univ. J.*, n.s. XV, 1953, 76–7
L.F. Brosnahan (1953) *Some Old English Sound Changes: An Analysis in the Light of Modern Phonetics*, in *Rev. Eng. Studs*, n.s. VI, 1955, 74–6

as B.M.H. Strang

B. Sundby (ed.) (1953) *Christopher Cooper's 'English Teacher' (1687)*, in *Eng. Studs*, XXXIX(1), 1958, 35–7

A Bibliography of Barbara Strang

C.L. Barber (1957) *The Idea of Honour in the English Drama, 1591-1700*, in *Mod. Lang. Rev.*, LIV, 1959, 88-9

J.A. Bennett (ed.) (1957) *The Parlement of Foules*, in *Durham Univ. J.*, n.s. XIX, 1957-8, 139-42

C.F. Hockett (1958) *A Course in Modern Linguistics*, in *Durham Univ. J.*, n.s. XXI, 1959-60, 135-9

J. Thirsk (ed.) (1958) *Suffolk Farming in the Nineteenth Century*, in *Notes & Queries*, n.s. VII, 1960, 195-6

A.G. Brodeur (1959) *The Art of Beowulf*, in *Durham Univ. J.*, n.s. XXII, 1960-1, 124-6

G. Shepherd (ed.) (1959) *Ancrene Wisse*, in *Durham Univ. J.*, n.s. XXII, 1960-1, 92

C.S. Lewis, (1960) *Studies in Words*, in *Durham Univ. J.*, n.s. XXIII, 1961-2, 45-7

R. Filipovic (1960) *The Phonemic Analysis of English Loan-words in Croatian*, in *Notes & Queries*, n.s. IX, 1962, 190-1

A. Vanvik (1960) *On Stress in Present-day English (Received Pronunciation)*, in *Durham Univ. J.*, n.s. XXIV, 1962-3, 47-8

S.I. Tucker (1961) *English Examined*, in *Durham Univ. J.*, n.s. XXIV, 1962-3, 46-7

A.C. Gimson (1962) *An Introduction to the Pronunciation of English*, in *Mod. Lang. Rev.*, LVIII, 1963, 548

A. Dent and D. Goodall (1962) *The Foals of Epona: A History of British Ponies from the Bronze Age to Yesterday*, in *Notes & Queries*, n.s. X, 1963, 233-5

S. Jacobson (1964) *Adverbial Positions in English*, in *Stud. Neophil.*, XXXVI, 1964, 376-8

U. Jacobsson (1962) *Phonological Dialect Constituents in the Vocabulary of Standard English*, in *Anglia*, LXXXII, 1964, 117-19

S.J. Kim (1963) *A Study of Concurrent Collocations of Noun, Adjective, Adverb plus Preposition/Adverb in Contemporary English*, in *Notes & Queries*, n.s. XI, 1964, 399-400

J.T. Waterman (1963) *Perspectives in Linguistics: an Account of the Background of Modern Linguistics*, in *Mod. Lang. Rev.*, LIX, 1964, 437

H. Spitzbardt (1962) *Lebendiges Englisch. Stilistisch-syntaktische Mittel der Ausdrucksverstärkung*, in *J. Eng. Germ. Philol.*, LXIII, 1964, 482-3

A. Martinet (1962) *A Functional View of Language. The Waynflete Lectures delivered in the College of St. Mary Magdalen, Oxford*, in *Durham Univ. J.*, n.s. XXV, 1964, 128-9

C. Barber (1964) *Linguistic Change in Present-day English*, in *Arch. Ling.*, XVII, 1965, 55-8

U. Bellugi and R. Brown (eds) (1964) *The Acquisition of Language*, in *Developmental Medicine and Child Neurology*, VII, 1965, 104-5

H.W. Fowler (1965) *A Dictionary of Modern English Usage*, in *Mod. Lang. Rev.*, LXI, 1966, 264-5

M. Girsdansky (1963) *The Adventure of Language*, in *Found. of Lang.*, III, 1967, 206

M. Joos (1964) *The English Verb: Forms and Meanings*, and F.R.

Palmer (1965) *A Linguistic Study of the English Verb*, in *Found. of Lang.*, III, 1967, 317–21
P. Roberts (1964) *English Syntax: a Programmed Introduction to Transformational Grammar*, in *J. Ling.*, III, 1967, 166–9
C.C. Fries (1965) *Linguistics: the Study of Language*, in *Found. of Lang.*, IV, 1968, 453–4
G. Leech (1966) *English in Advertising: a Linguistic Study of Advertising in Great Britain*, in *Lingua*, XIX, 1968, 316–19
I.I. Revzin (1966) *Models of Language*, in *Mod. Lang. Rev.*, LXIII, 1968, 134–5
F. Behre (1967) *Studies in Agatha Christie's Writings*, in *Stud. Neophil.*, XLI, 1969, 232–4
R.M. Jordan (1967) *Chaucer and the Shape of Creation*, in *Med. Aev.*, XXXVIII, 1969, 328–31
H. Aarsleff (1967) *The Study of Language in England, 1780–1860*, in *Found. of Lang.*, VI, 1970, 438–40
G.M. Miller (ed.) (1971) *BBC Pronouncing Dictionary of British Names*, in *Notes & Queries*, n.s. XVIII, 1971, 347–9
W.A. Shibles (1971) *Metaphor: an Annotated Bibliography and History*, in *Notes and Queries*, n.s. XIX, 1972, 344–5
M.F. Wakelin (1972) *Patterns in the Folk Speech of the British Isles*, in *Notes and Queries*, n.s. XIX, 1972, 269–70
A.J. Aitken *et al.* (eds) (1971) *Edinburgh Studies in English and Scots*, in *J. Ling.*, VIII, 1972, 346–7
R.A. Close (1968) *The New English Grammar, Parts Three and Four, 'How to Use the Verb'*, in *Found. of Lang.*, IX, 1972–3, 295–6
P. Wright (1974) *The Language of British Industry*, in *Notes & Queries*, n.s. XXI, 1974, 283
B. Foster (1970) *The Changing English Language*, in *Found. of Lang.*, XI, 1974, 455–6
J.W. Lewis (1972) *A Concise Pronouncing Dictionary of British and American English*, in *Notes and Queries*, n.s. XXI, 1974, 138–41
A.S. Hornby (1974) *Oxford Advanced Learner's Dictionary of Current English*, 3rd edn, in *Notes and Queries*, n.s. XXI, 1974, 378–9
C. Påhlsson (1972) *The Northumbrian Burr*, in *J. Ling.*, IX, 1975, 136–40
V. Adams (1973) *An Introduction to Modern English Word-formation*, in *Rev. Eng. Studs*, n.s. XXVI, 1975, 107–10
F.M.P. Liefrink (1973) *Semantico-Syntax*, in *Notes & Queries*, n.s. XXII, 1975, 28–30
R. Quirk (1974) *The Linguist and the English Language*, in *Rev. Eng. Studs*, n.s. XXVI, 1975, 365–6
E. Vorlat (1975) *The Development of English Grammatical Theory, 1586–1737*, in *Hist. Ling.*, III (3), 1976, 374–6
I. Robinson (1975) *The New Grammarians' Funeral, A Critique of Noam Chomsky's Linguistics*, in *Durham Univ. J.*, n.s. XXXIX, 1977–8 100–1
J.M. Williams (1975) *Origins of the English Language, A Social and Linguistic History*, in *J. Ling.*, XIII, 1977, 107–11
L. Todd (1974) *Pidgins and Creoles*, in *Mod. Lang. rev.*, LXXII., 1977, 135–7

A Bibliography of Barbara Strang

M. Cohen (1977) *Sensible Words: Linguistic Practice in England, 1640-1785*, in *Verbatim*, V (2), 1978, 13-14

J. Knowlson (1975) *Universal Language Schemes in England and France, 1600-1800*, in *Mod. Lang. Rev.*, LXXIII, 1978, 138-40

F. Behre (1973) *Get, Come and Go: Some Aspects of Situational Grammar*, in *Stud. Neophil.*, L, 1978, 148-50

D. Bolinger (1977) *Meaning and Form*, in *J. Ling.*, XIV, 1978, 347-52

G.A. Padley (1976) *Grammatical Theory in Western Europe, 1500-1700, The Latin Tradition*, in *Durham Univ. J.*, n.s. XL(1), 1978-9, 116-18

D. Woolf (1975) *Grundzüge der diachronischen Morphologie des Englischen*, in *Yearbook of Eng. Studs*, VIII, 1978, 309-11

V. Salmon (1979) *The Study of Language in Seventeenth-century England*, in *Mod. Lang. Rev.*, LXXVII, 1982, 408-10

R. Harris (1980) *The Language-Makers*; I. Scheffler (1979) *Beyond the Letter: A Philosophical Inquiry into Ambiguity, Vagueness and Metaphor in Language*, (eds) M. Ching *et al.* (1980) *Linguistic Perspectives on Literature*, in *London Review of Books*, II, no. 14, 1980, 17

A. Hughes and P. Trudgill (1979) *English Accents and Dialects, An Introduction to Social and Regional Varieties of British English*, in *Notes & Queries*, n.s. XXVII, 1980, 85-7

W. Nash (1980) *Designs in Prose*, in *London Review of Books*, III, 10, 1981, 19-20

S. Jacobson (1975) *Factors Affecting the Placement of English Adverbs in Relation to Auxiliaries*; ibid. (1978) *On the Use, Meaning and Syntax of English Proverbial Adverbs*, in *Stud. Neophil.*, LIII, 1981, 184-8

M.C. Alleyne (1980) *Comparative Afro-American: An Historical-Comparative Study of English-based Afro-American Dialects of the New World*, in *Yearbook of Eng. Studs*, XII, 1982, 264-6

G. Lakoff and M. Johnson (1980) *Metaphors We Live By*, in *Mod. Lang. Rev.*, LXXVII, 1982, 134-6

An environmentally friendly book printed and bound in England by www.printondemand-worldwide.com

PEFC Certified
This product is from sustainably managed forests and controlled sources
www.pefc.org
PEFC/16-33-415

MIX
Paper from responsible sources
FSC® C004959
www.fsc.org

This book is made entirely of sustainable materials; FSC paper for the cover and PEFC paper for the text pages.

#0084 - 290615 - C0 - 229/152/14 [16] - CB - 9781138917323